MW00633514

THE GERMANS OF CHICAGO

by

Rudolf A. Hofmeister

German Department
University of Illinois, Chicago Circle

ISBN 0-87563-113-4

Copyright © 1976
STIPES PUBLISHING COMPANY

Published by
STIPES PUBLISHING COMPANY
10-12 Chester Street
Champaign, Illinois 61820

To my family:
Pat
Rudy
Theresa

Contents

List of Tables

Preface

This study aims to present a general history of the Chicago Germans from 1825, when the first German settler was attested in the Chicago area, to the present time. It is not intended to be an exhaustive treatment, but rather an attempt to provide an indication of the German element's significant role in Chicago's history. Few people know that for a quarter of a century, from about 1875 to 1900, more first and second generation Germans lived in Chicago than any other ethnic group, causing several people to call Chicago, "one of the largest German cities in the world." This large number of Germans left a distinct Teutonic imprint on Chicago, which can still be seen in the names of many schools, streets, and monuments, despite efforts to eradicate it, especially during World War I. The attempts at blotting out the vestiges of German culture in Chicago are responsible for our failure to remember that without the Germans' presence in the city the Chicago Symphony Orchestra, the Museum of Science and Industry, Grant and Alexian Brothers hospitals, and many other familiar institutions in the city might not exist today. Despite its obvious importance, there has been no book in the English language about the German element's role in Chicago's history; and the last German book on the subject, *Chicago und sein Deutschthum*, appeared 75 years ago. Therefore, this study on a disregarded facet of Chicago's history hardly needs a justification.

No two authors would agree what the contents of a study such as this should be. In order to give a survey of the 150-year history of Chicago's German element, representative examples had to be selected and it may well be that much has been omitted which some readers would have liked to have seen included. On the other hand, in order to do justice to the German element's positive and negative contributions to the growth of the city, I may have discussed persons, activities, or events considered inconsequential by some readers. My task, undoubtedly, would have been easier if I had concentrated on a few of the many outstanding individuals or organizations of Chicago's German element rather than attempting to give a broad history. Such a selective treatment, however, would have presented a slanted picture.

A major difficulty of this study was to determine what constituted Chicago's "German element." Not infrequently, especially during war eras, some Chicagoans denied their German background, refusing to indicate that they were born in Germany or born of parents who had emigrated from Germany. For lack of information, these people could not be considered part of the city's German element. Since Germany's political boundaries changed repeatedly during the timespan dealt with, in this study only those individuals are discussed who in some way indicated that they were German. This, no doubt, includes some people who were actually born in German-speaking parts of Switzerland or in Austria. However, an effort was always made to ascertain where they were born; doubtful cases were excluded.

This book owes its existence to the Consulate General of the Federal Republic of Germany, which first suggested that it be written. I am grateful to the consulate for inducing "Inter Nationes" in Bonn to provide—as a contribution to the American Bicentennial—a grant to help defray the expenses of publishing this study. I would also like to thank Professor Robert R. Heitner, head of the German Department at the University of Illinois, Chicago Circle, who made many valuable suggestions for improving this work. I am especially grateful to Mrs. William F. Petersen who allowed me to use the private archive of her late father, Dr. Otto L. Schmidt, who was at the hub of Chicago's German element for well over forty years. I wish to acknowledge the courtesy and helpfulness of the staff of the Chicago Public Library, as well as that of the library staffs of the University of Illinois, Chicago Circle, the Chicago Historical Society, City Hall, and Newberry. Finally, I owe thanks to the large number of club secretaries whose innumerable informative pamphlets, programs, or reports of their various organizations could not be listed in the bibliography, as well as to the anonymous translators of the Chicago Public Library WPA project, whose work was used in this study.

Brookfield, Ill.
December 1975

Rudolf Hofmeister

Chapter 1

Introduction—Evidence for the German Element's Presence in Chicago

Many misconceptions about Chicago's German element exist for a host of reasons. Early misconceptions about the city's German element appeared in the *Tribune* of August 26, 1879 when it reprinted a speech by William Bross, Illinois's lieutenant governor after 1864 and long-time editor of the *Tribune*, who had given the talk on the previous day at the fifth annual German Old Settlers' Picnic at Ogden's Grove. He gave a survey of Chicago's German element which must be characterized as being more flattering than accurate. In stating that the *Illinois Staatszeitung* was founded in 1846 as Chicago's first German newspaper, Bross was only a little mistaken, for the German paper *Chicago Volksfreund*, with which he confused it, was founded in 1845. However, when he estimated that few Germans were present when he came to Chicago in 1848 and that no Germans came to Chicago before 1840, he was far afield from the historical facts. When he gave an account of the accomplishments of the Chicago Germans, he must have been in a jocular mood, for in addition to giving them credit for playing a crucial role in the American Civil War, which he characterized as "their ballots and their bullets were equally on the side of freedom," he mentioned only three more of their contributions to the Chicago scene. He asserted that the custom of growing full beards, introduced by the Germans, made Chicagoans appear more handsome, that the Germans' beer, being less potent than whiskey, had a salutary effect on sobriety, and that the beneficial influence of German music elevated the inferior position of American music.

Similar misconceptions, or giving the Germans credit for minor accomplishments while disregarding important ones, are found in sporadic accounts of the Chicago Germans in various local newspapers and periodicals. Often, in a good-natured, patronizing manner, something is mentioned about "Sauerkraut" or "Bockbier," and the legendary German "Gemütlichkeit" constitutes almost an obligatory part. However, a survey of the Germans' role in Chicago's history suggests that little opportunity existed to stress German "Gemütlichkeit" in such times as the era of persecution by the "Know-Nothings," adherents of the quasi-secret American party, which gained prominence in the 1850's and wanted to exclude non-native Americans from public office. There was little "Gemütlichkeit" in the tumultuous days during the Haymarket "Riot" in 1886, and the harassments during the frantic World War I years. On the whole, the much quoted German "beer, women and song" played a relatively small part in the total Teutonic imprint on Chicago. These misconceptions about the German element of Chicago seem to be a natural consequence of its general disregard.

The disregard of the German element, as well as that of other ethnic groups, in American history received public attention in one of Chicago's more memorable, if less spectacular, happenings during the "Roaring Twenties," the School Superintendent McAndrew controversy which culminated in McAndrew's ouster on March 21, 1928. During the trial, the defendant William McAndrew, realizing the futility of his case, read the daily newspapers in a "circus-like atmosphere of the courtroom" while Mayor Thompson's henchmen harangued him with trumped up charges of un-American conduct. McAndrew was convicted on the basis of former Congressman John Gorman's testimony that McAndrew had endorsed "un-American" history books, especially David Muzzey's *History of the American People*, which, according to Gorman, contained "false and insidious teachings of alienism." Gorman had been appointed by Mayor Thompson to bring about the ouster of McAndrew as part of the mayor's pre-election pledge to "bust King George in the snoot." When Gorman was hit with a $100,000 libel suit by Muzzey, and it became obvious that he was left "holding the sack" by city hall after he had accomplished his mission against McAndrew, Gorman, in an effort to avoid the damage suit, wrote a retraction of his former testimony. According to the *Tribune* of October 12, 1929, Gorman said that he had not even read Muzzey's book and that a careful study showed it to be well-adapted for use in public schools.

In the wake of allegations that history books provide the British rather than the American viewpoint, in 1927 several committees of Chicagoans investigated history books used in Chicago's public school system to see whether any of them distorted or disregarded historical facts. From this ensued a front-page story in the *Chicago Evening American* of February 23, 1927. A committee of the American Historical Society, composed in part of representatives from various ethnic groups, the Germans being represented by William Teichmann, Charles Richter, and Frieda Ackermann, charged that in Chicago's public schools at least three history books were used which exhibited "rank discrimination against Polish, German, Irish and French heroes of American history." These books, William Gordy's *A History of the United States*, William B. Guitteau's *Our United States*, and Lewis and Rowland's *The Silent Reader*, treat the Germans, as well as other ethnic groups, with "the contempt of silence and the venom of propaganda." They do not even give footnote notices to outstanding Germans who have had a crucial role in America's history, such as John de Kalb, who sacrificed his life for the American cause or Baron von Steuben, the founder of West Point.

Just as on the national level, the German element has been slighted on the local level. Few local historical accounts do justice to the Germans' part in shaping Chicago. For instance, Mayer and Wade's illustrated history, *Chicago, Growth of a Metropolis*, contains a few illustrations related to the German element and mentions the Germans twice. Yet, it seems to be one of the few history books that refer to the Chicago Germans at all.

The disregard of the Germans' role in Chicago's history is not limited to scholarly books, but also is present in other areas. Again and again one hears how many Poles there are in Chicago, but few people ever realize that at one time Chicagoans of German extraction were more numerous than any other nationality, including American. Whereas other ethnic groups operate cultural museums, such as Balzeka's Museum of Lithuanian culture, the Ling Long Chinese Museum or the Polish Museum, the Chicago Germans do without such a storehouse of culture and tradition. There are, of course, German cultural objects exhibited in Chicago museums, most popular, perhaps, the submarine in the Museum of Science and Industry, but if one searches in the Historical Society's museum for traces of the German presence in Chicago, not much can be found. Only the initiated know that this repository of local history has attained its excellence partly through the efforts of several Chicagoans of German extraction, such as Dr. Otto Schmidt, the society's former president and Charles Gunther, alderman and famous "Candy Man," whose priceless Americana collection was transferred to the Chicago Historical Society from "The Coliseum," which he had erected. This disregard is to be blamed partly on the Germans themselves, but also on other factors, such as coverage by the news media. When other ethnic groups organize public demonstrations, such as the Leif Erickson Parade or the Columbus Day Parade, a minimum of coverage by the news media is assured, but the annual German von Steuben Day Parade seems to be ignored.

All of these factors pertaining to the more or less obvious disregard of Chicago's German element add up to create a composite picture. This mosaic would seem to indicate that the German element had played a rather insignificant role in Chicago's making. However, a careful investigation of its role shows that it took a prominent, often controversial part in various facets of Chicago's history and contributed greatly to its development.

When Prince Heinrich of Prussia, the brother of Kaiser Wilhelm II, visited Chicago in March of 1902, most citizens read about his sojourn only in connection with a sumptuous banquet in his honor arranged by the corrupt First Ward aldermen "Hinky Dink" Kenna and "Bathhouse John" Coughlin at the elegant Everleigh "Club" at 2131-33 Dearborn Street, also known to the initiated as the world's most exclusive bordello. But there was also a more decorous reception of the royal visitor, a gala banquet at the dignified Germania Club, on March 3, 1902, at which many local dignitaries were present to hear Mayor Harrison praise "the approximately 500,000 Chicagoans of German ancestry who have contributed significantly to elevate Chicago to her present greatness."

In the 1900's when the peak of the German influx through immigration had barely passed and the more or less assimilated German constituents reached sizable numbers, the presence of the Germans was considerably more conspicuous than now. Then they received credit for their contributions not only at election time when scheming politicians sought to attract the large German voting block. It was also easier to notice their presence and whenever fair-minded Chicagoans cared to find out more about them, they did not need to search laboriously. The great number of Germans which the *Staatszeitung* of September 6, 1915 estimated to be some 700,000 first and second generation inhabitants left a decided imprint on Chicago.

This Teutonic imprint must have been extraordinarily pronounced, for it is still evident to the observant Chicagoan in spite of vigorous attempts to eradicate it. This occurred especially during the hysterical days of World War I, when in Ward Twenty-eight alone well over twenty streets with German names were supplied with less "offensive" ones. Likewise, names of schools which were an eyesore to "patriotic" Chicagoans received American names and thus, the former Bismarck School at 2010 North Central Park is now named General Frederick Funston School. Nevertheless, at least thirty-eight Chicago elementary schools still bear German names, such as Brennemann, Nettelhorst, and Steinmetz. Likewise, testimony of the German presence is still offered in streets named by or after Germans, such as Altgeld, de Kalb, Diversey, Germania, Goethe, Hirsch, Humboldt, Kemper, Kruger, Lehmann, Lessing, Lieb, Luther, Schiller, Schreiber, Sieben, von Steuben, Thomas, Wacker, Wieland, and Wolfram.

There are only a few of Chicago's suburbs, such as Schaumburg, Hanover Park, and Frankfort, which still show by their names that they were settled by Germans. Many of the originally German-named towns have been renamed, such as Chicago Heights, which was formerly known as New Strassburg or Elmhurst-Addison, which was named Teuto. The following is a list of Chicago area towns which were either settled or inhabited at their beginnings by Germans: Addison, Arlington Heights, Bensenville, Blue Island, Chicago Heights, Country Club Hills, Elmhurst, Flossmoor, Franklin Park, Hanover Park, Hillside, Hinsdale, Hoffman Estates, Homewood, Itasca, Libertyville, Lincolnville, Lindenhurst, Markham, Matteson, Morton Grove, Mount Prospect, Niles, North Aurora, Northbrook, Palos Hills, River Grove, Riverwoods, Sauk Village, Schaumburg, Schiller Park, Sesser, Skokie, South Chicago Heights, South Deering, Thornton, Villa Park, Westmont, Wheeling, and Winnetka.

Because it is difficult to efface the origin of monuments, commemorative plaques, or other historical markers, they retained perhaps the most massive evidence of the Teutonic imprint. After all, in order to obliterate their German nature the monuments' names would have to be changed or they would have to be destroyed. But changing the name of a monument like the Goethe statue would be absurd, and destroying it, though contemplated several times in 1918, would have been widely condemned as wanton barbarity. Thus, of all the monuments erected by the various nationalities in Chicago and vicinity, the number of German ones is the largest. In various parks, buildings and other public places, Chicagoans of German descent have dedicated monuments among others to the memories of John P. Altgeld, the "Anarchists" executed after the Haymarket "Riot," Beethoven, J.

W. Drexel, Goethe, J. Haas, Henry Horner, A. von Humboldt, Frederick Jahn, Lessing, S. Mizenberg, Fritz Reuter, Schiller, and Theodor Thomas.

Germans have been present and have helped to mold Chicago since its beginning. But it is a futile undertaking to establish the identity of the first German settler in the city or when he first arrived. The various garrison lists of Fort Dearborn usually contained a few German names. Thus, it is not surprising to find that at least three soldiers of German extraction saw action during the 1812 Massacre, namely Lieutenant Linai T. Helm and the privates John Simmons and August Mott, both of whom perished in the encounter between the soldiers of Fort Dearborn and the Indians. But the German soldiers of the Fort Dearborn garrisons and other short-term inhabitants, such as the Germans fur traders sent by John J. Astor, have played a negligible part in Chicago's development and will be excluded from consideration.

The first genuine German settlers in Chicago's immediate vicinity seemed to have come about 1825, for in that year the German H. Rothenfeld supposedly settled at Dunkley's Grove, now Addison, according to page 181 of the first volume of Pierce's *History of Chicago*. Within the city there must have been Germans by 1830. When the former Chicago Mayor "Long John" Wentworth addressed the second annual German Old Settlers' Picnic in Wright's Grove, reprinted in the *Staatszeitung* of September 6, 1876, he stated that "the first German who voted here was John van Horn whom I knew well and who was here already in 1830; the second was John Wellmacher, a baker, who made a nice profit by selling bread to the Indian settlers."

Ex-Mayor Wentworth listed fifty Germans whom he remembered as having come to Chicago by 1839. Of course, his list was not complete. It could not be since he most likely did not know all the Germans in the Chicago area. He could not have found documentary proof about their existence, for many of the early settlers left no documentary traces, or if they did, they most likely were destroyed in the Conflagration of 1871. From registration lists of the annual German Old Settlers' Picnics, which were held annually from 1875 to about 1915, from biographies, and various other accounts many names of early German settlers and their dates of arrival in Chicago may be gleaned. Since not only Americans, such as William Bross mentioned above, believed that no Germans were present in Chicago before 1840, but also historians of German background seemed to think that very few German settlers arrived in Chicago prior to 1840, the following list of German settlers in the Chicago area up to 1839 may be of interest. The dates given indicate the times when their presence in Chicago was first attested.

Amberg, Adam—1833
Asche, Wilhelm—1836
Aste, Christian—1837
Baier, Johann—1838
Baer, Lorenz—1836
Barth, Nicholas—1839
Baumgarten, Charles Peter and Moritz—1834
Baxmann, Johann—1839
Belz, John—1833
Berdell, Charles—1838
Berdell, Nicholas—1836
Berg, Anton and four brothers —1834
Best, Anna—1839
Beyer, B.A.—1836
Biermann, Christian—1836
Blasie, Bernhard—1839
Boas, Jacob—1836
Boeske, Heinrich—1834
Bohlander, Johann—1837
Bold, F.C.—1837
Bomino, P. Dr.—1837
Boos, F.—1837
Brandwell, Johann—1834
Brettmann, Johann—1839
Buchholz, Friedrich—1835
Burk, H. and M.—1837
Burke, Henry—1837
Busch, John—1839
Cachand-Ervendberg, Ludwig—1836
Cohen, Peter—1830
Diversey, Michael—1838
Dolese, John and Peter—1837
Donei, Fritz—1839
Eberhardt, A.—1833
Ebinger, Christian—1832
Ebinger, Heinrich—1834
Eitermann, Maria—1836
Ernst, Anna—1832
Escher, Jacob and Martin—1836
Falch, L.—1839
Fippinger, Michael—1837
Fischer, Diedrich—1835
Flosser, E.—1837
Forcht, J.—1837
Franzen, Hermann and three adult sons—1835
Frey, L.—1836
Frost, Georg—1837
Funk, Johann—1839
Gerber, B.—1834
German, F.—1837
Getzler, Anton—1839
Gherken, Heinrich—1836
Glasen, Johann—1839
Glos, Johann—1837
Goeden, Susan—1836
Graue, Friedrich—1834
Groll, Philipp—1839
Gross, Georg—1835
Gross, Jacob—1837
Haas, Solomon—1839
Haas, Wilhelm—1836
Harmann, William—1837
Harmer, H.—1837
Hauert, William—1837
Hettinger, A.—1839
Heymann, F.T.—1839
Hoffmann, Franz and Michael—1837
Holte, John—1838
Hondorf, John—1833
Horn, John van—1830
Horner, William—1833
Hueffmeier, Johann—1836
Huehn, Anna—1836
Huhn, Adam—1839
Jaeger, Josef—1839
Kaemper, Johann—1836
Kanizer, N.—1838
Kastler, Nikolaus—1839
Kessler, Franz—1837
Kleinhaus, Michael—1839
Klingmann, William—1835

Knopp, Adam—1837
Koehler, B.—1834
Krage, M.—1839
Krieter, Friedrich—1837
Kroeger, A. and K.—1837
Kruse, Friedrich—1838
Kuhl, J.—1837
Lampmann, Heinrich and J.—1833
Landmeyer, G.—1837
Landwehr, H.—1838
Langgut, Christian—1837
Lauer, Kaspar—1835
Lesemann, Karoline—1837
Letz, F. and J.—1838
Lobbeke, Friedrich—1832
Ludwig, Agnes—1835
Maas, Hubert—1839
Maerker, Wilhelm—1838
Mahler, J.F.—1838
Malzacher, M. and L.—1833
Mann, John—1833
Marbach, Joseph—1839
Marschall, Rosanna—1837
Mattern, Friedrich—1837
Mayer, Leo—1834
Meiners, Gerhard—1838
Merker, Heinrich—1836
Metz, Christian—1839
Meyer, Johann—1836
Meyer, Mathias—1831
Miguly, Rudolph—1839
Millemann, Jacob—1838
Miller, Josef—1835
Mueller, Jacob—1836
Mueller, Mathias—1838
Neudorf, Nikolaus—1839
Oberhart, A.—1837
Ott, Jacob—1837
Panakaske, A.—1837
Paul, John—1839
Periolat, Clemens—1837
Perrior, William—1839
Petrie, Philipp—1839
Pfeiffer, Casper—1839
Pfund, John—1838
Plagge, Wilhelm—1838
Plank, Johann—1832
Raber, John—1834
Raber, Philipp—1835
Rantze, Hermann—1836
Rehm, Johann—1836
Reis, Peter and N.—1839
Roth, J.—1839
Rothenfeld, Heinrich—1825
Russer, Georg—1836
Sauter, Charles and J.—1834
Sauter, Vincent—1839
Schaefer, L.—1836
Schall, Andreas—1839
Schaller, A.—1839
Schanck, L.G.—1839
Schmidt, Johann H.—1835
Schmidt, L.M.—1839
Schnaebele, Jacob—1835
Schneider, J.—1832
Schneitmann, L.—1835
Schuck, Henry—1839
Schuettler, Peter—1839
Schumacher, Joseph—1839
Speer, Charles—1839
Spohrer, K.—1833
Spoor, A.—1837
Spring, G.—1833
Stanger, D. and Ch.—1835
Steidle, Martin—1837
Stofer, J.—1837
Stose, Clemens—1833
Straussel, Martin—1839
Streicher, J.A.—1839
Strubler, Georg—1837
Stuenkel, Friedrich—1836
Sulzer, Konrad—1836
Sunderlage, Johann—1838
Suther, H.—1836
Tholser, A.—1837
Thuernau, Friedrich—1836
Trautmann, Philipp—1836
Uthe, Christoph—1838
Vaughan, Daniel—1834
Vogt, John—1839
Weber, John—1836
Weckler, John—1836
Wellmacher, John—1830
Wessling, Hermann—1838

Wiesenkraft, Charles—1833
Will, Philipp—1837
Wilmers, John—1838
Winkler, F.—1839
Wode, John—1833
Wolfinger, Th.—1837
Zalle, H.—1837
Zoliski, J.—1837

It must be pointed out that the individual names mentioned in the list above usually represent the presence of additional Germans. According to the Teuto Community Churchbook, kept by Ludwig Cachand-Ervendberg at Addison in 1838, the filial community of Lake View in Chicago was represented by nineteen households which constituted 67 souls. The family of Wilhelm Haas counted eight persons; that of Hermann Rantze and Konrad Sulzer each had six persons; and the household of Johann Hueffmeier, John Wilmers, and Philipp Trautmann numbered five members each.

Generally speaking, little is known about these early German settlers in Chicago. The "Deutsch-Amerikanische Gesellschaft von Illinois," a society of local historians of German descent, which flourished from 1900 to about 1936, tried to gather information about early German settlers. However, their harvest was meager, though they did gather some information about such men as Charles Sauter, the first German alderman of Chicago, elected in 1839, and Matthias Meyer, whom they considered to be the first German settler in Chicago. The secretary of the society, Emil Mannhardt, in the article, "The Oldest German Settlers in Illinois" in the January 1901 issue of *Deutsch-Amerikanische Geschichtsblätter*, asserted that Meyer was the first and only German in Chicago in 1832. Matthias Meyer was born in the vicinity of Frankfurt on the Main at an undetermined date. In 1825 he emigrated from Germany and came to Baltimore where he worked as a mechanic until the spring of 1831, when he came to Chicago to open a bakery. He died in 1856, leaving six children.

Actually, several other Germans preceded Meyer as settlers in Chicago, as may be seen in the list above. Johann Wellmacher and Peter Cohen came to Chicago as early as 1830. Wellmacher, born in Frankfurt on the Main, came as a seventeen-year-old youth to Pennsylvania, from whence he went to Galena, Illinois, to work in the lead mines. After he came to Chicago in 1830, he worked first at the Fort Dearborn bakery and then opened his own bakery under the name of Wellmaker and Co. He died a pauper in Joliet. Cohen came shortly after Wellmacher from Alsace. In the first issue of Calhoun's *Chicago Democrat* on November 26, 1833, he announced a sale of "winter clothing, provisions, groceries, and liquors" at reduced prices. He allegedly commited suicide in New Orleans around 1856.

At the second annual German Old Settlers' Picnic in September of 1876, a great number of early German settlers convened. They were listed according to the year of their arrival up to 1856 by the *Staatszeitung* of September 6, 1876 as follows:

1833— 3	1839— 8	1845— 17	1851— 39
1834— 5	1840— 12	1846— 51	1852— 71
1835— 3	1841— 5	1847— 46	1853— 60
1836— 9	1842— 16	1848— 40	1854—109
1837— 7	1843— 13	1849— 30	1855— 41
1838— 2	1844— 16	1850— 32	1856— 24
			Total—659

While this list shows that many early German settlers were still living by 1876, it does not show how many Germans were actually present in Chicago at any particular year.

The numerical presence of Germans in Chicago has frequently been misinterpreted. For instance, in a series of articles on recent immigrants to Chicago, the *Daily News* of October 21, 1974 asserted that "more newcomers came here from Poland than from any other country." This statement is true only for the times of immigration after World War I when the climax of German immigration had passed. In the overall picture, far more Germans than any other nationals have come to Chicago. This may be substantiated with figures from the federal and school censuses. As a means of comparison, the city's total population, as well as the number of Irish and Polish, are given whenever available:

Year	1843	1844	1850	1860	1870
Total Population	7,580	10,280	28,269	109,206	298,977
German	816	1,056	5,073	22,230	59,299
Irish	773	972	6,096	19,889	39,988
Polish				109	1,205

Year	1880	1890	1900	1904
Total Population	503,298	1,099,850	1,698,575	1,990,750
German	75,205	161,039	170,738	202,091
Irish	43,631	70,028	73,908	96,152
Polish	5,453	24,086	57,713	56,839

Year	1910	1914	1920	1930
Total Population	2,185,283	2,437,526	2,701,705	3,376,438
German	181,987	191,168	112,228	111,366
Irish	65,922	68,305	56,786	47,385
Polish		124,543	137,611	149,622

Year	1940	1950	1960	1970
Total Population	3,396,808	3,620,962	3,550,404	
German	83,424	56,635	70,153	31,430
Irish	35,156	29,804		13,766
Polish	119,264	94,009	70,894	55,711

These figures cannot be viewed as absolute values. As a result of Europe's ever changing political boundaries it happened that Europeans in the border regions east or west of Germany sometimes registered as Polish but at another time as German or at one time as German but later again as French. The 816 Germans listed for 1843 included also an indeterminable number of Scandinavians.

In order to give a more reliable picture, these statistics need to be interpreted. All nationalities listed above are foreign-born only. If second generation nationalities were included, that is children born to foreigners in Chicago, one could see that the German stock was predominant for several years in the nineteenth century. The *Chicago Arbeiterzeitung* of August 30, 1884, in the article, "A Large German City in America," pointed out that 209,631 Germans were in Chicago compared to only 143,000 "Americans" and 114,005 Irish. The *Abendpost* of April 22, 1892, cited statistics comparing Chicago's German stock of 1890 to other nationalities as follows: Germans—394,958, Americans—292,403, Irish—215,535 and Poles—52,756. The Chicago school census of 1898 still shows the Germans in the lead with 490,542 followed by 488,683 Americans, 248,142 Irish, and 96,853 Poles. But by 1909 the Germans had lost their lead in numerical representation, according to the estimate by the city statistician published in the *Daily News Almanac* for 1910 on page 509. Chicago's Americans constituted 699,554 inhabitants, followed by 563,708 Germans, 240,560 Irish and 173,409 Poles.

The enormous number of Germans present in Chicago can also be seen in the number of offspring born to them. The *Staatszeitung* of March 11, 1878 listed the number of births for the year 1877 according to nationalities of parents as follows: the total number of births were 11,152, of which the parentage was 4,518 German, 1,878 American, 1,625 Irish, and 234 Polish. The *Abendpost* of April 22, 1892 reported that of 23,021 births during 1891 in Chicago, 6,548 or twenty-eight percent were of German parentage, whereas 1,391 were of Irish, and 1,446 were of Polish parentage. The large number of German births caused the paper to state that "if the increase of our population is keeping up in the indicated proportions, Chicago twenty-five years from now will be predominantly German." Ironically, twenty-five years later, in the year of

1917, instead of thriving, the German element of Chicago was reeling under the effects of World War I. The prevailing anti-German sentiment caused many Germans to deny their background. This is reflected in the fact that within the six years from 1914 to 1920 the official number of foreign-born Germans dropped precipitously from 191,000 to 112,000.

The early as well as numerous presence of the German element was responsible for some German firsts in Chicago's history. This includes trivia, such as Chicago's first divorce in May of 1834 between Daniel and Angelina Vaughan, nee Hebert; the first street-car conductor, Adolph Mueller, who came in 1852 from Germany; and the first perfect bowling game with twelve straight strikes by Louis F. Ullrich, as reported in the *Staatszeitung* of January 5, 1899. However, the German element was also responsible for other, more significant firsts, as the following selected examples will show. The first police officer to die in the line of duty on September 18, 1854 was Kaspar Lauer, who had come from Germany about 1835. Some of the trades or professions practiced for the first time by Germans were as follows: first "iron manufacturer"—Clemens Stose in 1833, first brewers—William Haas and Konrad Sulzer in 1836, first brickmaker—Heinrich Lampmann in 1833, first professional musician—Nicholas Berdell in 1836, first grave digger—Heinrich Gherken, "Dutch Henry," about 1836, and first cafe proprietor—Frederick Burky in 1860. Probably the first rental library in Chicago was owned and managed by the German Edward Buehler on 111 Monroe Street, who placed a notice in the *Staatszeitung* of September 30, 1867, offering to rent illustrated periodicals and books on mechanics which were not to be had on the local market. Georg Schneider, the editor of the *Staatszeitung*, published Chicago's first Sunday newspaper, *Der Westen*, in 1854. The first "Linde ice machine" was brought to Chicago by F.W. Wolf in 1868, according to page 68 of the third volume of Andreas' *History of Chicago*. The first regular free Sunday concerts, not only in Chicago, but in the United States, were initiated by a group of German musicians in 1875. The Poor Handmaids of Christ, who had come from their mother house of Dernbach, Germany in 1875, opened Chicago's first day nursery in 1879. Among the firsts in the medical field, Dr. Christian Fenger, a veteran from the Franco-Prussian War of 1870-71, first introduced antiseptic surgery in Chicago at the Cook County Hospital and Dr. Otto L. Schmidt introduced the first X-Ray machine about 1893.

Chapter 2

Coming to Chicago – The Price Paid

A survey of the official immigration statistics reveals that the German immigration to the United States of America constitutes a total number considerably larger than that of any other foreign element. According to the 1972 *Annual Report* of the U.S. Immigration and Naturalization Service, by June 30, 1971 a total of 45,533,116 immigrants have entered the United States since their number and nationalities were officially recorded for the first time in 1820. Of this number 35,630,398 or 78.2 percent came from Europe. But of the European nations Germany holds first place in the number of emigrants, having sent 6,925,736 people. This number amounts to 15.25 percent of the total immigration to America. Then following in rank are Italy with 5,199,304, Great Britain with 4,804,520, Ireland with 4,715,041 and Austria-Hungary with 4,304,302 emigrants. The low numbers of 7,760 and 7,565 German emigrants to the United States recorded for 1972 and 1973 respectively stand in conspicuous contrast to the enormous mass of German immigrants in their heyday, the 1880's, when 250,630 people came in the single year 1882. This large number of immigrants for one year was surpassed a few times by three different nations in the twentieth century, namely by Austria-Hungary, Russia, and Italy, which had their respective record years of 338,452 in 1907, 291,040 in 1913, and 285,731 in 1907. In the nineteenth century only Ireland's 221,253 emigrants to America in 1851 came close to Germany's record number of 1882.

German and Irish immigrants constitute the major foreign element in the nineteenth century influx to America, but in comparison to Ireland, Germany had a rather slow start, sending only 7,729 people between 1820 and 1830, in contrast to Ireland's 54,338 for the same period. The 57,561 German immigrants registered for 1846 surpassed for the first time in history Ireland's number which amounted for that year to 51,752. However, Ireland did not relinquish its lead in the total number of immigrants until 1872 when a total of 2,557,607 German and 2,518,506 Irish immigrants were recorded for the period since 1820.

The total German immigration since 1820 by decades is as follows:

Period	Number of German immigrants to America
1820-30	7,729
1831-40	152,454
1841-50	434,626
1851-60	951,667
1861-70	787,468
1871-80	718,182
1881-90	1,452,970
1891-1900	505,152
1901-10	341,498
1911-20	143,945
1921-30	412,202
1931-40	114,058
1941-50	226,578
1951-60	477,765
1961-73	214,767
Total 1820-1973	6,941,061

From this chart it is obvious that the major influx of German immigrants occurred approximately between 1850 and 1900. In the nineteenth century no other nation comes even close to matching Germany's record decade 1881-90, amounting to 1,452,970. Ireland's 914,119 immigrants from 1851 to 1860 and Great Britain's 807,357 immigrants from 1881 to 1890 stand in second and third place, respectively. Only in the first decade of the twentieth century, when a total of 8,795,386 immigrants entered the United States, was this number surpassed by Austria-Hungary with 2,145,266, by Italy with 2,045,877, and by Russia with 1,597,306.

Until the end of the nineteenth century an open door policy existed with regard to European immigration. But persistent complaints by various groups and individuals about undesirable immigrants brought about the passage of the 1891 Act, which was to elevate the quality of immigrants by excluding criminals and obviously diseased individuals. Later rulings concerning moral and ideological traits of immigrants further delineated the acceptable immigrant. However, no official attempts were made to curb the quantitative influx of the European immigration until after World War I, even though the immigrants often served as convenient scapegoats for the diverse crises in the United States. Beginning with the 1921 Act, various numerical ceilings were placed upon immigration. Each country's quota was to be three percent of the nationalities present at the time of the 1910 census of population, which granted Germany 68,059 annual immigrants.

Dissatisfaction from various quarters with the 1921 Act brought about several complicated changes which reduced Germany's yearly number of immigrants to 51,227 in 1924, to 25,957 in 1929, and finally to 25,814 in 1952. After July 1, 1968 a ceiling of 120,000 was set for the Western Hemisphere natives on a first come first serve basis with no limitation on the number from any one country. Even though the immigration authorities interpreted the quota system rather loosely, at times admitting over 100,000 annual immigrants from Germany, as in 1950 and 1952, on the whole the quantitative and qualitative restriction on immigration throttled the influx of persons from abroad, and with it German immigration.

Chicago received a large share of the total German immigration, but for a variety of reasons it is impossible to ascertain the exact number. No adequate comprehensive records concerning the destination of German immigrants exist for the nineteenth century, when German immigration was at its peak. In addition to that, all immigrants were lumped together and the places of destination were listed only by states. For instance, we know that from 1855 to 1869 213,315 immigrants arriving at Castle Garden in New York listed Illinois as their destination, but we do not know how many of them were Germans or how many went to Chicago. Even when immigrants indicated their place of destination upon landing at the seaports, it meant little, since they often had no serious commitment to settle at the registered destination. The federal census and the Chicago school census reports show that the number of foreign born Germans in Chicago steadily increased from 5,073 in 1850 to 191,168 in 1914, but besides these figures few exact numbers are available.

The German Aid Society of Chicago, which was founded in 1853 to protect immigrants from exploitation, listed the number of German immigrants receiving aid. According to their publications in contemporary newspapers, they aided 1,757 German immigrants from April to September 1861 and helped 402 immigrants in October and November of the same year. In April and May of 1862, 498 German immigrants received help. In August 1867, 725 immigrants were aided by the society. The following chart for 1872 to 1931, based on the society's annual publications, shows how many families, children, and single persons received help, how much money was expended, and how many persons secured employment through the German Aid Society:

Year	Families	Children	Single persons	Amount of aid	Employment secured for
1872	648	1,620	580	$ 3,075.50	
1873	1,210	3,025	1,400	5,750.10	
1874	825	2,450	920	4,427.25	
1875	590	1,475	875	2,930.40	
1876	784	1,868	950	4,000.75	
1877	675	1,730	790	3,500.47	
1878	268	670	208	1,125.64	
1879	460	1,150	376	2,500.35	
1880	510	1,275	410	2,643.80	
1881	370	930	290	2,000.56	
1882	385	960	245	2,125.18	
1883	360	915	210	2,015.36	
1884	290	725	180	1,600.72	
1885	241	619	152	1,417.38	2,354
1886	148	416	167	806.65	2,599
1887	240	673	221	1,409.78	2,530
1888	267	691	189	1,560.91	2,249
1889	225	618	206	1,318.09	2,258
1890	371	981	254	2,160.08	3,097
1891	445	1,162	202	2,008.77	3,169
1892	450	1,287	177	2,754.43	3,353
1893	555	1,653	266	3,360.96	2,577
1894	1,173	3,545	571	5,442.75	1,620
1895	538	1,725	322	3,066.59	2,390
1896	471	1,447	301	2,833.54	2,606
1897	727	2,917	543	4,056.06	2,063
1898	908	2,376	568	4,793.38	3,188
1899	888	2,560	540	5,011.72	3,850
1900	748	2,284	457	4,158.40	3,477
1901	596	1,609	354	3,525.92	3,004
1902	582	1,647	488	4,060.44	3,694
1903	653	1,791	692	4,302.59	3,680
1904	753	2,045	873	4,349.05	3,069
1905	733	1,597	996	4,559.18	3,250
1906	762	1,937	653	4,362.96	3,642
1907	722	1,841	876	4,818.18	4,860
1908	1,462	3,809	1,443	7,663.29	3,858

(Table continued)

Year	Families	Children	Single persons	Amount of aid	Employment secured for
1909	1,128	3,137	1,006	5,837.13	5,134
1910	1,049	3,060	2,750	4,721.39	5,903
1911	894	2,488	4,139	5,238.48	5,143
1912	824	2,233	5,494	6,758.75	6,192
1913	673	1,834	3,045	6,229.21	4,749
1914	1,078	3,022	6,587	10,339.10	3,442
1915	1,250	3,234	7,982	13,015.38	3,527
1916	1,214	3,305	3,850	11,237.09	5,765
1917	913	2,791	697	9,809.06	4,598
1918	813	2,796	479	8,920.94	1,838
1919	716	2,666	544	8,318.19	1,918
1920	651	2,672	344	10,083.23	1,257
1921	776	2,973	373	10,403.97	1,228
1922	654	2,376	338	8,788.05	1,549
1923	603	2,204	226	8,440.93	1,574
1924	638	2,282	233	8,786.18	1,668
1925	627	2,161	256	8,524.33	1,714
1926	640	2,119	258	8,588.45	1,517
1927	801	2,776	305	10,689.17	1,206
1928	805	2,718	244	11,391.92	1,372
1929	613	1,843	225	8,444.51	1,327
1930	581	1,613	199	7,576.02	911
1931	862	2,081	178	10,384.13	874
	40,936	118,407	58,702	$321,992.78	136,843

Since not all German immigrants availed themselves of the German Aid Society's services, and since this society became a general charity organization after the Great Fire of 1871, their lists attest to the large number of Germans present in Chicago, but cannot serve as an index for German immigration to the Garden City.

The German newspapers of Chicago, especially after 1880, sporadically informed their readers about the German influx from abroad. One can read in the *Staatszeitung* of April 22, 1881, that from noon of April 19 to noon of April 20, 1881, 6,839 immigrants landed at Castle Garden in New York, seventy-five percent of whom were German. The newspaper ventured to guess that many of these Germans would come to Chicago. The *Arbeiterzeitung* of March 4 and June 3, 1882, assessed the total number of German immigrants coming to Chicago between January and May 1882, at over 104,350. The individual months were listed as follows: January—7,200, February—10,450, March—16,700, April—20,000, May—over 50,000. The *Arbeiterzeitung* further stated that only about one percent of the Germans remained in Chicago. On April 6, 1883 the same newspaper reported that in 1882, 712,542 immigrants, or 90.3 percent of the total U.S. immigration for that year came to Chicago. Of these, 229,986 were Germans, amounting to 91.8 percent of the total German immigration for 1882. The *Arbeiterzeitung* did not estimate how many of these German immigrants made Chicago their home, but did say that 226,000 total immigrants remained in Chicago permanently. Most of the Germans went on to the Western States. The *Staatszeitung* of December 8, 1891 reported that it was impossible to ascertain how many of the 33,000 German immigrants arriving in Chicago during 1891 stayed in this city.

In recent years the U.S. Immigration and Naturalization Service lists in its annual reports, in Table 12A, the destination of immigrants. These statistics make it obvious that Chicago and its metropolitan area attracts many Germans. Though the percentages vary somewhat from year to year, the following statistics for 1973 may still give a representative view:

Total German immigration to U.S.	7,565
" to Illinois	310
" " towns 2,500-99,999	198
" to Chicago	109
" to Peoria	1
" to Rockford	2

The Illinois towns between 2,500 and 99,999 inhabitants to which 198 Germans immigrated during 1973 must have included many Chicago suburbs.

In view of the veritable "Völkerwanderung" of Germans to the United States, especially during the years 1850 to 1890, one is led to ask about the compelling reasons that induced nearly seven million Germans to leave their homeland or, as nativistic opponents to immigration said, "to sell their birthright for a mess of pottage?" In particular, why did so many of them settle in Chicago?

One reason which is sometimes mentioned with regard to German immigration is the legendary "Wanderlust" of the German people. It is difficult to determine whether this innate desire for adventure impelled any people to come to the Garden City. Undoubtedly this romantic yearning for strange lands was present in a number of German immigrants, but Germans are known to be too levelheaded to make it even seem probable that such a vague feeling would be the sole determining factor for such a farreaching decision as emigration. In any case, little evidence could be found to support the "Wanderlust" factor, but there were other, more tangible causes for the immigration of Germans.

The reasons for immigration vary somewhat through time, but basic existential factors, such as overpopulation, unemployment, high taxes, and long, obligatory military service, have been by far the most important ones. The *Abendpost* of August 7, 1932 expressed this as follows: "Those immigrants whose alleged preference for America is the result of political and religious suppression constitute a mere minority. The majority come in quest of better opportunities for a livelihood." To the prospective nineteenth century German immigrant the United States proffered exceedingly compelling attractions, such as light taxes, cheap lands, the need for laborers and craftsmen, and, finally, the opportunity to attain a comfortable existence within a bearably short time.

These attractions were reinforced by glowing reports in articles and books about the New World which accentuated even more the poverty and want in the old fatherland. One of the most widely read, favorable reports about the Midwest appearing in book form in Germany was Gottfried Duden's *Report on a Trip to the Western States of North America*, which appeared in numerous editions after 1829. It was a mixture of fact and fiction written in an appealing style. Many German readers were absorbed with Duden's account of what must have seemed to most of them a paradise compared to their grim reality. It continued to have a great effect in swaying prospective emigrants to break with the past in spite of Duden's numerous critics who pointed out that he generously interwove his imagination into experience and that reality in the Midwest did not correspond to Duden's idealistic portrayal.

Many other more or less reliable *Emigrant Guides* were published during the nineteenth century for a German audience, such as Traugott Bromme's *Missouri and Illinois—A Handbook for Immigrants . . .* (Baltimore, 1835). Often these guides were written primarily for the financial benefit of the author, but some such publications seemed to have the sole intention of serving the immigrant by giving a balanced picture of the immigrant's prospects in America. One of these guides, published in Chicago in 1887 under the sponsorship of the German Aid Society, was Adolph Armack's and Charles Folz' *Nützliches und Belehrendes für deutsche Einwanderer nach den Vereinigten Staaten.* This forty-seven page pamphlet tersely and soberly informed the prospective immigrant by means of statistics of all that he needed to know about Chicago and the Midwest. Practical hints on how to best arrange the voyage, what to take along, and how to avoid being exploited are included. Conversion tables for measurements, weights, and money, as well as a list of the German Aid Society's services were intended to help the immigrant adjust during the first few weeks after his arrival.

Another important factor which induced innumerable people to emigrate were enthusiastic "America letters" by those who had ventured out first and succeeded. Often a positive account of a close relative or friend from the same town induced less courageous souls to emigrate also, especially since they knew that they could rely on the help of the earlier emigrants. Many letters praising the blessings of the New World must have been sent by Chicago Germans to the Old World, but few of them are extant, and it is a rare occasion indeed if one of them finds its way back to Chicago. The Chicago Historical Society is fortunate to possess such a letter, the more so, since it is an exceedingly informative one. This letter was written on December 28, 1856 by Jacob Gross to his brothers and sisters in Kadelburg, a small village close to the Swiss border directly north of Zürich. Jacob Gross, his wife, four teenage sons, and three daughters left their native town Kadelburg on June 5, 1855 and arrived in Chicago on October 14 of the same year. Presumably a brother by the name of Henry Gross had induced the Gross family to come to Chicago, establishing them at a place on North Wood Street near West Chicago Avenue. The Gross family found life in Chicago to their liking, as the following excerpts from the letter shows, taken from a reprint in the 1956 Winter issue of *Chicago History:*

> As to our present circumstances, we can truthfully say that they are good. In the summer we must pay $6.00, in the winter $4.00 for rent, but we have one and one-half quarter acres of land around the house. And besides raising vegetables for our own use, we sold $18.00 worth. We sold radishes for 10 to 12 cents and also early and late cabbage; a head of lettuce for 5 to 6 cents—much depends upon the kind—and German vegetable seeds are preferred. Potatoes always are dear—last spring they cost 10 to 12 shillings; and in the fall 4 shillings a bushel (about 3 sester). Green beans $1.00 a bushel. But not nearly so many vegetables are used here in this country. The war with Russia caused us to have expensive bread last year. A barrel of flour, 196 lbs., cost $9 to $10, and this year $6.
>
> As to our employment: I and Theodor make wood in the city.... Last summer we made hay on the prairies—a very good business to make money. Theodor wanted to learn a trade, but I could not spare him. Leopold is learning plastering and whitewashing and gets 10 shillings or 3 gulden a day, but without board. Otto is learning the butcher trade and gets 12 dollars a month and board—he is strong and has grown large. Jacob goes to school and on the side helps to

slaughter and earns 2 to 3 shillings a day and enough meat for our own use. Elise also visits the school when it is not too cold. Elizabeth was in a hotel until this fall and earned 12 shillings a week, but this winter she is at home learning to sew and iron so that she will be ready to take an English position in the spring. Marie and the wife do washing in the town—mostly for Kadelburgers. We all work and have good incomes, but also plenty of expenses.

It will take us awhile to be able to have again the many things that we gave away in Germany. Every beginning is hard. But we never have had to battle with Want and Hunger, and if the Good Lord lets us keep our health, we have good prospects. We now have 1 cow, 5 sheep, and 2 hogs. We feed the hogs with entrails and lungs from the slaughter house. When the snow is gone we let the cow and sheep run on the prairie—they come home again at night. Not once have we wished to be back; we are satisfied. But we do wish that all Kadelburgers had it as good as we. What we earn is ours. When we have paid $1.50, then our obligations are discharged. When we asked Marie whether she would like to go back home again, she answered: "no sir-ee—I have more meat than at home." She is very plump. The Kadelburgers visit us quite often. Not long ago Alexander came, too, to say farewell. He has gone to Iowa, perhaps to buy land; his business is doing well. Brother Wilhelm is quite successful now; in the fall he was not well for awhile. Also, things are better for Heinrich, in spite of the fact that he had quite a loss. Last summer all of his tools—worth about $120.00—were destroyed in a fire. He had work all winter at 14 shillings a day. He is well thought of and is secretary of his lodge . . . I so much wish, dear Brother, that I might have you here with me if only for eight days, in order to let you see the trading and selling in the town, for Chicago is the largest trading city in the world. There is such life and urge that one's life is in danger when one crosses the street! Besides eight railroads, there are 37 branch roads in the town, where daily over 200 trains go back and forth. Also, the biggest fruit and lumber trade in the world (for boards lie in the town and in the outskirts which would reach in the Kadelburg field from the village to Hamburg, house high! One can hardly realize it.) More than 300 ships wintered in the harbor. The city is growing so rapidly that an average of 3,000 houses are built yearly. Also, last summer a German Hall was built (on shares), which is four stories high and is to be used for a theater, singing and reading clubs, and school purposes.

Even though the city has more conveniences, we like it better in the outskirts. It is more healthful. We have good water from a well from which we draw up the water out of a pump worked by a crank —so easy every child can do it. Next spring, five acres of land next to us will be for rent. If possible, we shall want to rent it . . . One word in conclusion, I have often thought it over and sympathize with the many girls at home who have the money for the trip yet who stay there under such hard conditions. Now here, a woman who is the wife of only a tradesman has it better than the richest farmer's wife at home. She does nothing but the housework. Mornings and evenings the husband carries in the wood and water and other necessities. Sundays they go walking, and if they have little children, the man carries them and the woman walks *beside* him.

I shall conclude. Up to the present time we are enjoying the best of health, and hope that you are too. Wife and children all charge me with heartiest greetings for you. Each is expecting an early reply.

You are greeted by a sincere friend and brother,

Jacob Gross
Theodor Gross

(I wrote but Father dictated to my pen.)

Who can should do as I—
I marched away to the ocean's shore—
I trusted myself to the waves,
Not yet was my spirit broken,
Nor yet lay I in hateful chains,
Strength remained to save myself.
America welcomes me!
I shall stay in the faraway land.

Jacob Gross in Chicago,
State of Illinois
North America

Included with this letter was a print by Braunhold & Sonne, showing bustling "Chicago from the Lake." It is obvious that Gross tried to convey the idea that he did not make a mistake in coming to Chicago and that he would be happy to have his relatives come also. It is interesting to note that there must have been a colony of Kadelburg people in Chicago, which included relatives of Jacob Gross. Undoubtedly, letters such as this attracted additional German immigrants.

Immigration agents in America and in Germany hired by various companies or organizations also stimultated the general exodus to the New World. Ship and railroad companies had huge financial stakes in immigration and their commissioned agents were not overly scrupulous in their efforts to keep boats and trains filled with immigrants. Chicago bankers, real estate developers, and transportation companies collaborated to bring German immigrants to the Midwest. Already in 1848 promoters like the banker R. K. Swift and the real estate agents, Rees and Kerfoot, unsuccessfully tried to induce the Chicago City Council to buy 5,000 German and 5,000 English copies of a pamphlet entitled, "Railroads, History, and Commerce of Chicago," destined for distribution to prospective European emigrants. In the 1850's and 1860's Chicago bankers, such as Elias and Henry Greenebaum, and the firm of Hoffmann & Gelpke, distributed similar pamphlets for the purpose of attracting German immigrants. Elias (1822-1919) and Henry Greenebaum (b. 1833), who had come from Eppelsheim to Chicago in 1847 and 1848, respectively, set up a European Passage Department which brought thousands of German immigrants to Chicago and other places in America from the embarkation ports of Bremen, Hamburg, Le Havre, and Liverpool.

Innumerable German immigrants were brought to Chicago and Illinois by the real estate developer, Francis A. Hoffmann (1822-1903). In 1862 he was asked by the Illinois Central Railroad to colonize the area between Mattoon and Effingham, and parts of Marion, Washington, and Clinton Counties with German settlers. German place names of towns in those areas, such as Sigel, Teutopolis or Germantown, and Augsburg attest to his phenomenal success. A small town in Clinton County on Route 161 perpetuates his name as well as Hoffman Estates, northwest of Chicago.

It should also be mentioned that Chicago real estate developers for towns in the vicinity of Chicago attempted to attract German immigrants. The enterprising S. E. Gross, who owned Chicago's biggest real estate business at the turn of the century, employing some 185 salesmen, serves as a good example. Sixteen towns or localities were founded or developed by him, among them Humboldt Park, Dauphin Park, and Grossdale, now Brookfield. He sold mostly to Germans, accomodating them in every conceivable way, even transporting them in special trains, which were complete with their own bands, to certain subdivisions. The attractive German-English real estate advertisements in which Gross offered trim houses in his developments at reasonable terms of purchase attracted many German immigrants, whose ambition it was to own their own homes.

Other colonization projects undertaken by German groups or individuals in Chicago were also successful, such as New Ulm in Minnesota, which was founded in the 1850's by German workers and "Turners" of Chicago, or Brandsville in Howell County, Missouri, which was settled in 1895 by the Chicago German brewer Michael Brand (1826-97), who owned over 16,000 acres there. It is impossible to determine how many German immigrants destined for some of the above mentioned colonies remained permanently in Chicago, but their number must have been great. Many a newcomer waiting for a connecting train to his destination may have been enticed to stay in bustling Chicago rather than to venture into some unknown, lonely wilderness, especially when during his stopover compatriots offered companionship and comfort. Such was the case with William Rauen, who as former president of the North Avenue Business and Improvement Association, was interviewed by the *Chicago Tribune* on April 6, 1930. Rauen came to Chicago in 1882 with six other compatriots from Germany intending to go to New Ulm, Minnesota. When he was unexpectedly delayed by a "runner," he became immersed in a German settlement in Chicago. The familiar language and customs and sympathetic people dispelled his homesickness, prompting him to stay in Chicago, where he found, within five years, a rather comfortable existence.

Chicago, the flowering city on Lake Michigan, attracted many a German immigrant who hoped to find El Dorado. Its enormous growth provided many well-paying jobs to people of varying skills and professions. After 1836 the building of the canal attracted thousands of Germans along with the Irish. It was antiquated by the time it was finished and many railroad lines, the new arteries for faster transportation of passengers and cargo, needed to be built. Chicago, as the biggest railroad center in the New World, continued to provide well-paying jobs. New buildings needed to be erected, the city was to be rebuilt after the Great Fire of 1871, the stock yards provided jobs, new industries invited workers, and two well-published world fairs, in 1893 and 1933, attracted numerous Germans. Even after World War II thousands of Germans poured into the Chicago area in quest of a better economic future.

On the whole it may be said that the Ciceronian saying "patria est, ubicumque est bene" very much applied to the mass of the German immigrants. So much so that they often were exhorted by the Chicago German press to concern themselves more with cultural and political issues and less with culinary and potatory interests. However, there were other reasons for German immigration which deserve mentioning, because they brought a group of Germans who, though small in number, exerted a profound influence. They were political exiles from the different political regimes in Germany.

Approximately between 1815 and 1860 a rather small number of Germans arrived in America who were of signal importance to the understanding of the German element's role throughout the ninetheenth century. These political exiles, on the whole, were highly intelligent, well-educated people who became spirited leaders in various fields. This group included the so-called "Latin farmers" who, disillusioned with corrupt society, settled on Missouri and southern Illinois farms in an effort to go "back to nature." But since they knew more about Circe's guiles than about feeding hogs, and preferred reading Ovid to hauling manure, they invariably failed as toilers of the fields and returned to cities like Chicago that were more amenable to their intellectual pursuits.

After the Napoleonic yoke had been thrown off, a new spirit of reform and democracy pervaded Germany's young men, but their fraternities, through which they tried to exert a liberalizing effect upon the autocrats of the diverse German states and principalities, were crushed in ruthless persecutions after the example set by Prince Metternich, especially during the years 1817 and 1818. This relentless suppression of a free spirit motivated idealistic men to flee to America, some to dream about the eventual unification of Germany under a republican government, others to richly repay America's hospitality.

One of them was the eminent publicist Francis Lieber (1800-72), who sought political exile in America after having tried his luck in several European nations. Lieber was gravely wounded while he was serving under Field Marshal von Blücher at Namur in 1815. Shortly after, he was arrested for having composed several songs about freedom, and after several months of imprisonment he was forbidden to pursue his studies at Prussian universities. In 1827 he came to Boston, where he edited the *Encyclopaedia Americana* for five years. Among his outstanding works, perhaps the best known is *Code of War for the Government of the Armies of the United States in the Field*, which he prepared upon the request of President Lincoln.

Chicago at that time was too insignificant to attract men like Lieber or such outstanding educators as Carl Beck and Carl Follen, who came on the same boat in 1824 and started at Harvard University to introduce the German university system in the United States. The smoldering political unrest in Germany and the sporaic overt reactions in the 1830's brought scores of Germans to Illinois, where most of them first settled in St. Clair County on the Mississippi. There Gustav Koerner, who was to become immensely influential in Illinois and national politics, established himself in the County seat of Belleville after 1833.

But some political refugees began to notice the budding city on Lake Michigan and decided to settle in Chicago. Francis A. Hoffmann (1822-1903), who in spite of his youthful age was a political fugitive, came early in 1840 to Chicago to work in a hotel and a printing shop before he was offered a teaching job at the German

Protestant community in Dunkley's Grove, which is now called Addison. He led a variegated and phenomenally successful public life which saw him as a teacher, journalist, preacher, lawyer, real estate developer, banker, immigration agent, alderman, soldier, lieutenant governor of Illinois under Governor Yates from 1861 to 1865, American consul at Frankfurt and, finally, after 1873, as farmer and author in Wisconsin.

In the wake of the unsuccessful Revolution of 1848, innumerable outstanding men came to the New World with the first high tide of German immigration that brought 502,873 Germans between 1852 and 1854. The most famous of these exiles, popularly known as the "forty-eighters," was Carl Schurz, who came in 1852 to the United States to start a spiraling career as a public servant which culminated as Secretary of the Interior from 1877 to 1881 under President Hayes. On one of his numerous visits to Chicago, he described, in a letter of September 30, 1854 to his wife, his nocturnal experiences there in an apparently humerous vein. His narration offers a rare portrayal of early Chicago and a poignant expression of the immigrant's plight suspended between two nations. It is here reprinted from the winter 1966 issue of *Chicago History*, pages forty-seven to fifty:

> It was nearly midnight when we reached Michigan City [by train], and after two o'clock when we arrived in Chicago. Here my misfortunes began. I was taken to a hotel, but there was not a room or bed to be had. In vain I drove to a second and a third; everything full. By this time the omnibus which carried me had reached its terminus and I had to get out. The hour was now past three o'clock in the morning; yet dead tired as I was, I had to seek in a strange city, and afoot, some place where I might lay my head. Fortunately I had left my baggage at the railway station. So I wandered forth at random, and when I saw a bright jet of gas light, decided that there must be a hotel, which was true. Finally in a small public house I found a chance to sleep in the same room with another man. But inasmuch as my prospective bedfellow in his exterior was not to my liking, I had the energy, to me now quite inconceivable, to decline the offer and entrust myself anew to the night. Meantime it had become very solitary. I wandered from one street to another but saw no human being to whom I could direct a question. Still, the streets had living creatures, and very jolly ones. Chicago has 'wooden sidewalks' under which live millions of rats. These rats regard the streets at night as their domain, and in my presence made great use of their freedom. Rats of all sizes and colors, old and young, white and gray, played charmingly about my feet, and when I stepped on one and it squeaked, it seemed to me as if I ought to beg pardon. I roamed

around in this company until a tower clock struck half past three. Then, on one of the bridges, I sat down upon a curbstone to rest a bit. The rats gathered about me and I experienced something like what Heine did when he was stalled with the mail wagon in the Teutoburg forest, surrounded by wolves who spoke to him. A large rat, who seemed the oldest and wisest of all, stepped forward and began: (Heine's wolves could talk German, but American rats naturally spoke only English.)

'What do you want here, stranger?' said the speaker. 'Why didn't you stay with your lovely wife and child? Why did you come into this distant country, in the pursuit of wealth and earthly things? Fool that you are! How sweet would be your rest with your loved ones, and now you are sitting here on a cold stone, lonesome, and nobody cares for you! But you cannot sit here any longer! Move on, stranger, this is our time and you are in our way; move on!'

The gaze of the speaker was so determined and energetic that I considered it diplomatic to be polite. So I answered: 'Mr. Speaker and Fellow Rats. Though I am not accustomed to speaking to so large and respectable an audience in a language foreign to my native country, yet I feel myself compelled, by the reasonable sentiments expressed by your honorable and worthy leader, to venture upon a word or two. Mr. Speaker and Fellow Rats! I am exceedingly sorry to have trespassed upon your nightly rights and privileges by the unfortunate fact of my presence. But, gentlemen, you may be sure that I never should have taken such an indecent as well as dangerous course, if not beings of my own race, men with hearts of stone, had kicked me away from their doors and turned me into the deserted streets. I know, gentlemen, that you harbor feelings of kindness in your hearts and that you are not insensible to the sufferings of a distressed stranger, who in the vain pursuit of earthly things, as your worthy speaker expressed himself very appropriately, has improvidently left his dearest ones and threw himself into the wide world. Mr. Speaker and Fellow Rats! Deep regret creeps over my soul when I remember my dearest ones, and every one among you who happens to be separated from his spouse and offspring will readily understand my feelings in this respect. (Several rats began to swallow hard.) Now, my friends, I see it is not impossible to kindle the holy fire of sympathy in the hearts of pure children of nature and, trusting to the world-renowned hospitality of the noble rats of Chicago, I throw myself entirely into your arms, and as men have forsaken me, I will sleep among you as one of your own!'

The rats broke out in great enthusiasm and gave me three cheers. They quickly named a 'committee of arrangements,' and after a short private conference the speaker came to me and said:

'Sir! I am very sorry to have addressed you in a harsh and discourteous tone, and if any one among us has offended you we are ready to apologize in any terms which you may choose to impose

> upon us. Now, sir, by unanimous consent we have agreed to offer you all the honors of our hospitality, and I hope you will feel quite at home amongst us. There is no rat in Chicago who would not exert himself to the utmost of his power to show himself worthy of your noble confidence in our race. Now, sir, I take the liberty to invite you to take supper with us; then I will introduce you to my lady, and she will be happy to accommodate you in one of our best rooms. This is the way to my house; please, sir, step in!'
>
> Thereupon the speaker pointed out to me a knothole in one of the planks of the sidewalk only big enough to enable me to stick two fingers in it. I was about to fall into a state of high indignation, when I was awakened out of my slumber by a man, who told me that I had been on the point of falling off the curb, etc. I told him my story, and he guided me to a hotel in which I found a room. Aside from a small air-hole over the door, this room had no window. The walls bore evidence of bloody bedbug battles. One of my predecessors had obviously attempted to kill the bedbugs by squeezing them with his finger against the wall until they burst, whereby he probably gained his purpose. I, however, threw myself like a daredevil into the bed, hoping to sleep until ten o'clock, for already the hour of four had passed. But soon after six I was awakened by a vulgar rapping upon the door, and heard a voice calling to me that breakfast was ready. I would gladly have renounced my breakfast, but thereafter I could not go back to sleep (particularly as I now felt the bedbugs more strongly than I anticipated); so I went out to visit my cousin Edmund and learned that a short time ago he had gone to St. Paul, Minnesota, on business, and would be away for four weeks. (Later I found several friends of the olden time—lawyers and newspaper men—who received me with extraordinary friendliness.) I will write you about Chicago next time. This young city is one of the most marvellous phenomena of America, or indeed of the world.

Cousin Edmund, whom Schurz mentioned, was the well-known German-American lawyer E. Juessen (1830-91), who served as tax collector of Chicago from 1869 to 1871 and as American Consul General to Vienna from 1884 to 1888. He drew much fire from the American press for his attempts to start a national German political party in Chicago in May of 1871.

As is evident from Schurz's letter, many other forty-eighters came to Chicago, at that time the "marvellous phenomenon" of America, and assumed leadership among their compatriots. Though not so widely known as Schurz, their ranks included illustrious men that left a decided imprint on Chicago in many fields. The journalist Georg Schneider (1823-1905) fought in word and deed for the German Revolution and had to flee to America in 1849 after having been condemned to death by the authorities. In

1851 he became editor of Chicago's second German newspaper, the *Illinois Staatszeitung*. In that capacity he vigorously attacked slavery and converted many Germans to the Republican party. Historians give him much credit for helping to elect Lincoln, who rewarded him for his efforts with an ambassadorship to Denmark. Schneider occupied other prominent public positions, which included the office of city tax collector for four years, elector at large for Garfield in 1880, and president of the National Bank of Illinois from 1871 to 1896. Since 1896 his name is perpetuated in the Georg Schneider Elementary School on Hoyne Avenue.

Four other influential German journalists who eventually came to Chicago, Lorenz Brentano (1813-91), Wilhelm Rapp (1828-1907), Caspar Butz (1825-85), and Hermann Raster (1827-91), were either compelled to emigrate or fled to America as a result of their stalwart commitment to the 1848 Revolution. Brentano, sentenced to death as the head of the Party of Liberty in Baden, served the Union faithfully as owner of the *Staatszeitung* from 1861 to 1867. He was also a member and president of Chicago's school board from 1863 to 1868, American Consul to Dresden from 1872 to 1876, and served in the Forty-Fifth U.S. Congress. An elementary school on North Fairfield and a playground on North Washtenaw still bear his name. Wilhelm Rapp exerted great influence on Chicago's German element for over thirty years through his editorials in the *Staatszeitung*. Before coming to Chicago, he was a political prisoner in 1850 and 1851 at the fortress of Hohenasperg and later tried for treason. The roles of Caspar Butz and Hermann Raster among Chicago's German element are discussed in the chapters on literature and on the press.

Persons from all walks of life became political exiles for their involvement in the 1848 Revolution. So large was the number of political refugees in Chicago, that they organized the popular "Club of Old '48." When this club celebrated the 58th anniversary of the turbulent days of the uprising in one of the favorite meeting places of the Chicago Germans, Anbach's Garden, on June 20, 1906, Joseph Rudolph (1825-1909), an old forty-eighter who had come to the United States in 1849 and had been in various Chicago business enterprises since 1855, was the speaker. He pointed out that the ranks of the club's members had been decimated within the past few years and that little interest was shown the forty-eighters by the contemporaries.

The Nazi regime was the next era that brought immigrants from Germany, primarily for political motives, but also coupled with racial reasons. Laura Fermi tells in her book, *Illustrious Immigrants*, the story of the intellectual migration from Europe in the years 1930 to 1941. The impact of this group was felt mainly in the field of learning. From Europe alone well over 25,500 professionals emigrated between about 1930 and 1941. After the attack on Pearl Harbor, immigration from Europe dropped significantly, being limited mostly to persons who were waiting for visas or transportation opportunities in nations not directly embroiled by the ravages of World War II.

According to Laura Fermi, the German-born constituted the largest group, amounting to about forty-four percent, or more than 11,220. Their highest percentage was reached during the years 1933 and 1937, when they made up nearly sixty-six percent of the total immigrant intelligentsia. In 1933 and 1934 hundreds of German academicians were dismissed from universities and institutions of learning. 1,500 of them were listed on a detailed roster published with the assistance of the Rockefeller Foundation in 1936 and were consequently called to the United States. During 1940 and 1941 the immigration of intellectuals from Germany to America reached its lowest point, amounting to about thirty-three percent of the total "brain migration."

Many outstanding individuals emigrated to America during the Nazi regime. Henry Kissinger, the present Secretary of State, who came from his native Fürth in Bavaria as a fifteen-year-old boy, is a prominent example. A large number of the emigrants were attracted by the cultural and technological institutes as well as the various colleges and universities of the Chicago area, where they repaid the hospitality of their adopted homeland with invaluable service. It would be tedious to mention all outstanding savants that came to Chicago as exiles from the Hitler regime, but a few of them ought to be named to show the ubiquity of the German element in the various fields of learning. Several German-born scientists, among them Maria Goeppert-Mayer and James Franck, were instrumental in bringing about the historical act of releasing controlled atomic energy on December 2, 1942, by Enrico Fermi and his team, nicknamed "the suicide squad." The Nobel laureates James Franck (1882-1964) and Maria Goeppert-Mayer (b. 1906) came to Chicago from the University of Göttingen. Another German Nobel Prize winner who fled the Nazi regime was Konrad Bloch.

Following is a short survey of other outstanding professionals who came to Chicago as political exiles. Ringing names in the art of healing are Franz Baumann, one-time president of the Chicago Metropolitan Dermatological Society; William Becker, founder in 1949 of the Self Help Home for the Aged in Chicago; and Rudolf

Schindler, who wrote the basic textbook on gastroscopy in Chicago. Otto Struve, of German extraction, but having lived in Russia before coming to the United States in the early 1920's, elevated the standards in astronomy, which German exiles, such as Hans Rosenberg, continued to uphold. Arnold Bergsträsser, having emigrated from Germany in 1937, headed the Army Specialized Training Program for Soldiers at the University of Chicago after 1944. Before Ludwig Mies van der Rohe retired from the Illinois Institute of Technology in 1958, he had trained many American architects and had contributed much to the modern appearance of the Chicago skyline since his arrival from Germany in 1938. The Oriental Institute seemed to have attracted a large share of German political refugees, among them the archaeologist Erich Schmidt, the art historian Ludwig Bachhofer, the Assyriologists Arnold Walther and Arno Poebel, and the Hittitologist Hans Güterbock. The historian Hans Rothfels attempted in his book, *The German Opposition to Hitler*, to demonstrate that there was a popular opposition to the "Führer" in Germany and that a nation should not be judged solely on the basis of a few abysmal years of political piracy by a despot and his henchmen, but also on the basis of its cultural achievements throughout the centuries. Finally, among the political refugees that came to Chicago at one time or another must be mentioned the theologian Paul Tillich (1886-1965). In coming from a German to an American university, he had to "come down seven steps on the social ladder," as he himself stated, according to Laura Fermi. Nevertheless, though he could have returned to Germany, in 1962 he came to Chicago to crown his life's work with writing the momentous three volume opus, *Systematic Theology*.

Other reasons, though far less powerful than economic or even political factors, caused Germans to come to Chicago. Racial persecution forced many people to flee their fatherland, as could be seen in the discussion above of political refugees during the Hitler regime. Little evidence could be adduced which would suggest that wholesale religious persecution was a compelling reason. To be sure, Germans emigrated who had been dissatisfied with their acceptable mode of religious expression in their homeland, as the group of "Altlutheraner" or Saxon Lutherans who in 1839 came to St. Louis from Dresden under the leadership of their bishop Martin Stephan, but few of them came to Chicago, compared to those that came for economic reasons.

In the so-called "Kulturkampf" during Bismarck's era, when especially Catholicism was subject to imposed change, a number of people thought it advisable to emigrate, as for instance Albert

Evers from Warburg who was priest of Chicago's St. Boniface congregation after 1892, or Johann M. Schäfers from Westphalia, priest of Chicago's St. Martin's congregation. Missionary and humanitarian motives prompted several religious organizations to send their adherents to Chicago. This factor is especially important with regard to the founding of charitable organizations, hospitals, and parochial schools. For instance, the Poor Handmaids of Christ, sent from their motherhouse in Dernbach, Germany to establish a cloister in Chicago in 1875, soon were immersed in many humanitarian activities. In 1879 they opened the first day nursery in Chicago. They also founded and managed the St. Elizabeth Hospital, which was dedicated on October 13, 1887. After 1903 they were in charge of St. Anne's Hospital on 49th Street and Thomas Street. In addition, the Poor Handmaids of Christ taught at several institutions including those of St. Augustine, St. Heinrich, and Heart of Jesu.

From which parts of Germany did the immigrants come? When their origin is discussed, the causes for emigration must be considered. For instance, whenever a certain part of Germany suffered heavily under famine or the devastations of war, the detrimental economic factors of that region tended to cause the people to emigrate in quest of a better existence. Too little supporting evidence is available to show this direct correlation conclusively, but from areas such as Schleswig-Holstein, Prussia, and Baden, which were directly embroiled in the conflicts between Prussia and Denmark in 1864, between Prussia and Austria in 1866, and between Germany and France in 1870, a disproportionately large contingent seemed to have come.

It seems that prior to 1870 the majority of Germans arrived from North Germany. Interesting information is provided for 1838 and 1839 in the church records of the first Protestant community of Cook and DuPage Counties. It was comprised of the mother community Teuto, now Elmhurst-Addison, and the filial communities Schween's Grove-Dutch Bush, now Palatine, Dutchman's Point, now Niles, and Chicago. These records are printed in the fall 1901 issue of *Deutsch-Amerikanische Geschichtsblätter*. The pastor of the Teuto community, Ludwig Cachand-Ervendberg, counted among the 221 souls of his parish sixty-one heads of households of whom thirty-six came from the area Hannover-Westphalia, seven from Rhenish Bavaria, five from Württemberg, four from Alsace, two each from Hesse, Darmstadt, and Baden, one from Switzerland, and, finally, two from Pennsylvania.

In the late 1840's many Germans came from Schlewsig-Holstein, the land of contention between Denmark and Prussia, some of whom were mistaken for Scandinavians. According to the December 1954 issue of the *Chicago* magazine, John L. Peyton, a Virginia lawyer, described the immigrants to Chicago in 1848 as follows: "Those whom I now saw were wild, rough, almost savage looking men from North Germany, Denmark and Sweden—their faces covered with grizzly beards and their teeth clenched upon a pipe stem."

The following table, based on the figures on page 516 of Pierce's third volume of *History*, which lists the origin of Germans living in Chicago in the years 1870 and 1880 in percentages, still shows a preponderance of immigrants from North Germany.

	Percent of foreign-born population		Percent of total population	
Origin	1870	1880	1870	1880
Prussia	17.25	16.07	8.34	6.54
Bavaria	2.56	1.28	1.24	.52
Baden	2.24	1.05	1.09	.43
Mecklenburg	2.35	.94	1.13	.38
Hannover	1.71	.94	.83	.38
Saxony	1.17	.79	.56	.32
Württemberg	1.47	.69	.71	.28
Hesse	2.35	.36	1.14	.15
Hamburg	.22	.20	.11	.08
Nassau	.14	.05	.07	.02
Oldenburg	.04	.04	.02	.02
Brunswick	.06	.02	.03	.01
Weimar	.03	.006	.01	.002
Lübeck	.008	.004	.004	.001
Not specified	4.58	14.28	2.21	5.81
Total	36.19	36.71	17.49	14.95

Prussia's 17.25 percent for 1870 amounted to 24,938 immigrants. Of all the German states and principalities, Hesse seems to have experienced the greatest decline in the number of emigrants from 1870 to 1880. It is also noteworthy that these statistics reflect a tendency to disregard the individual German regions.

Together with Bismarck's efforts to unite Germany under a common political bond after the Franco-Prussian War, the immigrants began to consider themselves not as subjects of the various principalities but as citizens of the German Empire, and tended to indicate their place of origin as Germany rather than as its various subdivisions. Under the overlordship of a common political system, economic and political factors were being equalized in the diverse regions of Germany, and, consequently, the percentage of immigration became more uniform for the German states. Of course, it still happened that for a short span of time certain regions seemed to be more heavily represented than others. For instance, the *Arbeiterzeitung* of March 4, 1882 reported that the 10,450 German immigrants arriving in Chicago during February of 1882 came mainly from Westphalia and Alsace.

Certain cities, such as Berlin, Hamburg or Munich appear again and again as the place of origin for immigrants, but this is to be expected, since these large cities would naturally provide more immigrants than towns several times smaller. On the other hand, if towns, such as Eppelsheim or Wertheim, which are so small that one needs a big scale map to locate them, are mentioned several times as hometowns of immigrants, it happens mainly because a few prominent people stem from there. Eppelsheim in Rhenish Hesse was the birthplace of Harry Hart (1850-1929), founder of the world's largest ready-to-wear clothing firm of Hart, Schaffner and Marx, and of Elias and Henry Greenebaum, who established a bank in Chicago in 1854 and were the first of generations of influential financiers. From Wertheim on the river Main emigrated in 1864 the "father of Humboldt Park," Edward G. Uihlein, a prominent brewer and horticulturist, and in 1869 Dr. Ferdinand Hotz, who enjoyed international fame in the fields of ophthalmology and otology.

Though some German towns or cities may boast of having sent an extraordinary number of notable men to Chicago which, of course, would be reflected in and perhaps distort the picture of the reference works, the great mass of immigrants who are not listed in the *Who's Who* have come from the various geographical regions of Germany in numbers proportionate to the population density of those regions. This can easily be verified by a survey of the birthplaces in the membership lists in the annual reports of the "Schwabenverein," a club which was founded in 1878 under the motto "charity and Gemütlichkeit" and still flourishes. It celebrated the 97th annual Cannstadt Folksfestival at Buffalo Grove on August 17 and 18, 1974. In the number of members it is the foremost of all German clubs in Chicago. Since membership is not restricted to Swabians, as the name of the club might suggest, it is reasonable to assume that their members constitute a representative cross-section of Chicago's German element. If the birthplaces of the members are plotted on a map of Germany, the same picture of regularity spread throughout Germany is repeated.

The price of admission to the United States paid by the immigrants was at times exceedingly high. Even if they were inured by hardships in Germany to privations of all kinds, their self-imposed expatriation must have caused untold anguish to a great number of them. They relinquished relatives and friends, the dear sounds of their mother tongue, as well as familiar customs and mores. The immigrants did all this and more for the hope of a better future, if not for themselves, then at least for their children.

Many an immigrant would not have come to the final decision to emigrate, had he known of the tribulations that lay ahead of him during the trip alone. What in our modern age has become a pleasant day-long experience was until the advent of the steamships in the 1850's for the mass of German immigrants coming to Chicago an ordeal fraught with severe hardships. The voyage on sailing vessels lasted anywhere from forty days to about sixty days, according to the testimony of Chicago Germans. Just to mention a few examples, Jacob Manz (b.1837), owner of the biggest engraving company in Chicago at the turn of the century, embarked from Le Havre in 1855 and arrived forty-two days later in New York. Paul Juergens (b.1834), who owned a large jewelry business in the old Stewart Building on State and Washington streets, sailed in 1850 from Hamburg on the *Deutschland* to arrive forty-nine days later in New York. Finally, Justus Kilian (b.1830), a successful business man in diverse enterprises, needed fifty-eight days from Bremen to Baltimore in 1857. When steamships came into use, the duration of the trip was reduced considerably and with it the accompanying extreme privations. For instance, John Baus, a lieutenant on Chicago's police force, required seventeen days for the crossing in a steamer in 1851. Only rarely did Chicago Germans preserve for posterity their experiences of emigrating on steamships.

In an effort to have as large a margin of profit as possible, the ship companies which transported immigrants across the Atlantic, with few exceptions, crowded as many steerage passengers onto the sailing boats as possible. Mortality rates went so high that Congress was finally forced to secure some rights for the immigrants. For instance, in the Act of March 3, 1855 it commanded that at least two tons of space be allotted per immigrant, and forced the companies to provide proper food and ventilation during the long trip.

Even though these provisions were sometimes blatantly violated, the lot of the immigrants improved through the introduction of steamboats. By 1856 only three percent of the immigrants availed themselves of the steamboat, whereas in 1869 the mode of conveyance was 517 to 183 in favor of steamboats. A parallel significant phenomenon was the drastic reduction in the mortality rate, as Frederick Kapp demonstrated on page 241 of his book, *Immigration and the Commissioners of Emigration.* In 1868, 200 out of 180,449 steerage passengers died in 451 steamers, but 393 out of 31,953 steerage passengers died in 200 sailing boats. In other words, one of 902 steamship passengers died, but for sailing vessel passengers the death ratio was one to 81.

This death rate is by no means extraordinarily high in comparison to other years. In 1847 no less than 20,000 of the 234,968 total immigrants died during the voyage, according to page twenty-three of Frederick Kapp's book, *Immigration.* Compared to these staggering losses, the 1868 mortality rates for sailing vessels seem moderate. Nevertheless, 1868 proved to be a disastrous year for 544 America-bound German emigrants who embarked from Hamburg on the ill-fated sailing vessel *Leibnitz.* The following excerpt from the immigration commissioner's report of these emigrants' fate is reproduced here from page 189 of Kapp's book, *Immigration*, not only because many of the unfortunate voyagers intended to come to Chicago, but also because it vividly describes their intense suffering and illustrates the general background conditions on immigrant boats.

> The *Leibnitz*, originally the *Van Couver*, is a large and fine vessel, built at Boston for the China trade, and formerly plying between that port and China. She was sold some years ago to the house of Robert M. Sloman, and has since sailed under her present name . . . she left Hamburg, Nov. 2, 1867, Capt. H. F. Bornhold, lay at Cuxhaven, on account of head-winds, until the 11th, whereupon she took the southern course to New York. She went by the way of Madeira, down to the Tropics, 20th degree, and arrived in the Lower Bay on Jan. 11, 1868, after a passage of 61 days, or rather 70 days—at least, as far as the passengers are concerned, who were confined to the densely crowded steerage for that length of time.
>
> The heat, for the period that they were in the lower latitudes, very often reached 24 degrees of Reaumur, or 94 degrees of Fahrenheit. Her passengers 544 in all—of whom 395 were adults, 103 children, and 46 infants—came principally from Mecklenburg, and proposed to settle as farmers and laborers in Illinois and Wisconsin; besides them, there were about 40 Prussians from Pomerania and Posen, and a few Saxons and Thuringians.
>
> It is not proven by any fact, that the cholera (as has been alleged) raged or had raged in or near their homes when or before they left them. This statement appears to have been made by or in behalf of

those who have an interest in throwing the origin of the sickness on its poor victims. Of these 544 German passengers, 105 died on the voyage, and three in port, making in all 108 deaths—leaving 436 surviving.

The first death occurred on Nov. 25th. On some days, as for instance on Dec. 1, nine passengers died, and on Dec. 17, eight. The sickness did not abate until toward the end of December, and no new cases happened when the ship had again reached the northern latitudes; five children were born; during the voyage some families had died out entirely; of others, the fathers and mothers are gone; here, a husband had left a poor widow, with small children; and there, a husband had lost his wife. We spoke to some little boys and girls, who, when asked where were their parents, pointed to the ocean with sobs and tears, and cried, "*Down there!*"

Prior to our arrival on board, the ship had been cleansed and fumigated several times, but not sufficiently so to remove the dirt, which, in some places, covered the walls. Mr. Frederick Kassner, our able and experienced Boarding Officer, reports that he found the ship and the passengers in a most filthy condition, and that when boarding the *Leibnitz* he hardly discovered a clean spot on the ladder, or on the ropes, where he could put his hands and feet. He does not remember to have seen anything like it within the last five years. Captain True, who likewise boarded the ship immediately after her arrival, corroborates the statement of Mr. Kassner.

As to the interior of the vessel, the upper steerage is high and wide. All the spars, beams, and planks which were used for the construction of temporary berths had been removed. Except through two hatchways and two very small ventilators, it had no ventilation, and not a single window or bull's-eye was open during the voyage. In general, however, it was not worse than the average of the steerages of other emigrant ships; but the lower steerage, the so-called orlop-deck, is a perfect pesthole, calculated to kill the healthiest man. It had been made a temporary room for the voyage by laying a tier of planks over the lower beams of the vessel, and they were so little supported that they shook when walking on them. The little light this orlop-deck received came through one of the hatchways of the upper-deck. Although the latter was open when we were on board, and although the ship was lying in the open sea, free from all sides, it was impossible to see anything at a distance of two or three feet. On our enquiring how this hole had been lighted during the voyage, we were told that some lanterns had been up there, but that on account of the foulness of the air, they could scarcely burn . . . And in this place about 120 passengers were crowded for 70 days, and for a greater part of the voyage in a tropical heat, with scanty rations and a very inadequate supply of water, and worse than all, suffering from the miasma below, above, and beside them, which of itself must create fever and pestilence.

The captain himself stated to us that the passengers refused to carry the excrements on deck, and that "the urine and ordure of the upper-steerage flowed down to the lower." As the main-deck was very difficult of access from the orlop-deck, the inmates of the latter often failed to go on deck even to attend to the calls of nature. There were only six water-closets for the accommodation of all the passengers. They have been cleansed, of course; but the smell that emanated from them was still very intense, and corroborates the statement of the above-named officers—that they must have been in an extraordinary frightful condition . . .

There was not a single emigrant who did not complain of the captain, as well as of the short allowance of provisions and water on board. As we know, from a long experience, that the passengers of emigrant ships, with a very few exceptions, are in the habit of claiming more than they are entitled to, we are far from putting implicit faith in all their statements. There is as much falsehood and exaggeration among this class of people as among any other body of uneducated men. We have, therefore, taken their complaints with due allowance, and report only so much thereof as we believe to be well founded.

All the passengers concur in the complaint that their provisions were short, partly rotten, and that, especially, the supply of water was insufficient, until they were approaching port. We examined the provisions on board, and found that the water was clear and pure. If the whole supply during the voyage was such as the samples handed to us, there was no reason for complaint as to quality. But, in quantity, the complaints of the passengers are too well founded; for they unanimously state, and are not effectually contradicted by the captain, that they never received more than half a pint of drinkable water per day, while by the laws of the United States they were entitled to receive three quarts. Some of the biscuit handed to us were rotten and old, and hardly eatable; other pieces were better. We ordered the steward to open a cask of cornbeef, and found it of ordinary good quality; the butter, however, was rancid. Once a week herrings were cooked instead of meat. The beans and sauerkraut were often badly cooked, and, in spite of hunger, thrown overboard.

The treatment of the passengers was heartless in the extreme. The sick passengers received the same food with the healthy, and high prices were exacted for all extras and comforts. A regular traffic in wine, beer, and liquors was carried on between the passengers on the one side and the steward and crew on the other. A man by the name of Frederick Hildebrand, from Wirsitz, in Posen, who lost two children, paid 35 Prussian thalers extra for beer and wine to sustain himself and his sick wife. A bottle of rum cost him one dollar; a bottle of bad wine even more. "This extortion, at such a time, cannot be too strongly condemned," says Captain True, in his report, which confirms the information received by us from the passengers.

When the first deaths occurred, the corpses were often suffered to remain in the steerage for full twenty-four hours. In some cases the bodies were covered with vermin before they were removed.

There was no physician on board. Although we found a large medicine-chest, it was not large enough for the many cases of sickness, and was, in fact, emptied after the first two weeks of the voyage.

The captain seems to have been sadly deficient in energy and authority in matters of moment, while he punished severely small offences; as, for instance, he handcuffed a passenger for the use of insulting words; but he did not enforce the plainest rules for the health and welfare of his passengers. Instead of compelling them, from the first, to come on deck and remove the dirt, he allowed them to remain below, and to perish among their own excrements. Of the whole crew, the cook alone fell sick and died, as he slept in the steerage. Three passenger girls who were employed in the kitchen, and lived on deck, enjoyed excellent health, during the whole voyage.

The physicians above mentioned, to whose report we refer for particulars, most positively declare that it was not the Asiatic cholera, but intestinal and stomach catarrh (catarrh ventriculi et intestinorum), more or less severe, and contagious typhus, which killed the passengers. From what we saw and learned from the passengers, we likewise arrive at the conclusion that the shocking mortality on board the *Leibnitz* arose from want of good ventilation, cleanliness, suitable medical care, sufficient water, and wholesome food.

The present case is another instance of the mortality on board the Hamburg sailing-vessels, and increases their bad reputation. Of 917 passengers on board of two ships of the Sloman line, not less than 183 died within one month! . . .

The commissioner continued to produce statistics which show that the mortality rate of the Sloman line ships was exceedingly high and recommended that a physician be required on board of all emigrant vessels with more than fifty passengers, that the orlop-deck be eliminated, and that the penalty for dead passengers, amounting to ten dollars per death, be strictly enforced. Descendants of Frederick Hildebrand, who was mentioned in the example for extortion, still live in the Chicago area.

Many horror stories could be told about the ocean voyage which German immigrants to Chicago experienced. Most relate to sailing vessels, but a few steamships are also among the number. On June 12, 1866 the *Staatszeitung* contained a report by W. C. Boeckmann and Johann Colljung, recent German immigrants to Chicago, who had crossed the Atlantic on the steamship *England*, which left Liverpool on March 29, 1866. Of the 1,312 passengers, 667 died at sea or in quarantine at Halifax. About half of the 563 Germans aboard perished. The conditions were much like the detailed description above: food of poor quality, consisting mainly of spoiled fish and potatoes, overcrowded quarters with poor ventilation, and indescribable filth. In addition to that, Boeckmann's and Colljung's baggage was stolen at Halifax.

Once the sea voyage was over, Chicago-bound immigrants still had an arduous journey ahead of them. Detailed accounts of prerailroad journeys to Chicago are rare, but after 1853 the newly founded German Aid Society published periodic reports in the Chicago German newspapers which include accounts of their trips. There are numerous complaints about the unsatisfactory special immigrant trains which brought masses of people on indirect routes to Chicago. On September 9, 1867 the immigration agent Ernst Knobelsdorf commended the Baltimore and Ohio railroads for setting a good example in transporting immigrants from Baltimore to Chicago in two or three days, but he also reported that "the regular trip on an immigrant train from New York to Chicago takes from five to six days. Numerous unnecessary stopovers are made for the benefit of hotel keepers and saloonkeepers who pay railroad employees liberally for the 'opportunity of relieving the immigrants of their cash.' "

The trip on inland waterways was hardly better, as is shown in the following example, which was reported by the immigration agent in the *Staatszeitung* of August 6, 1857. A German girl, Amalie Schlichting, arrived in Quebec on June 20, 1857 on the sailing vessel *Roret Brigham.* Her trip to Sarnia on the St. Clair river lasted three days and four nights. There she was put on the steamer *Montgomery*, commanded by a certain gruff Captain Nichols, and finally arrived in Chicago on June 28. So many immigrants crowded the boat that there was hardly room to move and no place to lie down. The prevailing conditions on the boat were so bad that "if livestock had been transported the voyage would have to be described as cruelty to animals." When Miss Schlichting complained about her lost baggage to the captain and received no satisfaction, she launched a lawsuit against the ship line which was of no avail. Abuse and exploitation of immigrants were so widespread that the officers of the law had their hands full only to check blatantly criminal cases.

The story of the Franzen family, taken from the fall issue of the 1901 *Deutsch-Amerikanische Geschichtsblätter*, may serve as an example of a German immigrant family that surmounted onerous difficulties to attain the fulfillment of their fond dreams. In April of 1834, Hermann B. H. Franzen left his tiny hometown Schale in the district of Tecklenburg, some ten miles south west of Osnabrück, for Bremen to emigrate to the New World. We may assume that he was not happy with his lot in Germany, for he was already sixty-two years old, but nevertheless was willing to brave an uncertain future in a strange land. Franzen did not have enough money to pay the fare for his family, consisting of his wife Adelheid and five children, aged eleven to twenty-four. When a neighbor refused to lend him the lacking five dollars, a stranger gave him the needed amount. They landed in Baltimore, after a grueling voyage of fifty-eight days, on June 27, 1834. Since they had no money to continue their journey, they all hired out as laborers. His wife and the youngest son stayed with a farmer, where they worked for their room and board. Two daughters, who hired out as maids, received five dollars pay in advance which was used to pay back the debt to the generous stranger. The father and his two older sons worked for the Baltimore and Ohio Railroad Company for sixty-six cents a day, of which twenty-five cents were needed for room and board. After six weeks of work all three contracted a disease, incapacitating them for work. As soon as they had recuperated, the parents and the three sons started to walk with their few possessions for Cumberland, Maryland, some 130 miles away, where all of them hired out as stonecutters. For three months they found a primitive home in an abandoned mill, and when the two girls joined them, after having also walked there from Baltimore, all set out on foot to Wheeling, West Virginia. This time they traveled without their household goods, which they had sent ahead. From Wheeling they went by boat to Cincinnati. There they all found work, the oldest daughter, Anna Maria, married a certain Friedrich Schwerdfeger, and Mrs. Franzen succumbed to the hardships. After a nine month stay in Cincinnati, a compatriot who had settled in Addison, Illinois, convinced Franzen to go to the budding city on Lake Michigan, where he arrived in November of 1835. With his sons he worked in Chicago for two years at various odd jobs before he settled in Addison, where he and his sons attained a comfortable existence and respectability. On April 25, 1936 the *Chicago Daily News* had an article on a monument in Bensenville erected in 1934 to the memory of John Henry Franzen, the second oldest son of Hermann, a successful farmer and linseed oil mill operator.

"The immigrant is like an apple from which everyone takes a bite" was an often heard comment adapted from Gerhart Hauptmann's play, *The Weavers*. The immigrants certainly had cause to believe that everyone was out to exploit them. Most German immigrants were disgruntled about the poll tax, levied on them upon their arrival at Castle Garden. It varied from time to time, amounting to two and one-half dollars in 1867. But these "official robberies" were insignificant compared to robberies by unscrupulous individuals into whose hands immigrants fell again and again, in spite of warnings published in the *Emigrant Guides*. For instance, an ancestor of Robert Sweitzer, the Democratic mayoral candidate who ran against William H. Thompson in 1915, lost all his money to a sycophantic compatriot when he arrived in 1855 at Castle Garden in New York. Being unable to communicate with Americans, he trusted a seemingly friendly man who had emigrated earlier from his hometown Herbolzheim in Baden, to exchange German gold currency into American money for him. The compatriot disappeared and Sweitzer's ancestor was left with nothing but railroad tickets to Chicago, where he eventually worked his way up to a comfortable existence.

Many German immigrants claimed, that on their way to Chicago they were were cheated by railroad officials in excessive baggage charges, in higher than ordinary ticket prices, and in the unfair exchange of money. Upon their arrival in Chicago other agents boarded the trains to prey on them. The *Staatszeitung* of November 23, 1872 reported that on the previous day fifty-six Germans who had come on the 11 A.M. Milwaukee train had been cheated out of fifty cents each by an agent of the Parmelee omnibus company who posed as a railroad official. This company must have had aggressive agents, because a few months before, on August 16, 1872, the president of the German Aid Society, Georg Schneider, had to ask the police to protect the immigrants from them.

The worst offenders were the so-called "runners," a contemptible group of people, working on commission, who knew every trick to fleece unsuspecting immigrants. A contemporary description of runners follows, taken from page sixty-two of Frederick Kapp's book, *Immigration*:

> As soon as a ship, loaded with these emigrants, reaches our shores, it is boarded by a class of men called runners, either in the employment of boarding-house keepers or forwarding establishments, soliciting custom for their employers. In order the more successfully to enable the latter to gain the confidence of the emigrant, they usually employ those who can speak the same language with the emigrant. If they cannot succeed in any other way in getting possession and control over the object of their prey, they proceed to take charge of

> their luggage, and take it to some boarding-house for safe-keeping, generally under the assurance that they will charge nothing for carriage-hire or storage. In this way they are induced to go to some emigrant boarding-house, of which there are a great many in the city, and then too often under a pretence that they will charge but a small sum for meals or board. The keepers of these houses induce these people to stay a few days, and, when they come to leave, usually charge them three or four times as much as they agreed or expected to pay, and exorbitant prices for storing their luggage; and, in case of their inability to pay, their luggage is detained as security. Some of these runners are employed by the month, and some work upon commission. Where they are in the employment of the forwarding establishments or passenger offices, and receive a commission for each passenger they bring, they are, in many cases, allowed by their employers to charge all they can get over a certain sum for transporting the passenger to a particular place. This, it will be seen, stimulates the runners to great exertions, not only to get as many passengers as possible, but to get them at the highest possible prices. To enable them to carry out their designs, all sorts of falsehoods are resorted to to mislead and deceive the emigrant as to the prices of fare and mode of conveyance.

In Chicago runners were working for several notorious boarding houses, such as the Minnesota House or the Rock Island House, which are mentioned repeatedly in the newspapers. On March 28, 1882 the *Arbeiterzeitung* reported that the authorities had revoked the licenses of Fred Dietzsch and Charles Meyer, managers of the Minnesota House, for detaining a German couple several days against their will and then charging them an exorbitant sum for room and board. Five days later the same newspaper reported that "again a member of the ill-famed brotherhood of hotelrunners, one Nicolaus Schultz, has been caught red-handed at night. This scoundrel, working as solicitor for the Rock Island House, snatched away an immigrant's luggage on Saturday night and forced him to come to his hotel. When Mr. William Meyer, who had charge of the immigrants, objected, he was knocked down by the ruffian." The report ended laconically with, "the police took care of him."

The fact that new immigrants knew neither the language nor the customs of their adopted homeland was exploited in a variety of ways by the human sharks that preyed on them. On April 4, 1926, the Chicago newspapers warned of a swindler who posed as a police officer to extort money from recent immigrants. The Germans Frank Mengelhauer, Nick Riff and John Meininger, the latest victims, were "arrested" on a fake charge by the spurious detective who "dropped the charge" after having been paid twenty-five dollars bail.

Those German immigrants who did not know that the Chicago German Aid Society provided free employment service, sometimes fell into the hands of individuals who not only charged several times the legal fee, but also exploited the newcomers in other ways. The *Abendpost* of January 5, 1904 reported a stark case: Twenty-five new German immigrants came to police headquarters and requested the apprehension of the employment agent Louis Krampe, 135 North Clark, for obtaining money under false pretenses. According to their statements they were sold into peonage in the Mississippi oyster territory by the accused. Hermann Mueller of 6614 May Street, the leader of the complainants, was the only one of the Germans who knew English. They had answered an advertisement and declared themselves willing to go to Pensacola, Florida, to work there in an oyster packing plant, since they had been promised two dollars a day for males and one and one-half for females. Instead of being sent to Pensacola, they were transported to Bay St. Louis in Mississippi, where they opened oysters and for which they received one cent per pound of meat. After they had worked for three days, they came to the conclusion that the most efficient worker among them could never earn more than fifty cents a day. When they wanted to resign, the owner of the packing house, James Dunbar, who had paid five dollars per worker, intimidated them with violent threats. Finally, they managed to return to Chicago to confront the employment agent Krampe who refused to return to each more than five dollars of the ten dollars which they paid him. Nine similar complaints had been lodged against Krampe, but nothing could be done about the situation.

Even though the maximum "registration fee" which the employment agents could charge was fixed by statute at two dollars, various loopholes, such as private contracts, permitted rapacious employment agents like the above mentioned Krampe to charge with impunity exorbitant fees. Grace Abbott stated in her report on "The Chicago Employment Agency and the Immigrant Worker" that "fees are always higher when the applicant is unable to speak English." The language barrier was an unending source of troubles for the new immigrants. Not infrequently, German immigrants unable to express themselves in English were arrested and put into prison before they could settle in Chicago and adjust themselves.

Unexpected expenses and widespread defraudation made it the rule rather than the exception that immigrants were destitute when they finally settled in Chicago. Their untold suffering was not recorded unless they kept diaries, which rarely happened, or when the more sensational cases were reported in the newspapers. One such case can be read in the *Staatszeitung* of May 15, 1879. Coroner Otto L. Mann published the following account of an inquest in an apartment at 110 West 14th Street shared by the families of Casimir Wist and Joseph Reuben, recent immigrants from Germany. A three month old child that had been born to the Wists on board an immigrant ship, contracted a fever, and died on May 13. The corpse lay barely clothed on a makeshift table while children of the two immigrant families played about unconcernedly. There was no furniture in three bare rooms. The fifteen-year-old Wist son, a two-dollar a week apprentice at the wagon factory of the German Peter Schuettler, provided the only income for the two families. The men Wist and Reuben were employed by one of the railroad companies, but had not yet received any pay. Even though both families, with their combined seventeen children, had lived for the last few weeks on refuse food, such as throw-away meat from the stock yards, they appeared to be in good health and spirits. Little is known about the future lot of these two families other than that the newspapers reported of collections among the Chicago Germans for them which presumably helped to alleviate their hardships. Most likely after their temporary abject misery they found a comfortable existence in Chicago, which they preferred to their marginal existence in Germany.

Many German immigrants to Chicago, however, never found the El Dorado which they had hoped to find, especially during such hard times as the depression of the 1930's, and they strived to return to Germany, preferring a life of poverty among friends and relatives to a subsistence among strangers. One representative example may be found in the fate of a man identified only as Erich which was reported in the *Sonntagspost* of January 21, 1934. He was a twice wounded World War I veteran who came to Chicago in 1925, hoping to find a better existence for his wife and two children than the one eked out on his father's small farm in the Rhineland. At first his affairs went tolerably well, while he was working for the Western Electric Company. But in 1926 a lung disease incapacitated him, enabling him to find only occasional part-time jobs. In January of 1927 when Erich became too weak to work, the entire family was close to starvation and managed to survive primarily on a monthly donation of fifteen dollars by the German Aid Society. They eventually returned to Germany through the intervention of this society, which attempted to persuade the government to deport them as paupers.

There are many cases in which both the German Aid Society and the County agent tried to have indigent, disillusioned immigrants deported at government expense due to some technicality, such as nonreported disease or feeble-mindedness at the time of entry. It is obvious that sometimes facts were distorted to obtain deportation status. This clearly happened in the case of Katie Schultz, who was deported in June of 1913.

The essential facts about her are found in a letter of May 13, 1913 by Lydia Gardner, Director of the Immigrants' Protective League to a Mr. Roberts, Inspector-in-Charge of the U.S. Immigration Service. Katie, an eighteen year old German-Hungarian girl, came in August of 1912 to New York on the *S. S. Bordeaux*. In Chicago Katie seemed to have had health and adjustment problems and was pronounced feeble-minded to such a degree that she would be unable to protect herself. However, this seems highly unlikely in light of the numerous letters which she wrote to relatives and friends and the excerpt of the following letter of December 19, 1913 by Charlotte Klomser to Lydia Gardner which reported Katie's readjustment in a small Hungarian village where she was sent after her deportation. It is taken from page 426 of Edith Abbott's book, *Immigration, Selected Documents and Case Records:*

> Now Katie is as happy as a bird, she learns Hungarian so quickly that she will be able to speak it quite well in two or three months. She likes her work, is very diligent. The first to begin and the last to stop with the work. She is so clever that they are going to put her in a part of the factory where it is more difficult, but where she earns more money. His Excellency says that neither he nor anyone else could find why one would call her feeble-minded, she is quite bright and all are fond of her. Nor could I find her feeble-minded, she must have been shy and as she did not speak sufficient English I dare say they said so. It is a great blessing you found the poor girl and took so much interest in her, else she would have been lost entirely. I think it is more than hard for your government to send back such a poor girl, without any proper reasons. She has been operated on in Chicago and perhaps one thought she would not be able to earn her living. The poor mother had given her all her money, 400 crowns, to have her go to America to earn much money.

Of course, there were many reasons why Germans returned to their native land either as deportees or as emigrants. Many of the deported Germans had committed crimes or were undesirable in other ways. Some emigrated again, because they could not find a decent livelihood in America, especially when they came during economic slumps. Over an extended span of time the relationship between German immigration and emigration varies considerably. A few representative statistics will show this. They are taken from the respective years of the *Daily News Almanac:*

Year	German Immigration to U.S.	German Emigration from U.S.
1918	447	28
1919	52	26
1920	1,001	3,069
1925	46,068	3,648
1926	50,421	3,908
1927	48,513	4,748
1929	46,751	6,330
1931	10,401	3,369
1932	2,670	5,533
1933	1,919	5,131
1934	4,392	3,502
1935	5,201	3,530
1936	6,346	3,672
1937	10,895	2,340
1938	17,199	2,270
1939	33,515	4,211
1940	21,520	1,978
1941	4,028	1,758
1942	2,150	2

During part of the Great Depression of the 1930's the net number of Germans in the United States actually decreased. In the years 1932 through 1935 14,182 Germans immigrated to the United States, but 17,696 emigrated.

A large number of the returning immigrants could have found a good financial future here, but returned nevertheless for other reasons. As the statistics above show, so many of them returned at times that various individuals, for different reasons, expressed their concern about the exodus. These emigrants were severely criticized by Theodore Roosevelt, because "they regard the United States only as an international boarding-house while amassing riches." According to him, they failed to assimilate and took their savings out of this country, thereby weakening America's economy. The *Abendpost* of December 14, 1929 from an entirely different standpoint defended the emigrants in the editorial "The Exodus" by stressing that they were driven away by intolerant laws and by a thwarted value system. Reflecting on the Prohibition and the "Roaring Twenties" the editor asked, "can you blame them for their unwillingness to live in a country where the drinking of a beer or a highball, or the smoking of a cigarette is considered a serious transgression, while habitual, genuine criminals, allied with politicians, control large cities?"

The German newspapers repeatedly lashed out at the repressive Prohibition laws and blamed them as the main reason for the return of Germans to their homeland. Immediately before and after the Prohibition went into effect, they often reported of emigrating Germans and other foreigners who had become America-weary. The *Abendpost* of October 10, 1919 quoted J. Popper, head of the Chicago Internal Revenue Office as saying that every day for more than a month about one hundred aliens, among them scores of Germans, sought permission to return to their native land, primarily because temperance fanatics and self-righteous bigots "have finally managed to dig a grave for liberty."

Those German immigrants who throughout Chicago's history decided to stay in this city for better or for worse had to find themselves homes. Generally speaking, they aimed to settle, for a variety of reasons, close to compatriots who had immigrated earlier. There are also indications that they found homes in just about every part of the city and in many suburbs, and that the main settlements shifted through time.

It is not known when or where the first German settlements in the Chicago area originated, but according to later testimony several of them must have sprouted up in the 1830's in various locations of the metropolitan area. According to the article, "Early Chicago Printing," in the fall 1947 issue of *Chicago History*, a broadside of 1835, one of the earliest examples of Chicago printing, is extant which advertises "forty lots in Germantown to be sold at auction by Barrett, Brown and Brother." While this gives testimony to one of the real estate transactions during the feverish land boom between the Black Hawk War of 1832 and the beginning of the canal building in 1836, the location of "Germantown" cannot be assigned conclusively, since there were several German settlements which could have matched the vague appellation.

One of the early German settlements must have originated as early as 1825 at Dunkley's Grove, later called Addison, because in that year the German Heinrich Rothenfeld made his home there, according to page 181 of the first volume of Pierce's *History*. By 1838 the German pastor Ludwig Cachand-Ervendberg started to keep a record book of the first Protestant congregation Teuto in Cook and Du Page County.

The Teuto community attracted other German immigrants. A group from Schaumburg, North Germany, including the families named Sunderlage, Meyer, Greve, and Dammermann settled in the vicinity of Wildcat's Grove, which they renamed Schaumburg after their hometown. According to the *Tribune* of April 19, 1973, when Schaumburg was incorporated in 1956, the biggest voting block still consisted of about 100 German settlers who were in the habit of bringing their interpreter to village board meetings.

Lake View, which was annexed to Chicago on June 29, 1889, attracted countless new German immigrants. Until the turn of the century its inhabitants consisted primarily of Germans. Even today the largest foreign element of the Lake View area is German. Many of the streets there, named by or after Germans, have gradually been renamed, as for instance Montrose Boulevard, which received its original name, Sulzer Road, after Konrad Sulzer, who came to Chicago in 1836.

Some other Chicago areas reveal their German origin through their names, such as Humboldt Park, Schiller Park, Hoffman Estates, Hanover Park, and Frankfort, but scores of others, such as Blue Island, Homewood, Chicago Heights, formerly New Strassburg, and Lincolnwood, once Tessville, were also primarily German at their inception. Most German immigrants tried to locate themselves where earlier compatriots had settled, such as the above mentioned towns. Being immersed in an environment familiar in language, customs, and life style made the acclimatization of the new immigrants to Chicago less of a shock.

Nevertheless, not all German immigrants flocked to established German settlements, but spread throughout the Chicago metropolitan area. In fact, throughout the history of Chicago, with its changing numbers of districts, one could find Germans living in every single community area. The only exception occurs after 1970 in that four of the 76 Chicago community areas are not inhabited by Germans. According to the 1970 *Community Fact Book*, no Germans reside in the community areas thirty-six, thirty-seven, thirty-eight, and forty. This can perhaps be explained on the basis of the reduced number of Germans in Chicago, in comparison to earlier times, and also in the population shifts to the suburbs. A comparison of population and distribution statistics of 1930 and 1960 from Kitagawa's and Taeuber's *Community Fact Book* reveals that of the foreign groups the Germans predominated in thirty-six community areas in 1930, but that this number had dwindled by 1960, in sharp contrast to other nationalities:

Nationality	1930 Chicago population	Number of community areas in which nationality is predominant	
		1930	1960
German	111,366	36	17
Polish	149,622	16	26

(Table continued on following page)

Nationality	1930 Chicago population	Number of community areas in which nationality is predominant 1930	1960
Italian	73,960	8	8
Irish	47,385	5	12
Russian	78,462	3	6
Other		7	6
Total		75	75

By 1960 the Germans were more numerous in three community areas that had been dominated by other nationalities in 1930, as the following data show:

Community area	Nationality	1930 Percent	1930 Number	1960 Percent	1960 Number
Near North Side	German	9.6	7,657	2.7	2,026
	Italian	17.5	13,821	1.8	1,355
Woodlawn	German	7.7	5,055	.4	363
	Irish	7.9	5,254	.2	197
Riverdale	German	22.4	332	.8	106
	Russian	30.0	445	.7	80

This slight gain by the Germans is insignificant in view of the fact that they had lost their numerical lead in twenty-two community areas to other ethnic groups, namely eight to the Irish, seven to the Poles, three to the Russians, and two each to the Italians and Canadians.

A gradual population shift of nationalities is evident in these statistics for the city. Different ethnic groups settled in formerly German-dominated areas, such as Rogers Park, West Ridge, Jefferson Park, Dunning, and Austin, as the following comparison of the 1930 and 1960 population figures shows:

Community area	Nationality	1930 Percent	1930 Number	1960 Percent	1960 Number
Rogers Park	German	10.3	5,944	5.0	2,860
	Russian	6.1	3,477	11.9	6,756
West Ridge	German	16.8	6,660	5.6	3,609
	Russian	2.2	893	21.6	13,709
Jefferson Park	German	19.7	4,018	9.4	2,587
	Polish	15.7	3,222	15.5	4,239
Dunning	German	20.3	4,010	9.2	3,823
	Polish	8.0	1,566	10.6	4,443
Austin	German	10.9	14,344	4.6	5,787
	Italian	5.2	6,801	10.6	13,384

The Germans tended to move from the city into suburbs, such as Buffalo Grove, Elgin, Elmhurst or Maywood. German stock constitutes the dominant foreign element in the largest number of suburbs. This is confirmed by the following table based on the 1930 and 1960 population figures for towns over 25,000 in the Chicago Metropolitan area, taken from the 1960 *Local Community Fact Book:*

	Number of suburbs in which nationality is predominant	
Nationality	1930	1960
German	12	13
Polish	4	5
Czech	2	2
Italian	1	2
Russian	0	2

Three of the twelve towns with the highest percentage of Germans in 1930, Highland Park, Joliet, and Hammond, were dominated by different ethnic groups in 1960, which shows that the Germans are gradually replaced by newer immigrant groups in the suburbs also:

		1930		1960	
Town	Nationality	Percent	Number	Percent	Number
Highland Park	German	10.9	1,331	4.7	1,204
	Russian	.7	81	7.0	1,779
	Italian	6.3	768	6.0	1,539
Joliet	German	9.4	4,053	3.7	2,450
	Italian	8.9	3,808	4.5	3,016
Hammond	German	10.7	6,917	3.2	3,592
	Polish	10.0	6,426	6.2	6,978

However, of the five towns, Arlington Heights, Des Plaines, Oak Lawn, Park Forest, and Skokie, which were not listed by nationalities in 1930, in all but Skokie, the German element is the largest foreign group. The 1960 population statistics for towns over 25,000 reveal that the Germans settled more evenly in the metropolitan area than other foreign nationalities. The range in number of Germans is from 670 in East Chicago to 4,548 in Elgin, whereas the number of Czechs ranges from 69 in Elgin to 11,999 in Berwyn, that of the Poles from 291 in Elgin to 7,516 in Cicero, that of the Russians from 110 in Arlington Heights to 6,907 in Skokie, and that of the Italians from 285 in Park Forest to 4,499 in Cicero. Considering all Chicago suburbs over 25,000 inhabitants, we obtain the following comparative number of inhabitants from the various nationalities for 1960:

	Number of suburbs containing the numerical range indicated								
Nationality	69 - 291	325 - 457	547 - 679	734 - 864	927 - 1,085	1,109 - 1,627	1,703 - 2,663	2,950 - 4,548	4,933 - 11,999
German	0	0	1	2	2	5	7	7	0
Polish	1	5	2	3	2	2	3	3	3
Czech	10	6	1	1	0	2	0	2	2
Russian	9	4	4	1	2	1	2	0	1
Italian	1	3	6	5	2	1	3	3	0

These figures give a fairly reliable indication of the even distribution of the German element, but numbers alone might be deceiving, since the size of the various towns is not considered. If one looks at the distribution of foreign nationalities according to their percentage of the total population in the suburbs, one sees again that the Germans fall within a narrower range than other nationalities. The percentage range in the inhabitation of the Chicago suburbs by Germans is from 1.2 in East Chicago to 9.4 in Elgin, by Czechs from 0.1 in Elgin to 22.2 in Berwyn, by Poles from 0.6 in Elgin to 11.9 in Calumet City, by Russians from 0.4 in Arlington Heights to 11.6 in Skokie, and by Italians from 0.7 in Elgin to 10.6 in Chicago Heights. The percentage ranges of foreign groups in Chicago suburbs over 25,000 by 1960 are as follows:

	Number of suburbs containing the percentage range indicated								
Nationality	0 - 1.0	1.1 - 2.0	2.1 - 3.0	3.1 - 4.0	4.1 - 5.0	5.1 - 6.0	6.1 - 10.0	10.1 - 12.0	12.1 - 22.2
German	0	2	2	6	5	4	5	0	0
Polish	2	7	6	2	1	2	2	2	0
Czech	14	4	4	0	0	0	0	0	2
Russian	15	5	1	1	0	0	1	1	0
Italian	5	9	3	2	2	1	1	1	0

Chapter 3

The Interaction of Germans and Chicagoans of other Nationalities

The interaction between Chicagoans of German extraction and those of American and other nationalities was not always harmonious, but instead constituted a long history of friction, which culminated during World War I in widespread persecution, or in "hunting the hun," to use a popular term of newspaper parlance. Various reasons for strained relations between the nationalities came to the fore at different times, but always lurking at the basis of the friction were mutual misunderstanding and a reluctance to appreciate each other's national characteristics.

Often prejudiced opinions about Germans were expressed. As Bessie Pierce pointed out on page 182 of her first volume of *A History of Chicago*, in 1847 a "Yankee" thought that most foreigners in Chicago were "Dutch." They spoke very bad English and when they were speaking among themselves sounded like "cackling geese." On the other hand, many Germans, forgetting that the American ways seemed mighty attractive while they were still in Germany, were quick to criticize American customs and institutions, comparing them unfavorably to German counterparts instead of trying to understand and appreciate them within the American context. This was irksome to the native Americans and they frequently expressed in editorials and letters to the editor their indignation about the impertinence of the foreigners, particularly the Germans. The *Chicago Times* of January 22, 1872 stated in an editorial: "It is about time for Americans, no matter where born, to ask themselves whether they propose to submit to the insolent dictation on the part of foreigners? If they, in their distinctiveness as a separate nationality, do not like our American institutions and ways, let them return to whence they came. They are aliens, not Americans." Gradually the influx of Germans became so great that Americans were apprehensive that the American ways would be altered to such a degree that their cherished customs and institutions would no longer be acceptable to them.

The anti-German sentiment was fanned by the fact that Germans, as well as other aliens, often were held responsible for a variety of undesirable social conditions, for which they were assailed as convenient scapegoats. For instance, the *Chicago Times* of May 10, 1876 asserted that all the public grievances, unrest, and crime were attributable to aliens. In innumerable verbal assaults the rather uncomplimentary appellation "damned Dutch" was a favorite expression levelled at the Germans.

The long history of anti-German sentiment in Chicago is a major outgrowth of the general xenophobia. With the first arrival of Germans in Chicago about 1830, isolated instances of German baiting were recorded, but nothing extraordinary occurred until July 17, 1840 when the *Chicago Daily Democrat* published a petition of Illinoisans to the United States Senate and House of Representatives asking Congress to deprive all foreigners not already enfranchised of the suffrage right. Of the 250 signees from Cook County the majority came from Chicago. The Germans were upset about this attempt to limit their rights and later refused to vote for any man who had signed the restrictive petition, which prevented many a public office seeker from being elected.

The Germans believed they had reason to complain about discrimination in public affairs. On February 7, 1844, the alderman Charles Sauter (1802-82) presided over a German mass meeting which resolved that they must fight for their rights in the face of attacks by nativistic groups attempting to deprive them of public offices. A fighting spirit by the Germans could be seen on March 19, 1846, when thirty-four German citizens published a statement in the *Chicago Daily Democrat* in which they denounced the action of the city council that had refused to appoint Charles Baumgarten as street commissioner just because he had been born in Germany.

The "forty-eighters," articulate, well-educated Germans who either expatriated themselves voluntarily or were forced to flee for their involvement in the 1848 Revolution in Germany, were such outspoken critics of American ways that because of this even Germans who had immigrated earlier collided with them. Their difference of opinion was the so-called conflict between the old

"Grays" and the new "Greens." The "Grays," being accustomed to American ways, were disgruntled with the newly immigrated political exiles from Germany who unrestrainedly criticized social evils, such as slavery, and expected to effect sweeping changes in America which they could not bring about in their own country, and at the same time clamorously insisted that they had a right to the lifestyle to which they were accustomed in Germany. Emil Dietzsch, a contemporary of the forty-eighters, described their escapades on page 106 of Eugen Seeger's *Chicago:* "On Sundays they were in the habit of marching through the streets of the city to the strains of blaring bands, preferring to parade past crowded churches on their way to the picnic grounds, where they amused themselves to their hearts' content while guzzling enormous quantities of beer. In short, with more 'courage and vigor' than diplomatic consideration the German lifestyle was demonstrated in order to show the Yankees once and for all what it means to be a 'free German of backbone' and then they enthusiastically assured each other that it was 'just like in Germany.' "

The temperance advocates and many other Chicagoans, however, took a dim view of their boisterous Sunday activities. Their resultant, vigorous anti-German propaganda caused the Teutons many grievances. Minor skirmishes occurred, as for instance between the German "turners" and the Know-Nothings, but for the most part they were confined to free-for-alls preceded or concluded with a rock pelting of the windows at the Turnhall on Griswold Street.

Individual Germans found it difficult to protect themselves against the harassment of the mob and they organized for mutual protection such clubs and societies as the "Harugari" and "Hermann's Sons." According to the *Abendpost* of October 18 and November 24, 1897 the first order of Hermann's Sons was founded in Chicago on October 6, 1852 by Nicolaus Kastler, Anton Neubert, Mathias Krier, Frederick Schmitt, and Georg Baum after the model of the very first lodge in New York which was founded on July 1, 1840. When a prominent German was buried there in the spring of 1840 the long funeral procession on Chatham Street was pelted by rowdies with stones, snow and dirt with the object of splitting up the hated "Dutchmen," to pursue them in all directions, and to abuse them. A certain Georg Heiner, in an ensuing indignation meeting, gave the stimulus for forming a protective society named after the liberator of Germany from the Romans. Paralleling the prevailing persecution of Germans to that suffered by the Germanic tribes from the Romans, he thundered: "A

Hermann is needed to free us from the nationalistic claws." The resulting society of the Hermann's Sons increased enormously in number splitting up into countless lodges and suborganizations. In 1896 there were in Chicago seven chapters of Hermann's Sisters amounting to 865 members that had made themselves independent from the unsatisfactory overlordship of the Hermann's Sons, of whom 500 lodges existed in thirty-eight states totalling 33,000 members. In Chicago there were at least twenty-seven lodges with some 2,000 members.

The stage for the first serious clash between Germans and the Chicago establishment, known as the notorious "Beer Riot," was set in March of 1855, when the former city physician Levi Boone, a colorful distant relative of the legendary Daniel Boone, rode into the mayor's office on the anti-foreign Know-Nothing party ticket. The following summary of this conflict between "whiskey and beer" is culled from an anti-German report in the *Chicago Times* of August 5, 1877 and from the pro-German eyewitness account of Eugen Seeger, a German newspaper reporter, in his book *Chicago*, pages 111 ff.

Soon after Boone assumed office, the Germans became convinced that he was out to implement the Know-Nothing motto "America for Americans" by infringing on what they held to be their rights. On Saturday, March 17, 1855 Mayor Boone issued a proclamation notifying tavern keepers that the Sunday closing law would be strictly enforced by the police force, which was almost exclusively American. On Sunday, March 18 there were many violations of the order and the police "jugged" many a German innkeeper while they did not bother to arrest "respectable" American bartenders in such places as the "Tremonthouse" or "Young America" who sold the "nobler" whiskey.

In addition to this, on March 27, 1855 the liquor licenses for tavern owners were raised from fifty to 300 dollars and they were to be in effect only until July 1, 1855. Only few of the German innkeepers who catered primarily to workers were able to pay the exorbitant fee, and many were forced to give up their businesses. Others, however, defied the order and sold beer without paying for the license. Over 200 of the transgressors were arrested and a test trial of a few violators by Judge Henry Rucker was scheduled for April 21, 1855. The Germans insisted that the frequently flaunted "equal rights provided for by the constitution" were at stake and "if they yielded to oppressive laws that limited their liberties, they would soon be reduced to the same state of servitude as the unfortunate slaves in the South." Therefore, they decided to rally to the aid of their incarcerated compatriots.

A considerable number of Germans armed themselves with every conceivable kind of weapon and marched on April 21, 1855, as the trial was about to start, to the courthouse, complete with fife and drum, in an attempt to intimidate and to effect a favorable judgment for the innkeepers by Judge Rucker. But while they were massing before the gates of the courthouse, some fifty special police agents descended upon them, trying to disperse them with billy clubs. Chaos ensued. A German cigarmaker discharged a shotgun at Officer George Hunt, whose arm had to be amputated the next day. Peter Martin, a German shoemaker, threw away his rifle and ran for safety, but he was pursued and killed by a police officer. The number of killed and wounded could not be ascertained, but it was said that mysterious funerals resulted from the riot on the North Side. Some sixty rioters were apprehended and the rest dispersed into all directions.

The scattered mob gathered forces on the North Side, while the militia General R. K. Swift made battle plans by alerting some 200 deputies, and by placing two antique cannons at the corners of La Salle and Washington streets and of Randolph and Clark streets. However, an Irishman who was in charge of the Clark Street Bridge thwarted the Teutons' thirst for revenge by swinging the bridge open when they approached about three o'clock in the afternoon to cross it in their assault on the courthouse. After considerable shouting and hurling of bloodcurdling threats, the Germans retreated to their favorite inns where they washed down their outrage and damaged pride with their special brand of beer. It is interesting to note that none of the riot instigators was prosecuted whereas in the Haymarket "Riot" of 1886 the leaders were prosecuted and four of them executed for no more evidence of having inflamed the mob than in 1855.

Conflicts between Germans and Americans or foreign groups continued to flare up sporadically. Ever so often Chicago's papers reported about clashes between Germans and other ethnic groups. For instance, on August 17, 1872 the *Staatszeitung* retold a bloody fight between Germans and Irish and on March 7, 1873 it reported that in a fight between German police and Irish on Halsted Street near Esplanade Street the Germans Charles Koch and F. Reiner shot two to death while Koch was clubbed unconscious. The *Tribune* of May 15, 1893 informed its readers about a fight between Germans and Italians at Union and Ohio streets where the German Georg Schiessle was fatally stabbed by Vincent Cardoroni, which almost precipitated a race riot.

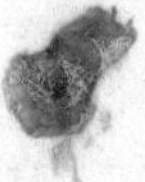

When the Franco-Prussian War was raging in 1870, repercussions were also felt in Chicago, for the enthusiasm with which many

Germans supported Prussia's cause was dampened by anti-German expressions of other nationals. When the Prussians were victorious, the Germans of Chicago staged on May 29, 1871 an elaborate victory parade or, as it was sometimes called euphemistically, a peace demonstration, because they felt that they also had conquered the prevailing anti-German feelings. The *Staatszeitung* of May 30, 1871 asserted that "the parade has the importance of a victorious battle against the prejudices and erroneous opinions of the other nationalities." The same report described in some 18,000 words the parade as the biggest ever in Chicago. Even newspapers which normally were critical of the German element, such as the *Evening Post*, readily admitted on May 30, 1871 that "the big procession was the longest and most impressive Chicago has ever seen." On the same day the *Chicago Times* conceded that "the Americans could not have done it" and that "the jubilee of yesterday was one that would not but excite the most enthusiastic admiration of all that witnessed its intricate picturesque but harmonious details." In spite of glowing reports in the newspapers, many Chicagoans resented the patriotic show of the Germans. They neither liked that May 29, a Monday, was declared a city holiday on which all public offices were closed, nor did they appreciate being awakened at 4:30 A.M. by drums, trumpets, and 101 cannon shots as the festivities began.

The situation was far from being harmonious. The *Staatszeitung* of June 1, 1871 reported that on North Clark Street a big inscription was displayed which read "Denmark mourns with France," that the Irish drove spectators from in front of their homes, and that a proclamation in English was circulated in 100,000 copies asking citizens "to stay at home and not look at this parade of despotism and of the murderers of liberty." Apparently this appeal caused at least one tragedy. The Bohemian Martin Benada refused to watch the hated "nemetz" when his fiancee Catherina, who worked with him in a tailor shop at 403 West 16th Street, asked him to accompany her to the parade. After Catherina went with another escort, Martin killed her and then himself.

The concerted efforts by the Chicago Germans to counteract the anti-German sentiment in a show of solidarity and strength were of little avail. Any Chicagoan who had a pronounced German accent was at a decided disadvantage. Eugen Seeger recounted in his *Chicago* on page 199 that during the Great Fire of 1871 a certain German named Kron was trying to transport in a handcart part of his property to safety on the West Side. On Canal Street a thief attempted to rob him of his possessions. A policeman happened to come by, but instead of helping the German, who was unable to express himself clearly, he arrested him without much ado while the thief carted off the booty.

The Germans, of whom some 50,000 had lost their homes in the fire, attracted much criticism in the aftermath of the conflagration for their opposition to the fire limit ordinance, which provided that only fireproof homes could be erected within the city limits. Even the *Staatszeitung* of January 16, 1872 spoke out against the "mob demonstration of the 10,000 Germans who stormed city hall," in order to show their dissatisfaction with the statute which, because of the high cost of building stone houses, would prevent them from owning homes. The legislator Wilhelm Massenberg stated in the *Evening Journal* of March 20, 1872, that in view of the fire limit agitation in Chicago he was almost ashamed to be a German.

The German element's conspicuous part in eliminating religious instruction from the public schools, in repulsing the temperance movement, in assuring less oppressive Sunday laws, and in the eight-hour movement provided fuel to fan the flames of the anti-German sentiment. The numerous clashes between the German workers and police often gave occasion to the capitalist-controlled press to picture the Germans as rabble-rousers. When in 1886 and 1887 the Haymarket "Conspirators" were convicted and executed as dangerous anarchists, the English language press did not tire of pointing out that the majority of the radical workers were German and attacking the German element as a whole. An interesting example is provided in the case of Martin Beem, a second generation German, born in 1843 at Pittsburgh, Pennsylvania, whose machinations came to light only after he had died in 1888. The impostor Beem denied his German background, as the *Staatszeitung* of May 14, 1888 asserted: "It is, indeed, true that Beem was a son of German parents, although he tried very hard to cover it up, and he understood not one word of German, or at least, he did not want to understand it." Nevertheless, the *Globe* of May 12, 1888, through him attacked the German element:

> This man Beem, who assumed the title of "General" without having any claim to it whatever, this member of the best social clubs, this pretended learned man, and ambitious politician, is now being exposed as a man not only without morals, but also without brains. One exception, however, must be admitted. Although he was insane, there was method in his insanity. He was a German. Of course, it can not be said that all Germans are crazy, but psychiatrists are of the opinion that there is a considerable tendency toward lunacy in

> the German blood. This opinion is confirmed by the large numbers of Socialists, Communists, Anarchists with which the German States are flooding the world.

In the face of harassment and blatantly insulting disregard, Chicago's German newspapers often contained editorials or appeals which took issue with the anti-German sentiment. For instance, the *Abendpost* of March 27, 1899 contained the following appeal: "Germans, come forth to today's meeting of protest at the Auditorium. Let us give a German answer to the propaganda of the Jingos and Anglophiles . . . Above all, the local German-Americans wish to proclaim and prove to the world that they are *bona fide* loyal citizens of this nation . . . " Again on July 18, 1910 the *Abendpost* in the editorial, "German National Character," took pains to explain: "The reason that 'Germans' are inclined to hide or even deny their nationality is to be found in the disposition of the Germanic races and also in the fact that they are more envied and hated than any other nationality."

The nadir in the history of the interaction between the Germans and Americans of Chicago, the hysterical World War I era, was ushered in by a glorious flash, the dedication of the Goethe monument on June 13, 1914. The Chicago Germans rallied every available club or society in an all out effort to obliterate foreboding omens of troubles with successful dedicatory exercises, which were to be crowned by the presence of President Wilson, who was personally invited by a delegation of prominent Chicago Germans. However, few of the high dignitaries deigned to grace the ceremony with their presence and even nature seemed to have forsaken the Germans, for the ceremonies had to take place in an abysmally dreary rain.

While America was embroiled in World War I as enemy of Germany, Chicago's German element received a staggering blow from which it has never fully recovered. This fatal period for the German element started with a seemingly insignificant happening, the assassination of Archduke Francis Ferdinand, heir to Austria's throne, at Sarajevo. The average Chicagoan who read about this political murder in the newspapers of June 28, 1914 discounted the incident as innocuous until July 24, 1914, when suddenly a report of Austria's forty-eight hour ultimatum to Serbia in the *Tribune* alerted its readers to the seriousness of the international crisis. Soon reports of the first armed clashes threw Chicago into a feverish pitch of activities. To a number of Chicagoans the distant war meant increased profits, reflected in higher prices of commodities on the Board of Trade, the price of wheat jumping from

83 cents on July 25, 1914 to $1.65 on February 2, 1915; and in reports, as the one of the Coudahy Packing Company of December 9, 1917, which listed gross sales of $184,811,000 for its past fiscal year, by far the largest figure in the company's history. On September 21, 1914 Charles G. Dawes, the president of the Central Trust Company, stated at a banquet of insurance underwriters that the United States was entering the greatest era of prosperity in its history.

For the foreign nationals whose native countries were embroiled in the war, however, the European clash signified an emotional turmoil. The School Census of May 4, 1914 indicates that Chicago's total population of 2,437,526 consisted in part of 876,288 foreign-born and another 754,570 with foreign-born parents. The Germans by far constituted the largest foreign group, amounting to 399,977, 191,168 born in the old fatherland and another 208,809 of German parents. The total number of the ten other largest national groups were as follows: Polish 231,346, Russian 166,134, Irish 146,560, Swedish 118,533, Italian 108,160, Bohemian 102,749, Austrian 58,483, Norwegian 47,496, English 45,714, and Canadian 44,744. The smallest foreign group consisted of 242 Mexicans.

Along with other war-affected foreign groups, the Germans held many patriotic meetings as soon as news of the war reached Chicago. On August 2, 1914 the newspapers reported that the German community of the North Side was full of German and American flags and that the patriotic pieces of the numerous bands propelled the masses into chauvinistic frenzies. The *Tribune* of August 4, 1914 reported that close to seven hundred Germans had registered at the German Consulate, eager to return for military duty in the fatherland.

On August 5, 1914 a mass meeting in excess of 10,000 Germans at the Auditorium listened to impassioned speeches by prominent German-Americans and resolved to send cables to the German and Austrian Emperors Wilhelm and Franz Joseph in which they pledged their support. At the same meeting the *Abendpost* and the Eitel brothers of the Bismarck Hotel gave $1,000 each to the local fund for the German and Austrian Red Cross which by February 1, 1915 amounted to $44,204 and by January 13, 1916 to $351,136. To foster and to demonstrate solidarity, Germans organized in societies such as the 1915 founded Teutonic Sons of America which, accordng to the *Tribune* of February 13, 1916, had over a million national members, with thousands of them in Chicago.

The initial enthusiasm was comparable to the one generated during the 1871 peace celebration of the Franco-Prussian War, but ominous clouds of anti-German sentiments were also present in that the speakers in the mass meeting at the Auditorium on August 5, 1914 stressed that they wanted "not favors but justice for the German cause." Already on July 31, 1914 the *Abendpost* had published many letters of Chicagoans, among them the prominent German-Americans Ernest Kruetgen, August Lueders, Lorenz Mattern, Oscar Mayer, and Jacob Kraft, who expressed their outrage at the biased newspaper reporting of the Anglo-American press.

Gradually the Germans' patriotic enthusiasm faded in the face of adverse reactions. The war progressed and newspaper reports of alleged German atrocities continued to appear and America's official neutrality was violated and infringed upon repeatedly by both sides. In spite of the fact that the *Tribune* on September 18, 1914 published a long dispatch from John T. McCutcheon in Aachen which asserted that there was no evidence for German atrocities, the anti-German campaign of American newspapers continued in full swing, as for instance, when the *Tribune* of December 28, 1914 published photos of the war front with captions such as "In this river thousands of Germans died like rats." Hatred of Germans was also instigated in many other ways, notably in movies. One such movie was "The Ordeal" which showed German soldiers decapitating children, raping women, and committing similar barbaric acts in the war, all of it portrayed in the last scene as having been a bad dream. Because it could incite race riots, this film was barred by Major Funkhouser of Chicago's vice squad on November 23, 1914, after it was shown in the Bijou Dream Theatre on State Street. Nevertheless, the *Abendpost* of December 28, 1914 reported that this very film was shown in Chicago as Christmas fare.

Meanwhile the friction among the various nationalities increased and engulfed most public institutions. Chicago's public schools were the first to be affected on a broad scale. On September 3, 1914, Mrs. Ella Flagg Young, superintendent of public schools, was compelled to issue an order forbidding the children from the various nationalities from settling their differences on school playgrounds.

Chicagoans of German extraction were frequently labelled with derogatory intent "hyphenated Americans," and in a variety of ways reacted against this slur. One of the more civilized examples of counteracting this insult may be seen in the following excerpt of an editorial in the *Abendpost* of December 31, 1914: "We are of German blood and heritage, but we are also citizens of the United States. We call ourselves German-Americans and every day we become more proud of this name. To us, the designation German-American seems proper and fitting. Nothing else would do. But other people do not agree with us. They deny us that right. They scoff at the implication of Germanism contained in the expression and call us 'hyphenated Americans,' which is to say, Americans with a mental reservation, or 'grade B' Americans."

Americans believed they had reason to question the loyalty of the Chicago Germans, or as they sometimes said, the disloyal "Dachshund element," when they read in the newspapers that Germans publically celebrated such occasions as the 100th anniversary of Bismarck's birth or Emperor Wilhelm's birthday. As a matter of fact, some Teutonic factions in Chicago were "more German than Germany." The emperor's birthday on January 28, 1915 passed officially unobserved in the old country, but members and friends of the Germania Club observed the Kaiser's birthday at their clubhouse in "a solemn and quiet celebration." There had been some controversy about the advisability of observing this celebration, but it was nothing in comparison with the storm that was raised over the celebration of Bismarck's 100th birthday on April 1, 1915. Pro and con arguments filled the German newspapers, of which the two most important ones were divided about the issue, the *Staatszeitung* being for and the *Abendpost* against the public celebration. In an announcement of March 1, 1915 in the *Abendpost* Ernst Kusswurm, president of the "Chicago Turngemeinde," stated that his "Turner Club" resolved not to participate in the celebration, giving the following reason: "The 'Chicago Turngemeinde' adheres to its traditional point of view that those who have taken the oath of American citizenship should refrain from celebrating in public any birthdays or anniversaries of foreign political leaders, regardless of their prominence." Some others who declined in the *Abendpost* to be part of the Bismarck celebration were C. G. Geleng, president of the Central Association of German War Veterans' Societies, and J. Danziger, director of the Chicago branch of the "German-American Nationalbund." However, the *Staatszeitung*, being for the celebration, appealed to its readers in several advertisements to participate by flaunting such slogans as "A united Germany is invincible! Dear fatherland, may your righteous cause lead you to victory!"

The Bismarck celebration took place at the Auditorium as planned on April 1, 1915 and over 4,000 listened to Congressman Henry Vollmer's assertions that a general anti-German movement had gripped the nation: "A slanderous and venomous battle is being waged against us. Whatever we may say or do, it will be misconstrued. When I, shortly before the beginning of the last session of Congress, probed into this thing, I found that a spiritual and physical campaign against Germany and Austria, and in favor of Engalnd and her Allies, had started in the United States."

The slanderous and venomous battle to which Vollmer alluded increased in intensity by leaps and bounds because of various reasons. One major factor was Germany's unconditional submarine warfare and the concomitant sinking of ships with American citizens aboard, such as the *Lusitania* on May 7, 1915. This not only precipitated America's eventual entry into the war, but also contributed much to the war hysteria that soon engulfed Chicago. The city was made painfully aware of the grim realities of the war, when the passenger lists of the torpedoed boats were released, for there were usually Chicagoans among the persons killed.

Agitators drummed up a feeling of preparedness in speech and writing. For instance, Henry Reuterdahl warned in the 1916 February issue of the *Metropolitan News* of an impending German invasion and alerted the people to be ready. In this milieu it is not surprising to find that on May 24, 1916 the Board of Education voted to introduce military training in all city high schools in the fall and that a few days later, on June 3, 1916 130,000 people marched for eleven hours through the Loop in a preparedness parade, the biggest demonstration in Chicago's history. The Chicago Germans served as convenient scapegoats to the inflamed tempers of the frenzied Chicagoans. Already on January 10, 1915 the *Sonntagspost*, commenting on "German Baiting in Chicago," had stated: "We Germans happen to be the most hated people in the world. Anybody who was ever dubious about that has had ample and frequent opportunity since the outbreak of the great conflict of nations to get rid of his doubt." This hatred of Germans was whipped into a feverish pitch through many factors and knew no bounds after America had declared war on Germany on April 7, 1917.

War hysteria was fanned to the utmost in many patriotic speeches and editorials. Anybody who dared to stand up for the Chicago Germans' interests was maligned as an infidel "German sympathizer" and this included Mayor William Thompson. When late in April of 1917 a French commission, headed by Rene Viviani, Minister of Justice, and General Joffre, hero of the Battle of the Marne, intended to visit Chicago, Mayor Thompson hesitated to invite them. He pointed out that only 3,681 French-born people lived in the city, but that Chicago was "the sixth largest German city in the world." This statement by "Kaiser Bill," as he was subsequently called, not only was taken up throughout the country, but also proved to usher in hectic, troublesome days for the mayor. The city council discussed on June 22, 1917 his impeachment, but dropped its demand for the mayor's resignation or impeachment on June 25, only to censor him again on June 28.

There were abundant war-related news reports in the Chicago papers to keep the city in a frenzied state for the duration of the war and even beyond that. On February 12, 1917 the newspapers were full of reports about the sinking of the Cunard liner *Laconia* and the fate of two Chicago women who perished with it. In March hardly a day passed on which not one sensational item was reported, as for instance, on the 12th President Wilson ordered the Navy to arm all ships, on the 21st the American steamer *Healdton* was sunk without warning, and on the 26th Governor Lowden ordered the mobilization of the Illinois National Guard.

Once the war was declared on April 7, 1917, much inflamatory news found its way into the newspapers, as some examples for a short span of time show. On August 19, 1917 an anti-war meeting by a pacifist group at Riverview Park was reported at which Max Eastmann, "Socialist firebrand," was one of the speakers. On September 1, 1917 Chicago police, acting under Governor Lowden's orders, dispersed a meeting of the pacifist group, People's Council of America for Democracy and Terms of Peace, but on the next day Mayor Thompson was reported as having defied Lowden by permitting the pacifist group to meet. This precipitated a crisis in that Governor Lowden ordered four companies of militia from Springfield to Chicago. The newspapers of September 4, 1917 informed that the city council resolved forty-two to six to condemn the mayor for permitting this meeting to take place. On September 5 and 6, 1917 one reads about raids by Federal agents at the headquarters and homes of five officers of the pro-German International Workers of the World and at the German *Chicago Arbeiterzeitung*, as well as the *Sozial Demokrat*, and a "radical" German bookstore at 817½ North Clark Street. Finally, on September 17, 1917 it was reported that William J. Bryan in a speech at the La Salle Hotel had declared that people who at this time insisted on their right of free speech to criticize America are not law-abiding citicens but promoters of anarchy.

Such war-related accounts continued to appear at a furious pace, and as if this were not enough to inspire hatred of Germans, fear was instilled through reports of suspected planned and accomplished sabotage or hostile enemy activities in the city or its vicinity. According to the *Tribune* of December 12, 1915, Hinton Clabaugh, head of the Chicago Division of the U.S. Secret Service, investigated a plot to blow up the Aetna powder works and the Gary steel plant. On August 19, 1917 "a mysterious fire" inflicted heavy financial losses on the Armour & Company ice plant. Chicagoans could read on November 16, 1917 that "2,000 at the Auditorium almost panic when a home-made bomb sputters without exploding in the aisle" during the first act of the opera "Dinorah." Not few readers suspected sabotage when they read a few days later on December 2 that thirty-nine soldiers were hurt when one of several troop trains returning to Camp Grant from Chicago was wrecked by a broken switch. "The worst crime wave in Chicago's history" constituted top news on February 9 and 10, 1918. It was combated with mass arrests of 1,000 known and suspected criminals, many of whom happened to be German aliens. When a ban on public gatherings was imposed from October 15 to 29, 1918, ostensibly to avert a "flu epidemic," many Chicagoans expressed the belief that it was done for the prevention of a catastrophe through sabotage.

Surprisingly often reports about hostile I.W.W. activities or alien arrests occurred. On September 28, 1917 Chicago's grand jury indicted 166 leaders of the International Workers of the World for sabotage, conspiracy, and plots akin to treason, of whom "Big Bill" Haywood and 99 others were found guilty on August 17, 1918. The papers reported on February 12, 1918 of the tarring and feathering of two Chicago German I.W.W. leaders John L. Metzen and Sezerion Oberdan at Staunton, Illinois. On September 4, 1918 it was reported that a bomb exploded in the Federal Building of Chicago, killing four and injuring thirty, and that police and secret service men suspected the I.W.W.

During these turbulent days, the Chicago newspapers were not models of objectivity. On July 11, 1918 they reported about the arrests of more that 5,000 Chicago draft evaders and unregistered aliens, but this number was reduced considerably to 1,137 on July 12, as happened quite frequently when initial, inflated figures were given. On February 6, 1918 Chicago newspapers reported that heavy losses of life occurred when the troop ship *Tuscania* with 2,173 Americans aboard was torpedoed in the Irish Sea, but subsequent reports reduced the number substantially. Moreover, reports of war-related news often were accompanied by inflamatory editorials, lashing out at the Chicago Germans, "the disloyal Dachshund element." Thus, the English language newspapers were responsible for a great share of the hatred of Germans. The German papers waged a strenuous campaign against them, trying to refute slanted arguments in their editorials and rectifying distorted figures, but it was all in vain, because only Germans were reading them, not those who needed to be influenced. They finally vented their anger and frustrations in impotent scoldings, as is evident in the *Abendpost* of January 18, 1919: "The American press of today is a cesspool. Its chief occupation is the condemnation of everything that is German or that has a German tint."

In addition to the hate-inspiring newspaper reports and editorials, there were numerous war rallies, speeches and other means of propaganda, which intensified the anti-German sentiment during America's participation in the war. A few days before the official declaration of war, two huge patriotic rallies were held at the Auditorium on March 31, and on April 3, 1917, at which Governor Lowden, former Secretary of War Henry L. Stimson, and Edmund J. James, president of the University of Illinois, generated enthusiasm of the masses by calling for a "just war against Germany's barbarity." Theodore Roosevelt did his best to arouse the masses against Germans in two addresses to capacity crowds at the Dexter Pavilion at the Stock Yards. In his fiery speech of April 28, 1917 he wanted to lead the fighting men in Europe against the "huns," and again on September 26, 1917 he denounced America's German language programs and press as detrimental to America's well-being.

To forestall harassment, many Chicago Germans tried their best to placate the overwrought community. They proved their loyalty in word and deed. On July 4, 1916 some 6,000 German-born Chicagoans attended a patriotic meeting at the Coliseum to pledge unconditional loyalty to America. Immediately after President Wilson's announcement of the break of diplomatic relations with Germany on February 3, 1917, the German Club of Chicago with about 2,500 members pledged absolute and unqualified support to the United States. On December 2, 1917 the *Tribune* informed its readers that the formerly pro-German teachers of the German Lutheran parochial schools met to decide that "Americanism undefiled" be taught and that classes be started and dismissed with singing the national anthem. The Germans pointed out that the honor lists of Chicagoans fallen in the battlefields of France showed a disproportionately large number of German names.

They employed logic, as contained in a letter to the editor in the *Abendpost* of August 22, 1918 by a certain Sophus Hartmann: "If one were to believe a certain kind of newspaper or certain plays which are now being performed, the morality and dignity of the German people must indeed have reached a low level. Are the German people supposed to have suffered sudden and complete degeneration? No, and no again, this is not true!"

All this was ineffective in averting hostilities, as were the praises and defenses of the Germans printed in German newspapers. When a man of German extraction attained a successful position, the German papers waxed enthusiastic in their praises. For example, they lauded Hermann Schuettler as the savior from the El Dorado of criminal vagabonds when he was appointed as chief of police on January 10, 1917. Dr. Georg Scherger, professor of history at the Armour Institute, bubbled over with enthusiasm for everything German in the following excerpt of an essay published in the *Staatszeitung* of January 19, 1915: "The German people are the most cosmopolitan in the world; they are wonderful. No language of the world is so flexible and fit for the translation of works of other languages as the German. Shakespeare is better known in Germany and his works are more often performed than in England. The Germans know our literature as well as we do. There is no educated German who will not speak four or five languages at least . . . " It was an ineffective attempt to bolster the Germans' morale in the face of impending disaster and, instead of appeasing the anti-German camp, may well have inflamed it even more.

The Chicago Germans represented a threat to Americans and were treated accordingly. The least that was demanded from the suspected enemy was "Americanization," described in the March 1919 issue of *Everybody's Magazine* by George Creel, chairman of the Bureau of Publicity, as a rather vague term which essentially meant blotting out the multifarious expressions of foreign cultures. Creel berated those zealots who forced their way to public attention at the beginning of the war by "hounding the foreign-born citizens of our country in order to Americanize them." A touching anecdote is told by him of a Bohemian woman to whose house "Chicago Americanizers" came, saying, "We have come to Americanize you and your family." As it turned out, her sons were not present and could not be "Americanized," because they had gone voluntarily to serve in the U.S. Army.

A popular demand from the Know-Nothing period, "America for Americans," could be heard again and again. A certain Paul H. Burglund, in a letter to the editor in the *Tribune* of September 15, 1918, recommended that the citizenship of all Americans of German descent be revoked for the duration of the war "to give us complete control of all offices in the country." While this was impracticable, offices and jobs were taken away from Germans. The prominent musician, William Boeppler, who was to serve as choral director of the Illinois Centennial Pageant at the Auditorium from October 7 to October 12, 1918, was forced to resign because of vigorous opposition to his German background. It did not help him to assert in the *Tribune* of September 21, 1918 that he was a full-fledged, loyal American. On May 3, 1918 Captain George Hull Porter, president of the Illinois Athletic Club, announced that all German employees had been discharged, and on May 16, 1918 the Chicago Athletic Association followed suit by announcing that it had dismissed eighteen enemy aliens. The German Aid Society reported on September 8, 1918 that innumerable unemployed Germans urgently needed to be supported by charity, because only 360 of a large number could be placed in 960 available jobs. Few, usually only those of German stock, were willing to hire Germans, as the *Sonntagspost* of January 5, 1919 pointed out in the editorial, "No Germans Need Apply Here."

War hysteria found some strange outlets. The *Abendpost* of November 21, 1918, reporting about a cargo of German toys held up in Holland during the war, described the senseless fears that people held concerning them. Stirred on by vigilante groups who had demanded a strict boycott of all German-made goods, women's organizations wanted to protect the American children from the "Hun-made drums." They expressed even fear that these toys were poisonous or germ carriers and would cause an epidemic among American children. Senator Henry Cabot Lodge introduced a bill specifying that dealers in German-made merchandise must post conspicuous signs over the entrance of their store, announcing "Dealer in German Merchandise," which, of course, would have been tantamount to financial suicide.

It was indeed a troublesome time for the Chicago Germans, as William Stuart recalled in his book *The Twenty Incredible Years* on page thirty-eight:

> 'Hunting the Hun' became a pastime. The propaganda of hate was on. Chicago was doing her part as a great American city which never had failed in a national crisis, but it was not enough for some of those beating the war tom-toms and repeating the stories of the 'German atrocities in Belgium.' Pictures that chanced to put the German people in a favorable light were ordered off the screen. Excited young women hunted out and denounced youths suspected of being 'slackers.' There was a demand that a page in the school histories that praised the Kaiser be torn out. 'Spies' were arrested . . . Every day there was a report that this or that prominent German had been sent to a federal prison—false reports but serving their purpose.

The Germans were frequently harassed and persecuted, especially if they were stubborn. One such case was reported in the *Abendpost* of August 12, 1918: "Fred Grimmie, fifty years old and living at 54 East 18th Street, refused to stand up as 'The Star Spangled Banner' was being played last night on the Municipal Pier. Neither would he do so when asked by Miss Beatrice Larson and Mrs. Mabel Latimer. The two women then called Seascout Edward Coleman, to whose request to stand up Grimmie paid no attention either. Some other seascout then seized the man and had him arrested." Nothing is known about Grimmie's future tribulations, but there were many cases of imprudent Germans who suffered, because they failed to adjust to war hysteria. The *Abendpost* of November 1, 1918 reported about August Weissensel, who, when arraigned before Federal Judge Kenesaw M. Landis, was told by him that a thief fighting in France was a better citizen than he ever was. Weissensel, a man of about sixty, had been in this country for forty years and was an American citizen. He had uttered "pro-German statements" and "tried to convert one of his sons to his own pro-German ideas." In sentencing Weissensel, Judge Landis decreed: "For the sake of your son who is serving in the army, I will impose on you only half of the punishment the espionage law provides for—ten years in the federal penitentiary at Leavenworth."

Because of turbulent conditions during World War I many German-Americans were taken into custody. On February 16, 1917, the *Tribune* reported that all persons suspected of being militantly pro-German were under surveillance and that in case of war these persons were to be detained in camps to protect Chicago's industries. As soon as war was declared against Germany on April 7, 1917, some sixty Germans were arrested for their alleged pro-German activities. Some of them were Gustav Jacobsen and Albert Wehde, both of whom were convicted on October 20, 1917 for conspiring to cause a Hindu rebellion in India; Adolph Germer, national secretary of the Socialist party; and William Kruse of the American Liberty Defense League. According to a report in the *Tribune* of June 1, 1918 Judge Landis asserted in a speech before the Illinois State Bar Association banquet at the South Shore Country Club that the "Kaiser's" agents penetrated everywhere in Chicago.

All the Germans interned during World War I, of course, were not agents of the "Kaiser." The *Abendpost* reported on March 12, 1919, that some 5,000 Germans had been interned during the war in camps at Fort Oglethorpe near Chattanooga, at Fort Douglas near Salt Lake City, and at a camp near Hot Springs, North Carolina. Among about 2,500 private persons interned were prominent people, many of them from Chicago. To name just a few, Adolph Payenstadt, Carl Heynen, and Hugo Schmidt represented German banks, while Dr. Karl Much and Director Kuhnhardt were famous musicians. According to the *Abendpost* of March 12, 1919, many of the private Germans in the internment camps were held without charge: "The government suspected them, however, and they were placed in custody merely as a precautionary measure. Those who were guilty of a crime were prosecuted. But there were cases to which the existing criminal laws did not apply. People who disregarded the ordinances issued by the president, professional agitators, propagandists, and foreigners who had made themselves obnoxious were also interned. In some instances people were interned upon their own request in order to protect them against threats or dangers."

At times, together with the internment of Germans, occurred the confiscation of property owned by individuals suspected of sympathizing with Germany's cause. On March 12, 1919 the *Abendpost* asserted that H. A. Seebohm, manager of a German-owned chemical factory, had been interned and that the factory was under the supervision of the U.S. Alien Property Custodian. The confiscated possessions were not properly returned to their owners after the war. The *Abendpost* of April 3, 1926 told of a demonstration in favor of the Mellon Bill, which dealt with returning the property seized during the war: "Yesterday's meeting of the delegates for the German Day celebration turned into a sharp demonstration of protest against the retention of German property confiscated during the war. Captain A. P. W. Siebel made a rather long speech in which he pointed out the illegality of the confiscations . . . " One of the most publicized cases of property seized from Chicagoans was that of the Schoenhofen family. This family is known not only for the enormous pyramidal mausoleum in Chicago's Graceland cemetery, but also for the large brewery business established by Peter Schoenhofen (1827-93), who came in 1855 from Germany to America. Since the family cultivated ties with Peter's native land, the authorities singled them out and confiscated their possessions. It is said that Graf Schenk von Stauffenberg, who carried the bomb into Hitler's bunker on July 20, 1944, was a descendant of Peter Schoenhofen.

In an effort to avoid persecution some individuals and organizations resorted to changing their names. The Germania Club, founded in 1865 to become one of the foremost social organizations still in existence today, yielded on May 9, 1918 to the signs of the time when its members decided unanimously to rename it "Chicago Lincoln Club." Ten days later the Eitel brothers followed suit in changing the name of the Hotel Bismarck to Hotel Randolph while Hotel Kaiserhof became Hotel Atlantic. Not only provocative business titles were changed such as "Kaiser Friedrich Mutual Aid Society" to "George Washington Benevolent and Aid Society" on November 11, 1918, but also common, unobtrusive family names. The *Abendpost* reported that on August 20, 1918 alone the following persons asked the court for permission to give up their German names and to assume others in their stead. Harry H. Feilchenfeld, owner of a poultry firm on 206-8 North Wells Street, became H. H. Field. Otto W. Mayer from 1013 Foster Avenue wanted to be called Mayor, while Hans Kaiser turned into John Kern. Emma E. Gutmann had tried Gutman, but found it necessary to change her name to Goodman. A Berta Griesheimer asked to be named Gresham and a Joseph G. Schuman, son of the German Wisconsin settler Schumann, changed to Shuman. Numerous other examples could be adduced by comparing spelling changes in a pre-war Chicago *Who's Who* to later ones.

Changing of names became a political issue in the mayoral elections of 1915 and 1919. Robert Sweitzer, the Democratic candidate, was accused in numerous editorials and by other candidates of having dropped the *ch* from his name. Carter Harrison let the German constituents know that Sweitzer was not really deserving their votes since he had denied his German background by assimilating his German name. Sweitzer was forced to publish in the Chicago German newspapers an account of his background which started out with the arrival of his German ancestors, named Schweitzer, at New York's Castle Garden in 1855.

Chauvinistic zealots did not stop with persecuting Chicago Germans, but they also wanted to obliterate every trace of the German imprint on Chicago. The least harm done in that respect was total disregard for the Germans' role in shaping Chicago, as happened in the Centennial Pageant in the Auditorium on May 11, 1918, where in scene five, the Allied Nations' Grand Finale, all nations appeared that had a part in Chicago's history. Such nations as Serbia or Japan were represented which had 629 and 269 nationals respectively living in the city by 1914, but Germany was not represented though 191,168 of its natives lived in Chicago, the largest number of Chicago's foreign-born inhabitants, followed in second place by Poland's 124,543. The only historical character of German extraction appearing in the pageant was Lieutenant

Linai T. Helm in the "Massacre of Fort Dearborn," but most likely only because the organizers were not aware of his German background. Disregard alone did not make the Teutonic imprint disappear in Chicago. There were other "patriotic" activities which were less innocuous, most notably those of vigilante groups such as the "National Security League, the Protective League, the Knights of Liberty, and the American Defense Society," which, according to the *Abendpost* of February 6, 1919, left a "permanent stain on America's honor by inciting the various nationalities to mutual hatred and violence."

The most obvious target of Germanism was the German language. Since its first introduction into the public school system of Chicago in 1865, the popularity of German as an academic subject has had its ups and downs, but no negative reaction was comparable to the one during the war years. Still on September 9, 1914 the *Abendpost* exhorted its readers, as it and other German papers had done frequently, to have their children instructed in German in the public schools from grade five on, "because the German language is destined to become the world language, and that he who does not master it to some degree at least, will suffer economic disadvantages or will have less chance of progress than those who understand and speak German." According to a report in the *Staatszeitung* of June 17, 1915 by Martin Schmidhofer, Superintendent of German in the public schools, 18,160 pupils studied German in 112 schools during 1914/15. 11,557 of these pupils allegedly were not of German background. But as the war progressed, a precipitous drop in the number of students taking German occurred until finally many schools dropped German altogether. Early in the school year of 1917 the *Tribune* of September 4 and 7 reported that Chicago's Board of Education had banned German in elementary schools, but that in high schools German continued to be taught as long as there was demand for it. Naturally, soon after, many high schools did away with German also. Some of the decisions to eliminate German were published in the papers, as when Glen Ellyn High School dropped all German classes on March 29, 1918. In September of 1918 a group of citizens headed by the DAR member Mrs. C. C. Bird circulated a petition to abolish German in the Oak Park High School and in River Forest Township High School. The *Abendpost* of January 16, 1919 showed comparative statistics of a few high schools to show how enrollment had dropped from September of 1918 to January of 1919:

High School:	September 1918:	January 1919:
Tuley	208	108
Austin	150	50
Crane Tech	200	45
Englewood	150	0
Fenger	104	0
Morgan Park	35	0
Tilden	25	0

By September of 1919, of this list at least Tuley High School had also dropped all German classes. It was only a small step further when Samuel Insull, chairman of the State Council of Defense, asked that the general assembly pass a law barring the use of any language but English in the Illinois grammar schools.

Concurrent with the general abolition of German in Chicago's schools was its widespread suppression in public life. Though officially German was never outlawed, common demand banished it. For instance, on August 31, 1918 the Chicago newspapers reported that the seven local German Freemason lodges were ordered by the State Grand Lodge to conduct their meetings in English. The three noncomplying lodges Germania, Lessing, and Waldeck were simply expelled. By April 1, 1918 the *Tribune* somewhat prematurely informed its readers that Chicago's German singing societies discontinued their Sunday afternoon concerts at which German songs had been presented.

Last ditch efforts to adhere to their valued cultural heritage were made by some German clubs until they were forced by mob action to cease their activities. The *Staatszeitung* of June 22, 1918 made known the almost violent prevention of a public concert with German songs, and at the same time asked for support of the newspaper or it would succumb, as it in fact did as a daily in the later part of 1918, being published as a weekly until 1925 under extremely adverse conditions. The *Abendpost* of September 9, 1918, in the editorial, "The Fight Against the German Language," gives an inkling of how demanding it was to cling to the use of German: "At a meeting of a local German women's lodge held not so long ago, an American-born member, both of whose parents were German, rose from her seat and demanded for 'patriotic reasons' that thenceforth all proceedings should be conducted in the 'American' rather than in the German language." The editorial continued to state that the American Defense Society had published a report in which it told of its success in its "defense" against the German language. The society proudly reported that fourteen states have forbidden the teaching of German in all of their schools, and that in sixteen other states a campaign was in progress to bring about a similar ban. One of the resultant letters to the editor by a certain E. Berger of Maywood on September 20, 1918 stressed that two-thirds of all local German clubs would cease to exist if only English were permitted.

This bleak picture for Chicago's German clubs, accompanying the suppression of the German language, apparently was not exaggerated in view of the fact that already on June 25, 1917 the *Staatszeitung* informed its readers of an alarming trend: "Nearly every day we are informed that another German-American society has given up its usual activities, that festivals, many of which serve charitable purposes, have been postponed, that meetings and conventions will not be held while the war lasts." It is true that many clubs or societies only suspended their activities during the war years until more auspicious times would be more conducive to their work, such as the German-American Historical Society, but for many German organizations the imposed inactivity was a fatal blow. Those of the eighteen local German lodges of the Independent Order of Odd Fellows that suspended their activities, rather than comply when they were ordered to use only English in their business meetings, did not resurface in more auspicious times.

At times the language question became more important than justice, as the *Abendpost* of November 10, 1919 pointed out in reporting about a damage suit dating back to 1916. A plaintiff, able to communicate only in German, had asked for an interpreter, but the judge refused to do so and appointed a language teacher for him, explaining that the case would be recessed until the plaintiff could speak English.

It is astonishing to find in Chicago still streets, schools, and monuments with German names, because for a time it appeared as if hysteria would blot out everything German, as a few of the more publicized examples will show. On March 28, 1918 students at Bismarck School on North Central Park demanded that the school's name be changed to its present name, General Frederick Funston School, and a certain Thomas A. Willoughby asked in a letter to the editor in the *Tribune* of March 17, 1918 for demolition of the German House in Jackson Park, which had been saved in response to a general request after the World's Columbian Exposition in 1893. On April 14, 1918 more than 1,000 Polish-Americans signed a petition, asking the city council to change all German street names. This was followed up on April 16 by a meeting at St. Hedwig School at which it was resolved that Alderman Adamowsky ask city council to change all German street names in

Ward twenty-eight, such as Berlin, Hamburg, Frankfurt, Coblentz, Lubeck and Rhine, which was promptly done.

Though trying vigorously, the zealots failed to effect a change in the name of Goethe Street. On December 17, 1918, Gold Coast residents, through their spokesman Fred A. Cary and Alderman Earl J. Walker of the 21st Ward, recommended to the city council that the name of Goethe Street be changed to Boxwood Place, "because nobody could pronounce it properly." They staunchly denied that the name's German origin was the reason for the proposed change, but when Alderman Coughlin's suggestion of Busse Place, after the former mayor (1907-11) of German extraction, was not acceptable to the petitioners, the true motivation for the attempted change became obvious. Comic relief in the fight for the name "Goethe Street" was provided when Aldermen John Haderlein and B. S. Schwartz proposed that, if the change could not be avoided, it ought to be called "Nutwood Street" to properly characterize adherents for the irrational change. All German clubs and even disinterested citizens strongly protested the proposed change, so that the city council on April 2, 1919 unanimously refused to alter the street's name which it had received in 1843.

Not only the name "Goethe Street" but also the Goethe Monument in Lincoln Park was an object of vexation to some Chicagoans in that it bore witness to Germany's culture, striking a discordant note in the "German barbarity" campaign. The *Staatszeitung* of April 16, 1918 stated that certain people living near the entrance of Lincoln Park on Diversey Boulevard had threatened to tear down the monument and cast it into Lake Michigan. One of the Park Commission's planned preventive measures included its temporary removal. On May 7, 1918 the Chicago newspapers reported that "two Americans" had smeared yellow paint on the statue and had left a placard demanding its immediate removal.

The Americanization process of many originally German organizations or institutions was in many cases so complete that people forgot their German origin. Few people realize that Grant Hospital was known as "German Hospital" before World War I, having been founded on December 17, 1883 by a group of prominent Chicago Germans. Likewise, hardly anybody knows that the Chicago Symphony Orchestra was composed almost exclusively of Germans in pre-war days. This world-famous orchestra, which has done more to eradicate Chicago's sinister image in the world than any other cultural institute, was founded officially in 1890 by the German Theodor Thomas (1835-1905), and had a precarious existence throughout the war era because of the predominant anti-German sentiment.

The first step in Americanizing the orchestra was made on February 24, 1913 when the trustees of the orchestra decided to change its name from "Theodor Thomas Orchestra" to "Chicago Symphony Orchestra" over the vigorous protests of its patrons, who favored the old name two to one, according to the Chicago newspapers. During the war the harassment of individual orchestra members began. In August of 1918 hardly a day passed on which the orchestra was not in the news. On the ninth of August four members were questioned about their alleged anti-American statements, and on the following day the Conductor Frederick Stock and the Manager Albert Ulrich were summoned by District Attorney Clyne for the purpose of Americanizing the orchestra. On August 13, 1918 Assistant U.S. State's Attorney Borelli questioned the following members in connection with alleged "pro-German statements: Alfred Guensel, flute; Otto Hesselbach, viola; Henry Woelfel, violin; Kurt Baumbach, flute; and Albert Ulrich, trumpeter and manager. Rumors circulated about cancellation of the American citizenship and possible imprisonment of Bruno Steindel, cellist.

According to a report in the *Abendpost* of August 17, 1918, attempts to break up the orchestra were so persistent that counter tactics had to be employed by the members. It included a public show of loyalty, which stressed that the musicians had subscribed 16,300 dollars to the third Liberty Loan while their wives had done extensive work for the American Red Cross. In addition to that, the orchestra's manager, Albert Ulrich, warned the members in a meeting at Ravinia Park on August 16, 1918 not to be foolishly provocative by saying: "If ever I hear the slightest disloyal or pro-German remark from anyone of you, I will report him not only to the orchestra society, but also to the Department of Justice, to make him pay for his foolishness. The times are too serious for foolish remarks of sentimental devotion to the old country, too serious for anti-American speeches of any kind. Speak the American language, so that every one can understand what you say; think before you say anything and always be aware of your duty toward the country we all love, the United States of America."

The *Abendpost* of August 17, 1918, which reprinted Ulrich's exhortation, reflected that this imposed show of loyalty seemed strange in view of the fact that Ulrich not only had a son serving in the navy, but also had been an American citizen since 1878. Of 91 orchestra members 88 were American citizens and two additional ones possessed their first papers. Nevertheless, after endless meetings, compromises, and even threatened libel suits, the Chicago Federation of Musicians on October 11, 1918 expelled the orchestra members Bruno Steindel, Otto Hesselbach, William Krieglstein, and Richard Kuss and on October 1, 1918 Frederick Stock had to resign as conductor for a period necessary to become a citizen. Stock was reinstated as conductor on February 28, 1919, even though he had not yet become an American citizen, which happened amidst much publicity on May 22, 1919. When the twenty-ninth orchestra season opened on October 17, 1919, Chicagoans, as if to recompense them for the troubles suffered, paid homage to Stock and the members of the orchestra in a long standing ovation.

When Chicago found out about the end of the war on November 11, 1918, after a false report of armistice on the seventh of November, the hostilities between Germans and Americans in Chicago did not cease abruptly. Still much incendiary news about German-connected anarchists or agitators circulated to keep passions high. According to the newspapers of October 14, 1919, hundreds of war veterans raided quarters of the International Workers of the World in South Chicago and burned piles of propaganda pamphlets. On January 1 and 21, 1920 the *Tribune* reported that close to two hundred anarchists and Communists were rounded up and indicted.

Exhibits of German war atrocities still fueled the hatred of Germans. A certain C. A. Koenig in a letter to the editor in the *Abendpost* of October 18, 1919 expressed his outrage about a "war relics exhibition," at Clark and Madison streets near the Morrison Hotel, where pictures were shown representing "the height of vileness and vulgarity." The examples described were such scenes as German soldiers nailing children to barn doors, and women with hands cut off surrounded by guffawing Germans.

It took a while before the German element gradually asserted itself again, even though there were early attempts to do so. For instance, Ernest Kruetgen, owner of a lithograph shop and Chicago's postmaster in the 1930's and 1940's, attempted to stage a public German Day festival in 1920, which proved to be a spectacular failure in that hardly anyone participated. Chicagoans of German descent were simply tired of persecution and avoided compromising situations. Typical is a letter of August 31, 1920, by Alfred de Liagre to Dr. Otto L. Schmidt, in which the twenty-one names of persons who contributed between $1,000 and $5,000 to the American Committee on the Study of the Causes of War, were coded to protect their identity and avoid possible harassment.

The American public still was incensed when anyone showed the slightest traces of German sympathies, as Professor William E. Dodd of the University of Chicago found out. He had stated that the vindictive peace terms imposed on the Germans were comparable to those imposed on the South after the Civil War for which he was subsequently assailed by Civil War veterans' groups. It is not surprising to find that many people of German background refused to contribute any money to such an unpopular undertaking as attempting to redeem Germany. For instance, when G. Fasting of Chicago solicited money from Charles Nagel, a highly prominent German-American of St. Louis, for the Neutral Commission on the Study of the Causes of War, Nagel declined to help by stating: "Unhappily, conditions in our country have been such that if a citizen bearing a German name has regarded anything in the German people as commendable, or has entertained doubts about the real cause of the war, his suggestions will be received with hesitation, if not suspicions."

Even though Chicago papers on October 6, 1923 flaunted captions such as, "100,000 Chicagoans gather on Municipal Pier to celebrate German Day and hear Mayor Dever explain why he is trying to stop the sale of beer," Chicago's German element was still reeling from the severe blows of war hysteria. A more realistic picture is portrayed two years later in the *Abendpost* of July 13, 1925 in a report of a demonstration by some 3,000 in Humboldt Park to show that "the German oak tree is still alive despite some devastating storms." Ernest Kruetgen appealed to the Germans to be proud of their background, asserting: "A German who denies his German descent is like Judas, the betrayer, and deserves to be despised by all respectable people."

German-Americans did not easily forget what they suffered for their Teutonic background. This was expressed by Georg Seibel in his German Day speech of August 13, 1933, when he summarized the persecution of Germans during World War I as follows: "This pride in our Germanic origin has caused us German-Americans great suffering during the bitter war years. Thousands were interned, beaten, ruined in business because they were German. German books were burned, and 'patriotic' women avowed never to buy German goods again. We were called barbarians and Huns; we were the 'scum of humanity' because we were German. The world had gone mad with war hysteria."

In the 1930's several German groups sympathetic to the Hitler regime in Germany contributed to the propagation of anti-German sentiments. Already in 1929 the Nazi periodical *Vorposten* was founded in Chicago to distribute, "News of the German Freedom Movement in America." The *Scandia* of January 18, 1934 reported on fascist organizations established by Germans, such as the Friends of New Germany, the "Bund der Auslandsdeutschen" (Association of Germans Abroad), the Brown Shirts, and a number of "front organizations" like The Stalwart Americans which, in spite of their American names, were nevertheless fascistic in their anti-Catholic, anti-Semitic, anti-labor, and pro-war propaganda.

Of these organizations especially the "Bund" and the Friends of New Germany were known as extremely troublesome, rabble-rousing societies. In 1936 the Friends became the "German-American Bund" and were also known under the name of German-American People's League. Fritz Gissible, "Gauleiter" (District Leader) of the Middle West for the Friends, became notorious for his rabid rantings about the "Fuehrer" and German nationalism. On August 12, 1933 he announced with a dramatic flair in the *Abendpost* that his organization would not participate in the German Day celebration of the World's Fair in Chicago, "because of the continual insults to the German flag and the Government of Germany." It was only the swastika flag which was banned, because it represented a party flag and was a symbol of anti-Semitism. This ban coincided with the wishes of the German group representing a large segment of Chicago Germans who generally opposed the activities of the fascist groups. Symptomatic of the sentiment of many Chicago Germans in this regard is the following warning against joining the "Bund" in the *Sonntagspost* of August 27, 1933: "To establish and maintain close cultural relations between German-Americans and their compatriots in the old country, we do not need any consolidation of American societies under the auspices of organizations which have headquarters in Germany, with statutes and bylaws controlled by a foreign government. We must make this clear because the 'Bund' which is composed of Germans who are citizens of the Reich and German colonials, with headquarters in Berlin, has made the announcement that it would not rest until all German-American societies had joined it. The *Sonntagspost* is of the opinion that the German-American societies are not a suitable object for the activities of the Berlin organization."

Though the "Bund" tried to consolidate the German element under its overlordship, the great majority of the German-Americans did not want to have anything to do with it. William Seabrook's book, *These Foreigners*, also gives testimony of the fact that only about ten percent of the German-Americans could be termed sympathizers of Naziism and that only one percent or less were "rabidly militant Nazi in a not nice way." In Chicago the Nazi movement never became as strong as in New York and even there it fizzled out after 1939 when the national leader of the "Bund," Fritz Kuhn, was convicted on a variety of charges and imprisoned.

According to Richard O'Conner's book, *The German-Americans*, page 452, "Unlike World War I, pro-Germanism was a dead issue in the United States by the time the country went to war with the Axis. No hysteria this time, except in regard to the innocent Japanese-Americans. How could there have been with an Eisenhower leading the second American expeditionary force against Germany, a Spaatz commanding the bombers which were pulverizing Germany, a Nimitz in command of the Pacific Fleet, an Eichelberger and a Kreuger commanding the two armies under General MacArthur?"

Of course, there were during World War II instances of German baiting in Chicago, just as there had been before, especially if the victims were known to espouse tenets of the Nazi Party, but in general the hatred was directed this time not so much against the German people *per se*, as against an ideology embraced and propagated by Hitler and his henchmen. Laura Fermi also points out on page 316 of her book, *Illustrious Immigrants*, that during World War II a drastic change in policy was evident since World War I, because many sensitive, war-related jobs were given to aliens which would have been impossible during the first armed clash of the nations.

Even today the German-American National Congress, founded in Chicago upon the instigation of Leonard Enders in 1958, devotes much effort in its monthly publication, *Der Deutschamerikaner*, to combating anti-German sentiment in America. This publication points out, for instance, that because of the excessive number of war movies, which depict Germans as the hated enemies, in war games of American children the opponents of "Americans" are usually "Germans" and not enemies of more recent wars. Even Bill Kurtis remarked on the Channel Two five o'clock news of January 24, 1975 that the Korean War and the Vietnam War have been practically ignored by the film makers in favor of the clash between Germans and Americans during World War II.

Chapter 4

A Group of People Suspended Between Two Nations

The German-American Chicagoans frequently were suspended in a strained relationship to both their native homeland and their adopted homeland. Specifically, their expressions of loyalty to either country became a cause for discord. There were, of course, individuals who felt no compunction to dissociate themselves completely from everything German to become "more American than Americans," but many German newcomers to America were in many ways still attached to their native land. Those German-Americans who did not want to sever their ties with the fatherland completely, but felt they owed it some loyalty, were often put into trying situations.

The officials of their native land often dealt with them in a stepmotherly fashion. This was exemplified by Bismarck, who was "possessed by a raving madness against America and German-Americans," according to the *Staatszeitung* of October 26, 1885. He allegedly expressed the opinion that "Germans once in America lose interest in their language and what is more, speak insultingly of Germany." Some Chicago Germans tried their utmost to convince Bismarck that the German-Americans "cling with all their love to the old fatherland and honor the Kaiser highly," as Professor Hoffmann did, according to the *Staatszeitung*'s sarcastic report of December 26, 1885. Bismarck deigned to become an honorary member of the Chicago German Veterans Club, when a delegation from this club sought an audience with the "Iron Chancellor" and assured him of their deep gratitude and loyalty.

The leaders of the Chicago Germans who tried to cling to and preserve as their precious cultural heritage the German language, customs and education, instead of venerating German autocrats, were made aware that they represented the forgotten Germans, whose interests were callously disregarded. There were few official expressions of gratitude for their selfless relief work in times of crises, such as during the Franco-Prussian War in 1870/71 or after World War I. On the other hand, when the German government would have been in a position to help relieve suffering in the United States, they turned a deaf ear. After the Great Fire of 1871 many Chicagoans of German extraction were made painfully aware of, and bitterly denounced, Germany's procrastination in sending aid in any form. Chicago Germans had to bear the brunt of criticism when no official condolences were extended from the German government at President Garfield's death in 1881 and at other diplomatic *faux pas* by Germany's authorities.

Most German-Americans felt obliged to and were anxious to demonstrate in a variety of ways loyalty to their adopted homeland. However, many American zealots believed that they were lax in repaying the hospitality of their new homeland, insinuating that they were putting the interests of their native country above those of America. Not infrequently German-Americans were forced into publically stating that in case of conflict of interests their loyalty would unhesitatingly be directed toward America.

Carl Schurz, who had fled from Germany as a "forty-eighter" and became Secretary of the Interior under President Hayes in 1877-1881, was often placed into a position where he had to affirm his loyalty to the United States. In March of 1872 the Republican Senator Mathew Carpenter of Wisconsin reproached him for his German birth, accusing him of being in "his innermost heart still a subject of Emperor Wilhelm." This slur followed in the wake of an incident at a congressional hearing a month earlier. In February of 1872, during a congressional inquiry into the American sale of arms to France during the Franco-Prussian War, Schurz was accused of "German sympathies." In the ensuing retort Schurz defended his German background, asserting at the same time his pride in being an American citizen. A short excerpt of his apologia follows, taken from page 227 of the 1922/23 issue of *Deutsch-Amerikanische Geschichtsblätter*:

> I certainly am not ashamed of having sprung from that great nation whose monuments stand so proudly upon the battlefields of thought; that great nation which, having translated her mighty soul into action, seems at this moment to hold in her hands the destiny

> of the Old World; that great nation which for centuries has sent abroad thousands and thousands of her children upon foreign shores with their intelligence, their industry, and their spirit of good citizenship; while I am by no means ashamed of being a son of that nation, yet I may say I am proud to be an American citizen. This is my country. Here my children were born. Here I have spent the best years of my youth and manhood. All the honors I have gained, all the aims of my endeavors, and whatever of hope and promise the future has for me, it is all encompassed in this my new fatherland. My devotion to this great republic will not yield to that of the Senator from New Jersey, nor to that of any member of this body, nor to that of any man born in this country. I would not shrink from any sacrifice to prove it, as I never did shrink from it . . . . This Senator also intimated yesterday that the German-born American citizens could not entirely forget their old fatherland. Possibly not; but I ask him, should they forget it? Does he not know that those who would meanly and coldly forget their old mother could not be expected to be faithful to their young bride? Surely, sir, the German-born citizens of this country have demonstrated their fidelity in the hour of danger.

Most German-Americans attacked for sympathies toward "Mother" Germany could not defend themselves as eloquently as Schurz did, but they demonstrated their fidelity to "Bride" America whenever they were propelled into the agony of choosing sides in a clash of interests, most notably during the two world wars. Ernest J. Kruetgen, a prominent German-American leader in the Chicago Centennial celebration at the "Lincoln Club" on November 10, 1918, described the German-Americans' plight during World War I, as follows: "Faithful and loyal Americans as the German-Americans are, they cherish the memory of their childhood days, their literature, and their music. A man may give his son for his adopted country, or may even shed the last drop of his blood for it, but the man who could change the love for his own, his native land into hatred could never become a good and trustworthy citizen of any other country."

No matter how loyally they performed their duties for America, the German-Americans, just as other ethnic groups, were often accused of shirking their fair share in the wars of their adopted homeland. Already during the Civil War, especially after the battles of Fredericksburg and Chancellorsville, German soldiers were defamed as the "Dutch cowards." This happened quite frequently in spite of vigorous retorts by German veterans of the American Civil War. For instance, the Chicago German soldier, Wilhelm Vocke (1839-1907), who later became a prominent Chicago lawyer, felt compelled to refute such attacks in the *Nashville Union* of June 10, 1863. In the Spanish-American War General Arthur McArthur infuriated the German element by deprecating the German-Americans' role in the wars of America, and during World War I German-Americans were disparagingly called "the disloyal dachshund element." However, objective studies demonstrate that the German-Americans have contributed their fair share to the wars waged by the United States, even when the enemy was the land of their origin.

The Chicago Germans on the whole have obeyed the call to arms conscientiously. In the garrisons of Fort Dearborn German names appear again and again. During the 1812 massacre, Lieutenant Linai T. Helm, a Pennsylvania German, was second in command while John Simmons and August Mott, soldiers of German background, perished. In the Black Hawk War of 1832 German soldiers also served. Of the Chicago militia that saw action in May of 1832 under Gholson Kercheval, at least one, John Wellmacher, was German and the militia sent from Michigan as reinforcement was commanded by the German J. E. Schwartz. At least four of the forty-three signers of the peace conference of 1833 were German, namely John T. Schermerhorn, Georg Bender, J. E. Schwartz and A. H. Arndt. Some of the German militia men may have settled in Chicago and vicinity. In any case, during the 1833 peace conference many of the individuals that claimed sums of money or tracts of land, such as Georg Hollenbeck, Nicholas Klinger, Thomas Hartzell and H. B. Hoffmann, were of German background. The Chicago militia between 1842 and 1848 consisted partly of Germans, and in 1847 almost all of its officers were of German extraction: Captains—J. B. Wier and Frederick Schäfer, First Lieutenant—Richard P. Denker and Second Lieutenant—Charles Kotz.

According to the lists in the first volume of Andreas's *History of Chicago*, many Chicago volunteers for the Mexican War were German, such as August Stempel, Henry Brunner and Frederick Wenter from the First Regiment and John M. Bauer, August Eberhard and August Seidler in the Fifth Regiment. In addition to those mentioned by Andreas, there were other Chicago Germans that served. One of them was Henry Budde, who saw action in the First Regiment under Captain Mowers in Company K and was wounded in his left leg in the battle of Buena Vista on February 22, 1847. In 1845 at the age of thirty years Budde had come from Hannover and worked as a lumberman until 1846, when he bought a sixty-acre farm in Niles township. After the Mexican War he bought an additional 160 acres and farmed there until he retired to Chicago in 1895.

Another German participant of the Mexican War was the mechanic, Dietrich L. Jürgens, who had emigrated from Germany in 1845 to follow a previously emigrated sister to Milwaukee. As an eighteen-year-old youth he came to Chicago in 1846 and joined the Third U. S. Infantry Regiment on March 3, 1847. Later he married an American girl and established a tool factory in Chicago.

At times the Chicago Germans' role in the Civil War was lauded. This happened, for instance, when the Illinois lieutenant governor and *Tribune* editor, William Bross, addressed the annual "German Old Settlers' Picnic" at Ogden Grove on August 25, 1879. According to the *Tribune* of August 26, 1879, Bross averred that the Germans to a man were on the side of the Union, that "their ballots and their bullets were equally on the side of freedom." However, often the Germans' role in the Civil War has been ignored. This happened in history books, as for instance in Paul Angle's *Pictorial History of the Civil War*, which mentions the German soldiers only once on page 58 to state that the German-American Franz Sigel, though rallying many Germans to the Union's cause, fought without distinction. However, he failed to add to the caption of a picture on page 198 that all officers of the 82nd Illinois Infantry Regiment instrumental in the fall of Atlanta were German-Americans. Even worse, the Germans have been attacked for their part in the Civil War.

After slanderous attacks of the Germans by the Know-Nothings, the *Staatszeitung* of July 20, 1863 retorted in the editorial "Copperhead Lies about Germans:"

> We hardly need to mention that these slanderous reports are nothing but a pack of lies. Germans are loyal citizens of the United States. The Teutons love the land of their adoption and the liberty they enjoy in it. They were the first to take up arms in defense of government and the Union. Germans snatched the state of Missouri from the clutches of the Secessionists and kept it in the fold of the Union, and on every battlefield Germans have proved their love and loyalty to the Union, the refuge of all who are persecuted and oppressed. The German citizens of this country who were willing to rise up against the tyrants of their former fatherland have no sympathy whatever for the rebellion of the slaveholders.

This favorable description of the Germans' role in the Civil War apparently corresponded to reality, for they in fact rallied wholeheartedly to the colors of the Union. So eagerly did the Germans obey the call to arms and swell the ranks of the Union Army that General Robert E. Lee of the Confederate Army allegedly asserted: "Take the Dutch (German) out of the Union Army and we could whip the Yankees easily."

The estimates of the number of Germans fighting in the Civil War vary considerably, but the fairly reliable statistical work of Benjamin A. Gould, *Investigations in the Military and Anthropological Statistics of American Soldiers*, published in 1869 from the records at the national and state capitals, puts the number of soldiers born in Germany at 176,817, which contrasts favorably with 144,221 Irish and 45,508 English fighting men. Albert Faust calculated in his *The German Element in the United States* on page 524 that, according to the relationship of volunteers to total population, the Irish furnished 5,169 men beyond the proportionate rate while the Germans conscribed 58,415 soldiers in excess of their proper share.

Of the total number of 176,817 German soldiers fighting in the Civil War, Illinois provided 18,140, of whom the majority came from Chicago. When after South Carolina's secession on December 20, 1860 ominous shadows of impending hostilities were cast, many Germans obeyed the call when concerned Chicagoans held a preparedness meeting at Bryan Hall on January 5, 1861. Some of the more prominent Germans present were Edward Voss, A. C. Hesing, N. Eschenburg, Julius Rosenthal, Lorenz Brentano, Ernst Pruessing, Georg Schneider, E. Schlaeger and Adolph Loeb. In addition, an exclusively German preparedness meeting at the German House was organized by Carl Haussner for January 8, 1861. After the poet Casper Butz and the orator E. Schlaeger instilled the assembled Germans at this meeting with patriotic fervor, elaborate recruiting plans were forged.

Many Chicagoans of German extraction fought in the Civil War. A. T. Andreas confirmed on page 196 of volume II of his *History of Chicago* that German fighting units were among the first to be ready for battle. By March 29, 1861 the *Staatszeitung* reported that from the "Chicago Turngemeinde" (Chicago Turners Community) alone forty "turners" had signed up for the Union Cadets which were to be part of the 60th Illinois Regiment. According to the *Staatszeitung* of May 5, 1861 the German companies "Turner Union Cadets," under Captain Kowalt, and Lincoln Rifles, under Captain Mihaloz, were at Camp Cairo, and at Camp Yates were the German companies from Chicago Union Rifles I, under Captain Robert Lippert, and Union Rifles II, under Captain Sten, the Washington Light Cavalry, under Captain Schambeck, and the Washington Light Infantry, under Captain Mattern. Schambeck's company, composed of 102 Chicago Germans who had served already in the Old Country, in their eagerness to see action, apparently left for war too early, because the *Staatszeitung* of July 1, 1861 reported that the government quarters at Cincinnati were not ready to receive them, so that they had to fend for themselves in securing meals and sleeping quarters. The same paper disclosed on July 14, 1861 that Christian Thielemann, who after the war was to own a theater on Clybourn Avenue, had lead a company, "a troop just as brave as Schambeck's boys," which also had to support itself on its way to the battlefield.

Schambeck's Washington Light Cavalry and Thielemann's Dragoons had been the first to follow Governor Yates's call for volunteers and formed the nucleus of the almost exclusively German Sixteenth Illinois Cavalry Regiment. An exclusively German infantry regiment, the Twentyfourth Illinois or the "first Hecker Jaeger Regiment," was organized at Chicago on June 18, 1861, where Colonel Hecker, the celebrated freedom fighter of the 1848 Revolution, addressed the soldiers at the flag presentation as follows, taken from page 196, volume II of Andreas's *History of Chicago*:

> Soldiers! Comrades! It is now twelve years ago, that I stood opposed in strife to the despotisms of Europe, and took up arms against them in behalf of freedom and independence. I now take a solemn oath to here defend the same. If we shall come to any engagement with the traitors to liberty, I will be your leader. I, on foot, will ask you to follow me; and if I fall, I only ask you to bring me back from the field, having avenged me. My hair is gray, the last hours of my life are not far off, but the arms I have taken up for our dear adopted country shall only be laid down with life. I will lead you to victory. Will you follow this flag?

Indeed, the Germans were eager to follow the flag of their adopted homeland, and on July 8, 1861 the ten German companies of the Twenty-fourth Illinois Regiment were mustered into service, headed by the captains Thomas Lang, Georg Heinrichs, Anton Sten, Leopold Becker, August Mauff, August Kovats, Julius Standan, John van Horn, Henry Ried and Ferdinand Rolshausen. In its more than three years of service it saw action in many battles, such as Perryville, Stone River, Dutch Gap, Chicamauga and Missionary Ridge.

Frederick Hecker resigned from the Twenty-fourth Regiment in December of 1861, and upon returning to Chicago organized the "Second Hecker Jaeger Regiment," the 82nd Illinois Regiment, which again was composed exclusively of Germans. Chicago Germans enthusiastically supported Hecker's recruiting efforts. The colorful sheriff, A. C. Hesing, funded Company B, known as the

"Hesing Sharpshooters," and the banker Henry Greenebaum recruited twenty-three men for Company E and stimulated in patriotic speeches pledges for more than $11,000. The 82nd Regiment was attached to the U. S. standing army on October 23, 1862 under the captains Anton Brun, August Bruning, Jacob LaSalle, Mathias Marx, Robert Lender, Frederick Weber, William Neussel, Emil Frey, Alexander Weid and Joseph Gruenhut.

In addition to the Sixteenth Cavalry Regiment as well as the Twenty-fourth and 82nd Infantry Regiments, there were other fighting units composed primarily of Chicago Germans. The Forty-third and Forty-fourth Infantry Regiments, as well as the First and Thirteenth Cavalry Regiments, were almost exclusively German. The Chicago German newspapers reported again and again that German companies were being recruited or leaving for battle, as for instance on May 24, 1864, when the *Staatszeitung* reported that 300 German-Americans had signed up for Peter Schimp's company and that August Ries and Joseph Schulte were the recruiters among the turners.

Of course, many Chicago Germans served in other than purely German regiments. For instance, the American Consul to Bremen, Dr. Theodor Bluthardt (1837-1906), who had been a prominent public servant of Chicago, served as Assistant Surgeon of the First Illinois Cavalry Regiment and was severely wounded at Lexington. The eighteen-year-old twins Charles and Frank Affeld served in Battery B of the First Illinois Light Artillery Regiment and the journalist, General Hermann Lieb, later Cook County clerk, served in the Eighth Illinois Infantry Regiment.

The list of fatalities for the German fighting units were long. Lorenz Mattern recollected about 1900 that of the 1,000 men who joined the Twenty-fourth Illinois Infantry Regiment with him, over 600 were missing when he was discharged in 1864. Soon after the German companies had left Chicago to fight in the Civil War, reports of casualties appeared in the German newspapers of Chicago. The *Staatszeitung* of November 5, 1862 reported grim, but familiar news, the death of another turner. This time it was Bernhard von Hollen, a twenty-four-year-old "turner" from the First Hecker Regiment, whose upper arms had been shattered in the Battle of Perryville and who was promoted to lieutenant hours before he died on October 28, 1862. Of the "Chicago Turngemeinde" (Chicago Turner Community) alone, fourteen were killed on the battlefields, five died as prisoners in Andersonville, and four drowned, as the *Abendpost* of September 18, 1927 reported in an account of a celebration during which a commemoration tablet perpetuating their names was placed in the "North Side Turnhalle."

The only Chicagoan killed at Fort Donelson was a private in Taylor's Light Artillery, Oscar Beckers, who was born at Aachen and came to Chicago as a stone cutter in 1854. According to page 272 of the second volume of Andreas's *History of Chicago*, Beckers's dying words were, "Go back, boys, and man the guns, I die for Liberty!" The *Tribune* of May 13, 1877 reported that at Waldheim Cemetery, now Forest Home, alone about 100 German-American Civil War soldiers were buried.

Soon after the Spanish-American War, General Arthur McArthur insisted that a German name in the regimental lists was a curiosity. Numerous Civil War veterans of German extraction considered this an outrage and together with other groups interested in repulsing attacks upon the good name of America's German element commissioned an investigation which conclusively demonstrated that, just like in other wars, the German-Americans had furnished more than their proportionate share of fighting men during the Spanish-American War. Many of the soldiers were Chicago Germans. It is interesting to note that in the 1958 spring issue of *Chicago History* on page 121 a picture of soldiers in Camp Thomas at Chicamauga Park, Georgia, waiting to be sent to Cuba, portrays a Chicago German, the quartermaster sergeant Arthur C. Lueder, who later became Chicago's postmaster.

Already on April 25, 1898, the day after the Spanish government had declared war, the *Abendpost* reported that prominent Chicago Germans, such as Karl von Wolfskeel and Wilhelm Reisenegger of the City Map Department had asked Governor Tanner's permission to organize a German sharpshooter battalion. Moreover, a German volunteer regiment was being recruited in wards 13, 14, 15 and 16. The enthusiasm generated among Chicago Germans induced many men to volunteer for service, so that by April 30, 1898 the *Abendpost* had announced that Captain Bloch intended to form a new battery since the artillerist contingent was so large.

Not only young men, but also veterans signed up for service. For instance, the former Prussian officer Frank Bielefeld, who had also fought in the American Civil War, decided to lead the "German Turner Regiment." So great was the Germans' eagerness to serve that not all of them could be accommodated in German fighting units. Many Germans, such as the second lieutenant Robert Lippert, entered the Seventh Illinois Regiment, known as the Irish Regiment. On June 18, 1898 the *Abendpost* reported that a delegation of Chicago Germans, headed by F. J. Dewes, Wilhelm Vocke and Georg Schneider, had sought an audience with Governor Tanner to induce him to call to the front the impatient German-American regiment commanded by Colonel Schumm.

In the meantime Chicago papers of June 6, 1898 headlined that Professor James T. Hatfield had resigned his position as head of the German Department at Northwestern University to enlist as a common sailor in the navy. His reports from the war in the 1902 spring issue of *Deutsch-Amerikanische Geschichtsblätter* gave testimony of the meritorious, but unappreciated service of German sailors on American battleships.

Strangely enough, almost at the same time that Hatfield volunteered, the eminent German Professor Hermann E. von Holst, head of the History Department at the University of Chicago, strongly opposed war with Spain, for which he was so severely attacked that on June 19, 1898 President Harper of the University of Chicago was obliged to defend openly his right for freedom of speech.

Many Chicago Germans did see action in the short war, but more perished from disease than from hostile activities. The *Abendpost* of September 7, 1898 stated that of 1,334 Chicago German-American volunteers only 1,167 were accounted for and that at least fifty-three had died at Montauk Point.

Not until World War I were the Chicago Germans put into a position of having to fight against people of their own blood. Many of the 191,168 foreign-born and 208,809 second generation Germans of Chicago in 1914 openly expressed their support for the German cause in gigantic patriotic demonstrations, as the Chicago papers reported almost daily after the beginning of World War I in August of 1914. On August 5, 1914, for instance, over 10,000 German-Americans in the Chicago Auditorium resoved to pledge in telegrams to the German and Austrian Emperors their unconditional support. However, as diplomatic relations deteriorated between Germany and the United States, the Chicago Germans feared that they would be called upon to fight against their own people. This apprehension became a reality when the declaration of war between the two countries was announced on April 7, 1917.

To be sure, there were news of German war resisters and draft dodgers. According to the *Tribune* of May 2, 1921, there were 17,000 "slackers" in Chicago of whom one German, Hans Jacob Zimmermann, was arrested on May 27, 1921. As one Chicago paper sarcastically stated, he "claimed he could not kill a fly" and had spent the war reading Tolstoy's works on his father's farm north of the border in Alberta. However, by far the majority of those Germans called upon to prove their loyalty to their adopted homeland obeyed the painful call to the colors for the fight against people of their own blood.

The ensuing agony of having to fight against their own people was expressed in the Lincoln Club's Chicago Centennial celebration of November 9, 1918, by its president, Ernest J. Kruetgen, who stated that, "just as Lincoln called Americans of the North to fight against their brothers in the South to preserve the Union, so have Americans of German blood been called upon to take part in our country's struggle against the people of their own races."

The German newspapers of Chicago were eager to point out to Americans that the Germans were not shirking their military duty. On September 1, 1918 the *Abendpost* stated that a particular troop in France contained forty-one percent volunteers of German descent, and on September 17, 1918 it reported that the well-known war correspondent of the *New York Times*, Charles H. Grasty, had asserted on September 5, 1918, that "one out of four American fighting men had a German name" and that "we have no better soldiers."

The German papers did not tire of stating that the leader of the "American Expeditionary Force to France," General John Pershing, had come from German ancestry with the name of Pfoerschin and that Chicago's flying ace, Eddie Rickenbacker, was a second generation German whose former name had been Reichenbacher. In the editorial, "The Rejected Stone of the Building," the *Abendpost* of May 7, 1919 printed a formal recognition of the German-Americans by the United States government, stating that "the registrants of German parentage rallied to the colors loyally by the thousands." The editorial also cited numerous case histories of loyal Chicago Germans, such as August F. W. Siebel, who had been born on the island of Rügen in 1877, and after coming to Chicago had served not only in the Spanish-American War, but also commanded a company of the 132nd U. S. Infantry Regiment in France during World War I. In addition, the *Abendpost* contrasted an example of German and "American" loyalty to the United States' cause by relating how a local "pure" American politician, whose son was a draft dodger, had advocated the defamation of German-Americans after he had been defeated by a German opponent whose sons had joined the American army voluntarily. That Chicago's German constituents did their full share of military duty during World War I may be seen without a doubt in a survey of Cook County's honor roll listed for the respective war years in the *Daily News Almanac*. At least a fourth of the fallen soldiers bore German names.

During World War I, as in other military clashes, the Chicago Germans also supported America's cause financially, as a German Club's *Bulletin* (volume III, page 9) pointed out: "The German Club of Chicago in the matter of Liberty Loan purchase, under the direction of Mr. Henry Zander, exceeded by far such staunch patriotic organizations as the 'Hamilton Club of Chicago.' " The Central Loan Committee gave a summary on May 3, 1918, of the Third Liberty Loan subscription by nationalities as follows: Germans—$18,000,000, Polish—$9,500,000, Italians—$8,500,000, South Americans—$5,825,000 . . . . Even though from this source it seems as though the Germans had purchased the most bonds among the foreign nationalities, the *Abendpost* of April 20, 1919 reported that in the Fifth Liberty Loan drive, the Germans were in third place behind the Czechs and the Poles, because many did not admit that they were German. In exhorting its readers to pledge as much as they could to buy Liberty bonds, the same paper on May 5, 1919 pointed out that the Germans had given much, but were not usually given credit as Germans, but rather were entered in the records as nonclassified nationals.

During World War II the Chicago Germans' loyalty to the United States on the whole repeats the same pattern. However, mainly because of decreased immigration there were not as many first and second generation Germans in Chicago as during World War I. Moreover, the more remote German ancestry minimized the divided loyalty factor. Chicago's German element furnished its fair share of fighting men during World War II, as a survey of the regimental lists and the honor rolls of the fallen soldiers reveals.

Chapter 5

The German Element's Role in Public Life

The Chicago Germans' role in politics and their presence in the municipal government is exceedingly interesting. German newspaper editorials and political leaders of German extraction frequently commented on the disproportionately small representation and unfair allotment of municipal offices to the German constituents of Chicago. A few typical complaints published in Chicago newspapers should suffice to demonstrate some of the Chicago Germans' displeasure with the disregard of the Teutonic element in public offices.

On January 7, 1893 the *Staatszeitung*, as a mouthpiece of the German-American Club, lashed out against those who were elected by promising to consider the German contingent, but then allegedly broke their promises: "The German American Club considers the deliberate procedure by which its recommendations were nullified and shelved to be an absolute disregard of the German people, which comprises exactly one-third of the voting strength of Cook County." In the same year the *Abendpost* of November 27 asserted: "The German voters are barely represented in the city government. On the other hand all departments except the judicial are headed by men of Irish blood." On October 18, 1925 the *Abendpost*, as part of a report on an anniversary celebration of the German Club in the Cameo Room of the Morrison Hotel, reprinted a speech delivered by William Rothmann, who belabored the point that "Chicago's German element takes very little part in the administration of state, city and country. Only a few, like Edward Litsinger, Judge Theodore Brentano, Charles Dieters, Arthur

Lueder, and a few more represent the German element in public life, while one-third of the city's population is of German blood." Finally, the April 1966 issue of *Der Deutsch-Amerikaner*, the official organ of the Chicago-based German-American National Congress, reported that the office of Postmaster of Chicago was in danger of being given to a non-German. To avert its occurrence it urged a letter-writing campaign to Mayor Richard J. Daley, stressing that "this office was in the last years the only noteworthy position held by a German-American."

Some of the complaints about the unfair representation of Germans were repeated so often that they became devoid of meaning. For instance, the *Abendpost* of January 17, 1927 reported that when Edward Litsinger, the Republican candidate for mayor of Chicago, spoke before 500 members of the German Lutheran Welfare Society, he asserted that the German element never wielded the influence it deserved and that before him only once was an American of German descent candidate for mayor. Presumably he referred to Arthur C. Lueder, who had been the Republican candidate for mayor in 1923. However, he was not aware of the fact that Robert R. Sweitzer, the Democratic candidate for mayor in 1915 and 1919, also liked to mention in his campaign speeches that before him no other German-American ever was mayoral candidate of Chicago. None of them apparently knew that before Sweitzer at least twelve Chicagoans of German extraction had run for mayor, the first one being Dr. Ernst Schmidt in 1879 on the Socialist ticket, and that one of these candidates, Fred A. Busse, was elected to serve from 1907 to 1911.

It is, of course, impossible to investigate for every year the relationship of inhabitation or voting strength to representation in public life of the German element in Chicago's history. A few representative years in the nineteenth century, when the Chicago Germans tended to see themselves as a separate ethnic group, will give some idea about the German element's ratio of population to representation. The *Staatszeitung* of April 22, 1868 listed all German aldermen from Chicago's sixteen wards as follows: Ward Three Charles G. Wicker, five—John Raber, seven—James H. Hildreth, twelve—C. J. Kasselmann and John Buehler, thirteen—Georg T. Beebe and Georg K. Schmidt, fourteen—Theodor Schintz and Louis A. Berger, fifteen—John Herting, and sixteen—Georg B. Manisur. Considering that in 1870 Chicago's 59,299 German-born citizens constituted 19.83 percent of the city's total population, it seems that their share in the number of aldermen, amounting to eleven of the total thiry-two, was more than adequate. However, one must remember that the aldermen listed above include those of remote German ancestry and that the percentage of Chicagoans of German extraction was much higher than 19.83, amounting to at least one-third of Chicago's population, according to statistics in Chicago's German newspapers.

By 1871 the total number of aldermen in Chicago amounted to forty, but the number of Germans among them was reduced to eight, listed as follows for the various wards: ward six—Michael Schmitz, seven—William Battermann, eleven—Hermann O. Glade, fifteen—John Buehler, sixteen—Georg K. Schmidt, seventeen—Louis Schaffner and Theodor Schintz, and twenty—Gustavus A. Busse. The *Staatszeitung* of May 13, 1871 pointed out that the city council was composed of seventeen Americans, thirteen Irish, eight Germans, as well as two English and that in only four out of twenty committees Germans presided, namely Schintz in the judicial committee, Schmidt in that of the streets and alleys of the North Side, Busse in that of harbors and bridges, and Battermann on the markets committee.

Not only the city council representation of Germans was disproportionate, but also their relative number on Chicago's police force, according to the *Staatszeitung* of April 20, 1871. Even though there were 14,000 more Germans than Irish in Chicago, the city employed only 131 German policemen, but 158 Irish policemen. The newspaper held that if a strictly proportionate standard were used, Chicago's 53,000 Germans would be represented by 165 policemen, whereas the 39,000 Irish would have 110.

More and more Germans were eliminated from the police force, as the *Staatszeitung* of July 16, 1873 substantiated by quoting the official books of the police board. During the business year of 1872, 139 new officers were appointed and 85 discharged. Of the 139 new ones only fifteen were German, but of the 85 dismissed, thirty-three were German. Even more striking are the figures given for the police personnel change from July 9, 1873 to July 15, 1873: of 38 new appointees only three were German, but five of eight who left the police force were German.

In the city council the number of German aldermen also declined steadily. On April 12, 1881 the *Staatszeitung*, while commenting on the loss of a few council seats held previously by Germans, bitterly stated in the editorial, "The North Side Is Now Irish," that "everybody had believed that the North Side was German, however, the last city election proved that the North Side is an Irish district. Considering the nationality of the elected officials, it does not leave a shadow of doubt in our mind that this is absolutely true."

By 1893 the number of Germans on the city council and also in other public offices was at a conspicuous ebb, causing the *Staatszeitung* of March 18, 1893 to state in an editorial that "the same impertinence which was shown of the Republican party last fall has now been adopted by the Democrats. It may be recalled that the Republicans selected Hertz as coroner. He was a Scandinavian and they tried to pass him off as a German." The Democratic party nominated twenty-one Irish-Americans, but only four German-Americans as aldermen.

This disregard of the German element found expression in much public disapproval by German spokesmen, which gave the *Tribune* of March 21, 1893 cause to wonder why the Teutons were upset. A glance at the school census population figures and the voter registration statistics gives the answer. In 1893 Chicago's German population amounted to 405,822 in contrast to the Irish 169,048. In addition, the number of registered German voters had increased steadily to become twice that of the Irish. In 1886 there were 81,733 total registered voters in Chicago of whom 42,710 were American, 14,556 German and 11,988 Irish. The next largest voting block, the English, consisted of 2,441. But by 1892 the total number of voters was 258,069 of whom 130,435 were American, 47,005 German, 23,578 Irish, and the Swedes were next in rank with 10,838 voters.

The German newspapers frequently blamed the Irish for the decline in the number of Germans in public offices, accusing them of intimidation quite frequently. In reporting on the treatment of Germans who favored Washington Hesing over Carter H. Harrison in the primaries, the *Staatszeitung* of February 28, 1893 reported that a certain precinct captain named H. W. Robinson had issued the order "let no German vote or if he does, challenge his vote." It continued that "in wards five, six, fifteen, and eighteen nobody with a German name was allowed to vote and that many votes were simply thrown away. 'Boss' Farrell of ward twenty-two allegedly told his 'infamous gang' that the ward must be won for Harrison 'regardless of cost' and the 'gang' did its best to the utmost satisfaction of its leader." The *Abendpost* of April 31, 1893 reported of a political meeting of Germans in "Arbeiter Halle" in Ward Twenty-two, at which Irish agitators forced the speakers to talk English, for they did not want to listen to anything "Dutch." It pointed out that the Irish had only 210 voters in Ward Twenty-two in contrast to the 2,577 German voters, and asked its readers whether they would let themselves be beaten at the polls by Captain Farrell with his 210 followers.

The *Staatszeitung* of March 20, 1893 described the dominion of the Irish over the Germans in some of Chicago's wards. It asserted that in the Tenth Ward 2,285 Germans were forced to be subservient to 830 Irish, because Jack Cullerton, "Chick" Curran, and other Irishmen dominated them. The *Staatszeitung* told its readers that in Ward Fifteen 3,054 Germans were submissive to 575 Irishmen who were able to advance as aldermanic candidates Pat Mooney and Mike Ryan. It expressed outrage that while there were 19, 737 Germans, 9,393 Irish, and 3,906 Bohemians in West Town, yet the Democratic town ticket showed as political candidates three Irish, one Bohemian and no German.

Again and again it was asserted that the German element suffered unfair representation in all public affairs, not only in the number of public offices, For instance, the *Abendpost* of September 21, 1898 reported that Governor Tanner had slighted the Germans when he invited participants to the ceremony of naming the new battleship *Illinois*. He extended invitations to many clubs, but failed to invite the "Germania Maennerchor" and the "Schwabenverein," Chicago's foremost German clubs. Of 150 prominent Chicagoans invited, a disproportionately small number was of German extraction, namely John P. Altgeld, Franz Amberg, William Boldenweck, H. Eurich, Charles Guenther, E. Mandel. T. Ochne, M. Rosenfeld, J. Rosenthal, A. M. Rothschild, W. C. Seipp, M. Ullrich, and Otto Young.

At times the disproportionate representation of the German element in public affairs has been blamed on its aloofness from politics and its apathy in public issues. This certainly was true for a great many Germans, perhaps more so than for other ethnic groups, but there have been many Chicago Germans who have shown vigorous interest in the various levels of governments and public life. According to page 154 of Andreas' first volume of *History of Chicago*, the German element first asserted itself as a factor in municipal affairs on March 19, 1846 when thirty-four Germans denouced in the *Daily Democrat* the city council's refusal to appoint Charles Baumgarten as street commissioner, allegedly because he was a German. Of course, some Germans took part in municipal affairs before 1846, even though, as the Germans occasionally complained, not in proper proportion to their numerical presence.

It may be that as early as in the August 2, 1830 election, when Chicago was part of Peoria County, Germans were voting at the house of James Kinzie, the polling place for the Chicago precinct. Of the thirty-two voters, John Mann, Peter Frique and Joseph

Bauskey may well have been German, as sometimes has been surmised, but we know nothing about them. Another 1830 voter, John van Horn, despite his Dutch name, was apparently German. The *Staatszeitung* of September 6, 1876 reported that "Long John" Wentworth, Chicago's ex-mayor, in addressing the second "Annual Picnic of Old German Settlers" on September 4, 1876 in Wright's Grove verified that the "first German that voted here was John van Horn, whom I knew well."

Seven years later, the rosters of Chicago's six wards for the mayoral election of May 2, 1837 contain of 709 total voters the folllowing list of Germans. This list is based on the first volume of Andreas' *History of Chicago*, and on Emil Mannhardt, "Die ersten beglaubigten Deutschen in Chicago," in *Deutsch-Amerikanische Geschichtsblätter*, I, 4 (1901), 38-48. Sometimes the names are so distorted that they can hardly be recognized. For instance, Martin Steidle was listed as Martin Stidel, and Peter Dolese as Peter Dolsey in Andreas' history: Ward One—H. Burk and Peter Cohen; Ward Two—Anton Berg, F. C. Bold, John Dolese, Peter Dolese, Louis Malzacher, A. Panakaske, Martin Steidle, Clemens Stose, A. Tholser, Thomas Wolfinger, and H. Zalle; Ward Three—Henry Burke; Ward Four—Christian Aste, Georg Frost, John Wellmacher, Phillip Will, and G. Berg; Ward Five—Moritz Baumgarten, M. Burk, L. Frey, and H. Harmer; Ward Six—Peter Baumgarten, F. German, E. Flossner, J. Forcht, Franz Kessler, J. Lampmann, A. Oberhart, J. Schneider, A. Spoor, J. Stofer, and J. Zoliski.

The first German who held a public office in Chicago was apparently Clemens Stose, about whom little is known other than that he came to Chicago in 1833 from Pennsylvania after he had immigrated from Germany as a ten-year-old boy, that he established a blacksmith shop in 1833 to become one of the city's first three blacksmiths, and that he died about 1880. He was elected alderman in 1839 from Ward Two, which at that time was located west of Clark Street on the South Side, where a German settlement was located along Wells Street from Washington to Lake streets.

After Stose no Germans were elected to municipals offices until 1843 when the shoemaker Charles Sauter and the farmer Joseph Marbach were elected aldermen of wards two and six respectively. Of Marbach we only know that he was one of the founders of the Catholic St. Joseph Church in 1846, but about Sauter the basic facts of his life are known. He was born in the vicinity of Stuttgart on October 30, 1808, learned the shoemaker trade, and came with his family to Chicago in 1834. Sauter mixed readily with Americans, for he sang in the Trinity Church choir and joined the second company of the volunteer fire department. The Chicago Historical Society Museum still possesses a fire bucket which bears Sauter's name. According to the *Chicago American* of March 2, 1843, he must have been prominent among the Germans, because he presided over one of their mass meetings. After moving to New Strassburg in 1845, he became the first and only postmaster of this suburb, which later became part of Chicago Heights. Sauter held several other public offices, such as County commissioner, town supervisor, assessor and justice of peace before he died in 1877. In 1900 a certain Ferdinand Jones, who had known Sauter, gave the following account published in the *Deutsch-Amerikanische Geschichtsblätter*, volume I, page 43:

> In reference to Charles Sauter, I am pleased to say that I knew him well in early times. He was in company with his brother Jacob in the shoe business at No. 212 Lake Street. As public spirited citizens they were prominent and influential. Charles Sauter was a fine looking fellow, blond and athletic, always prompt at festivals and fires, and popular with both old and young, both foreigners and natives. After a residence in Chicago of about ten years he removed to New Strassburg and died on May 18th, 1877, aged 66½ years. I have no special incidents connected with his life here but it would not be difficult to gather interesting accounts from some of the early 'boys'—such as Charles Stoce, Gen. Frank Sherman, Judge Bradwell, Groft, Fergus, and others.

Other Germans that entered public offices in 1843 were the painter William Wiesenkraft, who was elected police constable for three years. He was the nephew of Charles Wiesenkraft, who had come to the Chicago area in 1833, and after whom part of Niles was named "Wiesenkraft's Point." In the same year the milliner Anton Getzler became County treasurer.

One more early German office holder, Michael Diversey (1810-69), elected alderman from Ward Six in 1844, should be mentioned, because he left a great imprint on Chicago. He came in 1838 with his wife to Chicago, after having emigrated from Germany in 1836, and bought William Ogden's share in a brewery in 1841 to become partner of William Lill in a thriving business on Chicago and Michigan avenues. In 1861, when they sold 44,750 barrels of beer, their brewery covered two entire blocks and provided employment for over 100 workers. But Diversey did not only take care of the Chicago Germans' physical needs, but also worried about their cultural needs. In 1845 he headed a drive to establish a new German school in New Buffalo, commonly referred to as the "Dutch Settlement" on the North Side. This drive culminated on January 30, 1846 when the city council ordered "that the Mayor and Clerk issue a deed, under the seal of the city, of the school house in the Dutch settlement, to Michael Diversey and Peter Gabel executing a note to the school fund for $110 payable in twelve months."

Diversey was a generous founder of the Catholic churches St. Peter and St. Joseph in 1846 and St. Michael in 1852. The latter was named in honor of Diversey's patron saint, because he had donated the land for the church. With his business partner he also donated five acres to the McCormick Theological Seminary. It should also be mentioned that in 1856 he became the publisher of the German daily paper *Der Nationaldemokrat*. On December 12, 1869 the *Chicago Evening Journal* published the following eulogy:

> Colonel Michael Diversey died in this city yesterday. The deceased was a member of the well known firm of Lill & Diversey. He came to this city in 1838, and many years ago served very acceptably as Alderman. While all of our citizens will hear of his death with great regret, the German Catholics will mourn his loss with deep and abiding sorrow. He contributed liberally toward all their charitable and religious enterprises. The ground upon which S. Michael's Church was built was donated by him and he gave largely to help build St. Joseph's and St. Peter's churches. He did much toward assisting the poor, and in all respects was a man who will be generally missed by the community of which he was an honored and useful member.

His name is perpetuated not only in a magnificent monument in St. Boniface Cemetery, but also in Diversey Boulevard on the North Side.

Perhaps the first most important issue in which the Chicago Germans had a crucial part was the defeat of the Nebraska Bill in 1854 and the subsequent surge to power of the Republican party with the election of President Lincoln in 1860. The entire affair is exceedingly involved and might best be summarized by the following excerpt of the article "The Germans of Chicago and Stephen A. Douglas in 1854" by F. I. Herriott, who made the Chicago Germans' role in the slavery question the object of several studies. It is reprinted from page 381 of volume twelve of the *Deutsch-Amerikanische Geschichtsblätter*:

> Among the elements and forces that suddenly came together in January 1854, producing the 'tornado' in opposition to the passage of the Nebraska bill that so astonished and enraged Senator Stephen A. Douglas, the Germans constituted a factor of great potency—much

> **more influential than their mere number in the population would suggest and more important than has been realized by American historians. The opposition of Germans to the passage of that celebrated measure was instant, direct and positive; and so pronounced was their antagonism that it became, in the writer's judgment, a decisive consideration in critical junctures in the passage of the bill through Congress. Moreover, the tremendous disturbance thereby resulting among the Germans was a major cause in disturbing their political alignments; shaking and almost shattering their loyalty to the Democratic party, with which three-fourths of the Germans were then affiliated, inducing secessions in large numbers in 1856; and it set in motion among them the forces in opposition to slavery that made the Germans a determining factor in the overthrow of the Democratic party in 1860 and in the exaltation of Abraham Lincoln.**

Lincoln was aware of the importance of the German voters, who before 1856 had belonged almost exclusively to the Democratic party. In order to convert and hold them to the Republican party, he bought at least one German newspaper, the *Springfield Staatsanzeiger*, edited by Theodor Canisius. The Chicago-based *Illinois Staatsanzeiger* also exhorted its German audience to switch to the Republican party in the fight against slavery, causing wholesale conversion which in turn helped elect Lincoln.

It must suffice to mention one more case in which the concerted efforts of Chicago's German voters decided the outcome of an election. That was the nation wide election in November of 1892 in which the Democratic party scored important victories, putting a Democratic governor into office for the first time since 1852. The *Staatszeitung* of November 10, 1892 was probably not exaggerating when it summarized the German role in the election as follows: "How did it happen that the State of Illinois, the Republican stronghold in the West, elected a Democratic president, a Democratic governor, a Democratic legislature, and Democratic state officials. The Germans made it possible. 'The Germans did it,' thus reply friend and foe." The newpaper also published a message from the newly elected Governor Altgeld: "Extend to the Germans, through your paper, my sincere thanks for what they did. I shall never forget it. Credit is due to the *Staatszeitung* for having done its share in gaining the victory." Of course, Governor Altgeld was not the only one who expressed gratitude to the Germans for helping to elect him. Just about every official who received a substantial share of the Germans' votes was careful to thank them, as Fred Busse did in the *Abendpost* of April 3, 1907, after he had been elected mayor of Chicago: "I thank the Germans from the bottom of my heart, for they have stuck with me faithfully."

Most public office seekers in Chicago and Illinois wanted to make sure that they were on the good side of the German constituents. There was and is hardly any significant gathering of Germans in Chicago at which not a few politicians were and are conspicuously present. At the dedications of the more than a dozen German monuments in Chicago, city officials were usually present. For instance, when the Schiller monument in Lincoln Park was dedicated on May 15, 1886, Mayor Carter H. Harrison did not fail to utter such old vote getting slogans as how he "appreciated what the Germans have done for Chicago." The dedication of the Schiller monument had been planned for May 9, 1886, the anniversary of Schiller's death day, but was postponed because of the repercussions of the Haymarket "Riot" which had occured on May 4, 1886.

When prominent Germans observed private celebrations, public servants frequently showed up, as, for instance, when the *Abendpost* reported on October 7, 1931, that Mayor Cermak with incumbent consorts came to the 75th birthday celebration of the German musician Karl Bunge to hold a speech, assuring the numerous well-wishers of German descent his eternal gratitude for their part in Chicago's development. Usually the high city officials who attended German affairs, such as the annual German Old Settlers' Picnic, were invited, but at times politicians did show up without invitations to turn a festive or cultural affair into an opportunity to attract votes. This happened on December 18, 1927 when Mayor William H. Thompson attended the German Theatre and "greatly enjoyed himself even though he does not understand German perfectly," according to the *Abendpost* of December 19, 1927. But during the intermission Mayor Thompson also lashed out at school Superintendent William McAndrew, whom he described as a "subject of King George who will fly" in his "fight against the British Lion," and he did not fail to remind his audience that during World War I he was called "Kaiser Bill" for his pro-German attitude.

Frequently Chicago Germans took the pre-election campaign promises by office seekers seriously, and were disappointed when these promises were not fulfilled. The German newspapers often warned them not to let themselves be used. Typical is the following excerpt from the *Staatszeitung* of August 14, 1886: "Unfortunately, many Germans are taking these flattering, hollow phrases for serious, fall for it and after the election are ignored and turned away by the same political bosses who previously begged their votes for job promises."

At times opportunistic office seekers, in their eagerness to attract the German votes, went to extremes and were usually castigated by Chicago's German press for it. This happened especially if the political candidates had previously antagonized the Germans by denying their own German background or by disregarding the German element in a number of ways. For instance, the *Staatszeitung* of May 30, 1876 in a vitriolic criticism of Andrew Shuman, editor of the *Evening Journal*, pointed out that he had been a willing tool of the anti-German Know-Nothings in that his paper had insulted the Germans more consistently than any other Chicago newspaper. Now that he had been nominated for lieutenant governor by the Republicans and needed the German vote, he stressed that his ancestors had immigrated from Bremen and that he was of German extraction, forgetting his former denial of his German background, which included changing his name from Schumann to Shuman.

The events surrounding the mayoral election of 1915 form an interesting chapter in Chicago's history in which the pro-German attitude and German extraction became decisive campaign issues. On January 27, 1915, the *Abendpost* in the editorial, "The Missing *ch*," stated: "Mr. Carter Harrison has developed quite an affection for the German element of Chicago . . . . That is only natural because without good will there will be no vote, and without the German-American vote there will be no election of Mr. Harrison." The editorial continues giving evidence of the mayor's attempts to appear pro-German by attending German affairs and by making flattering speeches there. But then there is an objection: "Up to that point we do not object to Mr. Harrison's campaign tactics and efforts to show himself off as a pro-German candidate, but if he goes so far as to put a little German flag on his coat lapel as he did the other day, and to grant some of his friends an interview in German and then to joke about his German linguistic talents, all we can say is that he displays extremely bad taste."

The *Abendpost* was extremely irked, because Harrison conjured up an apparent pro-German attitude on the one hand, whereas on the other hand he attacked his German-American opponent Robert Sweitzer, whose name somehow changed to a less obvious German spelling: "Nor do we think it is nice of him to assert that one of our group is not being a true German-American just because the *ch*, which according to Harrison should be included, is missing from his German name. We do not have to stand for that. Many a good German in this country has to consent to the lopping off of a *ch* from his name and other Anglicizing cures, whether he wants to or not." According to the *Abendpost* of February 24, 1915, William H. Thompson obtained in the nomination election 87,060 votes out of a total of 176,000 Republican votes, winning with a majority of 2,305 over his opponent, Olson. Of 289,669 Democratic votes cast Sweitzer polled 182,534, defeating Harrison by a margin of 77,551 votes, which caused Harrison to observe, "The sentiment was with me, but the sediment was with Sweitzer."

Thompson, realizing how important the German-extraction factor was to obtain votes, had his Campaign Manager Pugh, who had offered his speedboat *Disturber IV* to the English after the start of hostilities between Germany and England, spread rumors that Sweitzer, having been raised as a stepson, was really of Irish ancestry. This was counteracted by several public affirmations on Sweitzer's part that he was indeed of German stock. The *Abendpost* of February 12, 1915 contained a long account of Sweitzer's background, stating that his father came in 1855 as a seven-year-old boy from Herbolzheim in Baden and had a "typical" immigrant's fate which included dastardly exploitation by a compatriot runner, and in the *Sonntagspost* of March 28, 1915 a German-American Citizens' Committee confirmed Sweitzer's German ancestry. In addition to these public testimonies, he sent leaflets dated April 3, 1915 to the Chicago Germans, reaffirming his German extraction. He also urged the readers to give "a fitting answer to the defamers of Germany" by electing a German-American mayor for Chicago, which "has a larger German population than any city in the world excepting Berlin and Vienna, but has never had her fair share of German-Americans in public office." The Germans voted for Sweitzer in large numbers, but he was nevertheless defeated, partly because the general population did not want to endorse his implied Germanism. When Sweitzer ran against Thompson again in 1919, he was not as widely endorsed by the German element as before because of Thompson's pro-German sentiments. Symptomatic of the changed situation is an account in the March 28, 1919 *Abendpost* of a March 17 political meeting by the German-American Citizens' Alliance. Seventy-six delegates, representing 5,500 German voters, endorsed Thompson with sixty-seven votes and Sweitzer with eight votes, because "Mayor Thompson protected the Germans during the troubled war times."

Chicago German-Americans have occupied positions in all public offices. The following list shows the first occupancy of the more important public offices by Chicagoans of German extraction.

LIST OF THE FIRST OCCUPANCY OF IMPORTANT PUBLIC OFFICES BY CHICAGO GERMANS

Office	First occupant	Installed	Office created
Alderman	Clemens Stose	1839	1837
County Treasurer	Anton Getzler	1843	1831
City Treasurer	Anton Getzler	1847	1837
City Clerk	H. W. Zimmermann	1851	1837
City Attorney	Arno Voss	1852	1837
School Agent	Elias Greenebaum	1856	1840
County Superintendent of Schools	J. F. Eberhard	1859	1831
City Marshal	Jacob Rehm	1859	1842
Sheriff	Anton C. Hesing	1860	1831
State Lieutenant Governor	Francis Hoffmann	1860	1809
City Collector	Georg Schneider	1862	1862
President of the Board of Public Works	John G. Gindele	1863	1861
County Coroner	Dr. Ernst Schmidt	1864	1831
County Clerk	E. S. Solomon	1865	1831
President of the Board of Education	Lorenz Brentano	1867	1857
President of the County Board of Commissioners	Dr. J. T. Bluthardt	1869	1850
Fire Marshal	Matt Benner	1873	1858
Chief of Police	Jacob Rehm	1873	1871
City Comptroller	Charles H. Schwab	1886	1857
State's Attorney of Cook County	J. M. Longenecker	1889	1889
Governor of Illinois	John P. Altgeld	1892	1809
Postmaster of Chicago	Washington Hesing	1893	1831
Mayor of Chicago	Fred A. Busse	1907	1837

Some public offices were occupied relatively late by Chicago Germans, as for instance, the office of postmaster, which was held for the first time by a citizen of German extraction in 1893, over sixty years after it was instituted. Washington Hesing (1849-97), the son of the colorful owner of the *Staatszeitung*, A. C. Hesing, held this office until 1896 when he resigned to become a mayoral candidate. After 1893 the office of postmaster was occupied for many years by German-Americans, Arthur Lueder (1921), and Ernest Kruetgen (1933) alone serving over twenty-two years. Of course, the proportion of Germans occupying different public offices varied. For instance, there were comparatively fewer city attorneys than city clerks of German extraction, but in most public offices, as that of county clerk, selected arbitrarily here for 1837-1934, a sizable number of Germans held office: John G. Gindele, 1869; Hermann Lieb, 1873, 1874-78; A. F. Klokke, 1878-80; Henry Wulff, 1886-94; P. Knopf, 1894-1902; J. F. Haas, 1906-10; R. M. Sweitzer, 1910-34.

At the present time many Chicagoans of German background may be found in a variety of public offices. *The Sun Times' Midwest Magazine* of August 18, 1968, devoted to the Germans in Chicago, gave a partial list of some of them, including eleven state representatives and three councilmen, as well as the U. S. Senators Charles Percy and Everett Dirksen. Whenever they attended such affairs as the Steuben parade or German Day, Percy liked to mention that his maternal grandmother was born in Stuttgart, Germany, while Dirksen habitually rumbled a few phrases of "Plattdeutsch" which his German mother had taught him. The *Midwest Magazine* reporter also interviewed the gregarious funeral home director John Meiszner who, in addition to being a member of forty-three clubs, was also an active Republican, serving as U. S. Marshal of the Northern Illinois district from 1969-73. Meiszner, whose father had come to America in 1911 from St. Georgen in Southern Germany, characterized the current political activity of Chicago Germans as follows: "In Chicago the German interested in public life wants to keep his independence and prefers to sit in the background and pull the strings."

The mayor's office is the single public office which was held by no more than one Chicagoan of German extraction, occupied by Fred A. Busse in 1907-11—if Theodor Schintz is excepted, who was acting mayor in 1869 while John Rice was in Europe. But to be sure, there have been many unsuccessful German mayoral candidates, the first one being Dr. Ernst Schmidt, the famous humanitarian, who was the Socialist Labor party's candidate in 1879. Since then many of this party's candidates were of German extraction: Georg Schilling, 1881; Henry Ehrenpreis and Michael Britizius, 1893; Johann Glambock, 1897; Henry Sale, 1903; and Adolph Karm, 1919. Democratic mayoral candidates of German extraction were Frank Wenter in 1895, Washington Hesing in 1897, and Robert Sweitzer in 1915 and 1919. Besides the successful candidacy of Busse in 1907, other Republican candidates were Arthur Lueder in 1923, Emil Wetten in 1935, and John Hoellen in 1975. After he had accepted the Republican nomination in Fall of 1974, John Hoellen, alderman from the 47th Ward, was humorously lauded in a commentary by Joel Daly on Channel

Seven for his candid appraisal of the slim chance for success. The former Governor John P. Altgeld was a candidate on the Municipal Ownership ticket in 1899.

The second generation German Fred A. Busse (1866-1914) was Chicago's first four year term mayor. Before he was elected top official of Chicago on the Republican ticket in 1907, he held several public offices, beginning with clerk of Northtown in 1891, assistant sheriff, member of the 39th and 40th legislature, two terms as state senator, state treasurer, and postmaster of Chicago. When Busse assumed office, he reduced expenses by cutting patronage jobs. For instance, in May of 1907, he eliminated seven "cowcatchers" from the city payroll whose salaries totaled $5,400, because in all of 1906 the work of the seven "city cowboys" consisted of impounding one horse.

Busse should also be remembered for initiating some important permanent changes in the city, most notably the execution of the Chicago Plan. In November of 1907 Mayor Busse instructed the Board of Local Improvements to begin work at once on the Burnham Plan, which provided for interconnected boulevards, wider streets, and a generally smoother flow of traffic. Almost two years later, on November 1, 1909, he appointed the eminently successful Charles Wacker, a second generation German, as chairman of the Chicago Plan which had recently been advanced by Chicago's Commercial Club. During 1908 and the following year he ordered three investigations to determine whether a Chicago subway ought to be built. In November of 1910 Busse approved ten percent pay increases for policemen and firmen to raise the maximum monthly salaries for patrolmen to $100 and those of firemen to $103.75.

In the opinion of Chicago's aristocracy, Mayor Busse committed a *faux pas* when in 1908 he secretly married a woman whom most people considered to be a mulatto. Ben Hecht in the collection of stories, *Gaily, Gaily* bluntly stated: "Busse has put the city's nose out of joint by marrying a Negress." Perhaps this explains a peculiar episode in Chicago's history. When Busse, still convalescing from appendicitis, could not be present at the cornerstone laying of the present city hall on July 20, 1909, none of four living ex-mayors, Washburne, Swift, Harrison, or Dunne, appeared at the ceremony. Busse, who had owned a coal business, died insolvent in 1914, allegedly leaving his wife only fifteen cents so that she was forced to work as an elevator operator in city hall.

The Chicago Germans who became Illinois governors were John P. Altgeld in 1893, Henry Horner in 1933, and Otto Kerner in 1965. In addition to these, some others may have had German blood ties, as for instance, Richard Ogilvie, who had some German forefathers on his mother's side, according to several reports in the *Abendpost* during 1968. Of these governors undoubtedly John P. Altgeld was the most outstanding one.

John Peter Altgeld (1847-1902), the "greatest governor in Illinois' history," according to the present Illinois Governor Walker, was born on December 30, 1847 in the small town of Niederselters, near Wiesbaden in Hesse, from where his parents emigrated to Mansfield, Ohio early in his childhood. During the Civil War he served some 100 days, participating in the James River campaign. After the war he taught school for several years, but also prepared himself for the legal profession and was admitted to the bar in 1869 in Savannah, Missouri.

In 1875 he transferred to Chicago, where he gradually established a good reputation as an able barrister. From 1886-91 he was superior court judge in Chicago. During his time as judge several factors made it evident that he was on the side of the exploited. Typical is an account in the *Abendpost* of January 11, 1890, reporting that the lawyer Joseph Kennard (who obtained $3,000 compensation in a damage suit for a Miss Hawblick, a working girl who became permanently crippled as a result of having been run over by a cab of the Chicago Hansom Cab Company) demanded $1,750 for his services. Indignant, Judge Altgeld "gave a lecture of disapprobation to the youthful leech and advised him in no uncertain terms to decrease his demand substantially," which he presumably did. Altgeld also showed his deep concern for the downtrodden when he published in newspapers and periodicals articles, such as "Protection of Non-Combatants," in the *Chicago Evening Mail* of April 26, 1886 or "Slave Girls of Chicago," in the *Chicago Times* of September 9, 1888. In 1890 they were published in book form under the title *Live Questions*.

When Altgeld campaigned for governor on the Democratic ticket, he visited in a "Walker-like" campaign all Illinois counties, relying on the people, rather than on the party machine, and he was elected with a margin of 23,000 votes over the incumbent Joseph Fifer. In becoming Illinois' governor, he not only was the first foreign-born citizen to hold that office in Illinois, but he also was the first successful Democratic candidate since 1852. As in his past careers, as governor he stood up for the rights of the oppressed.

One of his first and also most crucial official acts was the careful scrutiny of the Haymarket "Riot" trial documents to decide the fate of the imprisoned Fielden, Neebe, and Schwab. In the view of some pro-pardon people, this deliberation took too long.

When the prominent defense lawyer Clarence Darrow, as a pro-pardon spokesman, urged Altgeld to delay his decision no longer, the governor explained his situation in a statement, revealing his uncompromising nature, as Darrow recalled on page 101 of his book, *The Story of My Life*: "You seem impatient; of course, I know how you feel. I don't want to offend you or lose your friendship. But this responsibility is mine, and I shall shoulder it. I have not yet examined the record. I have no opinion about it. It is a big job. When I do examine it, I will do what I believe to be right, no matter what that is. But don't deceive yourself; if I conclude to pardon those men it will not meet with the approval that you expect. Let me tell you . . . from that day, I will be a dead man."

In granting the pardon on June 26, 1893, Altgeld stated in a scathing criticism of the judicial process observed during the 1887 trial that he freed the "conspirators" not out of magnanimity or because they had been sufficiently punished, but because the evidence clearly indicated that they had been the victims of an unjust legal process. As he indicated to Darrow, he knew that he would be "a dead man" when he granted the pardon. Indeed, he was not mistaken, for the storm of indignation over his clemency which broke over his head was swift and abusive. His friends began to call him John "Pardon" Altgeld, but his enemies termed him the gamut of unprintable names. In Naperville a group of "righteous" citizens hanged him in effigy. Even preachers lashed out at Altgeld, as the *Staatszeitung* of July 4, 1893 reported: "And now comes the bigoted little preacher of the Grace Methodist Church, 'Dr.' McGates from Jersey City Heights, N. J., stating: 'Illinois stands discredited with the threefold A's—Altgeld, Aliens, and Anarchists.' "

True to his campaign motto "Equal rights for all, privileges for none," Altgeld not only guaranteed the rights of the downtrodden, but he also curtailed the accustomed privileges of the capitalists, and in the ensuing war of attrition, he was crushed. Before he became governor he was independently wealthy, owning six Chicago buildings, of which the sixteen story "Unity Building" was "the best furnished office complex" in Chicago. However, when he died in 1902 he was a poor man. On the evening of his death day he gave in Joliet an impassioned speech on behalf of the exploited South African Boers, after which he collapsed and died.

After Altgeld had stated his position in the pardon message, he stoically kept silent on the matter and let the fury of abuse run its course. When one of Altgeld's friends exhorted him to ward off the "vile slanders heaped upon him by the press," he prophetically stated: "Remember this about any slander. Denial only emphasizes and gives added importance to falsehood. Let it alone and it will die for want of nourishment." Though vilified in office, he became a martyr for the oppressed. When his body lay in state at the Chicago Public Library, the newpapers of March 13, 1902 estimated that some 25,000 paid him the last respects, and people came in flocks when an Altgeld memorial service was held at the Auditorium on April 20, 1902, at which Clarence Darrow was the principal speaker.

The *Abendpost* of March 11, 1907 reported on a memorial service at the Garrick Theatre in which Altgeld was celebrated as a champion of the downtrodden who initiated humane social reforms, such as the parole system or decent treatment of the insane at Bartonville. At this service, Mayor Dunne asserted that "Nobody has been more abused and suspected in the state of Illinois than John P. Altgeld, because he fought the power of capitalism," but he also conceded that "this is the first time that in Chicago the memory of a politician is honored five years after his death." The fact that Chicagoans erected a monument to him in 1915 in Lincoln Park stands in contrast to the title of Harry Barnard's biography, *Eagle Forgotten*, adopted from the following poem by Vachel Lindsay:

THE EAGLE THAT IS FORGOTTEN
(John P. Altgeld. Born December 30, 1847; died March 12, 1902)

Sleep softly . . . eagle forgotten . . . under the stone.
Time has its way with you there, and the clay has its own.

"We have buried him now," thought your foes, and in secret rejoiced.
They made a brave show of their mourning, their hatred unvoiced.
They had snarled at you, barked at you, foamed at you day after day.
Now you were ended. They praised you, . . . and laid you away.

The others that mourned you in silence and terror and truth,
The widow bereft of her crust, and the boy without youth,
The mocked and the scorned and the wounded, the lame and the poor
That should have remembered forever, . . . remember no more.

Where are those lovers of yours, on what name do they call
The lost, that in armies wept over your funeral pall?
They call on the names of a hundred high-valiant ones,

A hundred white eagles have risen the sons of your sons,
The zeal in their wings is a zeal that your dreaming began
The valor that wore out your soul in the service of man.

Sleep softly, . . . eagle forgotten, . . . under the stone,
Time has its way with you there and the clay has its own.
Sleep on, O brave-hearted, O wise man, that kindled the flame—
To live in mankind is far more than to live in a name,
To live in mankind, far, far more . . . than to live in a name.

Nevertheless, Altgeld's name is perpetuated in monuments, parks, university halls, schools and other public buildings not only in Chicago, but in cities throughout Illinois, surpassed only by a few Illinoisans.

Chapter 6

The Clubs of Chicago's German Element

The presence of the German element in Chicago is perhaps most evident in the activities of its various clubs. Since the story of the Chicago Germans is mirrored in the history of their clubs, a survey of the activities of various German clubs affords an additional view of Chicago's German element. In the ninth annual "Steuben Parade" on September 21, 1974 some forty-one German compatriotic, singing, sports and sundry other clubs provided over 190 units for the spectators to watch along State Street. Most of Chicago's German clubs usually exert themselves to make a success of this parade, as well as of the annual German Day activities, held in 1975 on July 12 and 13. According to an interview in the *Tribune* of June 23, 1966, the former president of the German Day Association, Joseph Gies, asserted that 138 German-American groups of the Chicago area sponsored the 1966 German Day. Reliable statistics of the number of German clubs in the Chicago area are nonexistant, because some of the minor ones do not bother to announce their activities. With the present low number of Germans in the Chicago area it would be surprising to find more than 100 German clubs.

Whatever the present number of German clubs in the Chicago area may be, it is a far cry from former years. In 1935 when the major influx of German immigration had passed close to fifty years, the *Abendpost* on July 6 published a roster of at least 452 active German clubs in the Chicago area. They were thirteen compatriotic or local groups, such as the Palatinate Club; five united choruses, such as the United Male Choruses of Chicago; twenty-three ladies' choruses, like "Almira Damenchor;" fifty-nine male choruses, such as "Orpheus Männerchor;" five mixed choruses, like "Eintracht" (Harmony); twenty-five sport clubs, such as "Chicago Kickers;" eleven "turner" clubs, such as "Chicago Turngemeinde;" seven veterans' clubs, like German Veterans' Association of Chicago; over 100 mutual benefit associations, like Workmen's Sick and Death Benefit; 73 lodges of freemasons, odd fellows, Hermann's Sons, and "Harugari;" two professional clubs, namely the German Medical Society and the German Press Association; and 129 sundry organizations, such as Columbia Ladies' Club or the Kolping Society.

The Germans seem to be fond of organizing clubs, if one may believe John Meiszner, past president of the Germania Club and member of forty-two others, who stated in an interview in the *Sun Times* Sunday edition of August 18, 1968: "Put three Germans together and in five minutes you'll have four clubs." The first Germans who arrived in the Chicago area in the 1830's and 1840's to settle with compatriots in the North Side's "Dutch Settlement" or in the "Teuto Community" in the western suburbs most likely organized groups, perhaps singing clubs, to foster companionship and to spend leisure time pleasantly, but no records of their activities are extant.

Perhaps the earliest German club documented in Chicago was the "St. Peter Verein." Benevolent in purpose, it was organized on November 15, 1847 by some members of the St. Peter Catholic community on the South Side. Charles Baumgarten was its president, Christian Lohn its vice president, Peter Kerich secretary, and Jacob Weidzel treasurer. About a somewhat later club, the "Chicago Leseverein" (Chicago Reading Club), little else is known besides that it was founded in 1848 for social and educational functions and that it still existed in 1852, for it extended an invitation to a ball on November 1, in the *Staatszeitung* of October 22, 1852.

More is known about the "Robert Blum Lodge, No. 58" of the Odd Fellows, a German organization next in time. When it was established in October of 1849 under the charter members V. A. Boyer, John Fischer, Philip Friedrich, Georg Funk, Gottfried Laugheinrich, John M. Pahlmann, Joseph Schlereth, Peter Schmitz, Frederick Schott, and Frederick Singer, it became the first foreign language lodge in Illinois. This caused the Grand Master to reflect at the 1849 Grand Lodge session in Peoria as follows, taken from page 515 of volume I of Andreas's *History of Chicago*:

> As it is the established policy of the Order to allow lodges to work in other languages than the English, I requested the secretary to send for six copies of the books in the German language, as more would probably be needed. I am happy to say that I have none but good accounts of the working of this lodge. Since this occurred I have doubted whether it was the true policy to have lodges working in foreign languages—whether our duty to our country does not require us to use all our influence to Americanize all foreigners among us as soon as possible, and afford them no facilities for their being satisfied or comfortable without conforming to the genius, institutions and language of the land.

Apparently the Grand Master's misgivings about a German lodge did not prevent other German Odd Fellow lodges from being established, for in January 1857 "Harmonia Lodge, No. 221" was instituted by Germans of the West Side with the charter members John A. Boerner, F. W. Forch, Louis Hientz, John Hofmann, Charles Ippel, Georg Petermann, Charles Rietz, August Schenkoweitz, Konrad Schertel and John Smith. By 1871 at least ten other German Odd Fellows lodges existed, having been founded as follows:

German Odd Fellows lodges founded between 1866 and 1871

Lodge	Number	Year founded
Goethe	329	1866
North Chicago	330	1866
"Hoffnung"	353	1867
Northwest	388	1869
Garden City	389	1869
Hutten	398	1869
Lily of the West	407	1869
Douglas	432	1870
Lincoln Park	437	1870
Syria	451	1871

Chicago's first German Freemason lodge, the Germania Lodge, No. 182, organized on April 16, 1855, was the state's first foreign language Masonic lodge which caused an enormous controversy at the Grand Lodge session on October 2, 1855. In fact, the old dispensation for the Germania Lodge was revoked, and only after various resolutions was a new charter granted, permitting the use of German to the charter members A. Boyer, Frederick Brandes, Frederick Burky, Georg Glaessner, Georg P. Hansen, J. G. Higgins, August Otto, F. Schoenwald, and Rudolf Woehrly. Soon there were other German Freemason lodges, the "Accordia Lodge, No.

277" being next in 1858, Lessing Lodge, No. 557 followed in 1867, Herder Lodge, No. 669 in 1870, and "Waldeck Lodge, No. 674" in 1871.

In addition to lodges, Germans established sundry other organizations in the 1850's as follows: the "Männergesangverein" (Male Singing Club) in 1850; the "Chicago Turngemeinde" (Chicago Turner Community) in 1852; "Hermann's Söhne" (Herman's Sons), founded in 1852 by N. S. Kastler, Louis Appel, Georg Braun, Jacob Schmitt and Matthias Krier; the "Schneider Verein" (Taylors' Club) and the Schreiner Verein" (Cabinetmakers' Club) in 1853; the "Deutsche Gesellschaft" (German Society) also in 1853; and the "Freie Sängerbund" (Free Singers' Association). According to a document of March 11, 1854, published on page 78 of the *Deutsch-Amerikanische Geschichtsblätter* of 1908, the "Freie Sängerbund" had on March 11, 1854 forty-eight members under the presidency of H. Marwedel. In addition to these clubs, by 1857 the following German clubs existed in Chicago: "Sozialdemokratischer Turnverein" (Social-Democratic Turner Club), "Wagner Verein" (Wheelwrights' Club), "Junge Männer Verein" (Young Men's Club), "Germania Brüderbund" (Germania Fraternal Association), "Verbrüderung Deutscher" (Fraternal Society of Germans), "Verein für Kunst und Wissenschaft" (Society for Art and Science), and "Chicago Arbeiterverein" (Chicago Workers' Club).

Perhaps the most significant pre-Fire German club was the "Verein für Kunst und Wissenschaft," because it was responsible for the erection of the "Deutsches Haus" (German House), a focal point of the German community until it was destroyed in the Great Fire of 1871. This club was founded by some members of the "Männergesangverein" in 1853, having as president Carl Sonne, secretary Charles Dandorff, and as treasurer Francis A. Hoffmann, but after the Great Fire it was no longer active. The "Chicago Turngemeinde" was also important in its agitation against slavery and it generated many other Chicago "Turner" clubs in its long history.

Another important German organization of that era must be mentioned, the "Deutsche Gesellschaft," which was founded in spring of 1853 by the veterinarian Albert Borcherdt, who organized a group of Germans who had grouped together to help the victims of a disastrous train wreck. At first the "Deutsche Gesellschaft" was intended primarily to aid German immigrants against exploitation, but later it became a general benevolent society, which still exists under the name "German Aid Society" as Chicago's oldest German organization headed by Joseph Martini, who emigrated from Germany in 1923 from Brilon some forty miles east of Dortmund. But most of the other pre-fire German clubs were rather ephemeral, as was the fate which most clubs of the German element suffered.

As the Germans poured into Chicago, the number of their clubs mushroomed, but few of these clubs ever attained much prominence. For example, within a few days in March of 1900 the *Staatszeitung* announced two new German clubs. On March 5th the newly founded Bavarian Women's Society of the Town of Lake, under the presidency of Mrs. Lina Schumacher, announced that it would cultivate Bavarian customs and give sick benefits, while on March 20 John Bless, president of the recently established club "Immenschwarm," laconically stated that his club would "cultivate German customs." These and other clubs, such as the German Waiters' Society, which, according to the *Staatszeitung* of October 6, 1892, had just celebrated its seventh annual ball, did not cause many ripples and were not mourned when they disappeared from the Chicago scene.

Chicago's German newspapers often lamented the fact that the German element's many different societies were detrimental to its well-being in that no concerted efforts could be exerted toward some common goals. Eugen Seeger stated on page 109 of his *Chicago* that there were not only compatriotic clubs such as Hessians or Bavarians, but that there were also city clubs, such as "Frankfurter," "Hamburger," and even "Dummsheimer" (Citizens of Dumbham). It is obvious that compatriotic clubs which restrict membership to a limited geographic region would barely vegetate or cease to exist altogether when a significant drop in immigration occurred. There are, of course, exceptions, for Chicago still has compatriotic clubs, such as the "Rheinischer Verein" or "Saarländer Verein," but these clubs usually do not limit membership to origin. In fact, one apparent compatriotic club, the "Schwabenverein," is one of the most flourishing German organizations in Chicago. Contrary to what one might assume from its name, the "Schwabenverein" does not restrict its membership to persons from Swabia, but accepts persons from everywhere.

Since the "Schwabenverein" is one of Chicago's most important German clubs in a number of aspects, it deserves more than just a passing mention. The first official news about the formation of a proposed Schwabenverein was an announcement in the *Staatszeitung* on March 27, 1878, requesting all persons interested in establishing such a compatriotic club to come to Karl Taxis's inn on State and Adams streets. Of the twenty-three men responding to the call, officers were elected. Ernst Hummel was chosen president, Gottlieb Federer as vice president, Franz Demmler as secretary and Louis Glanz as treasurer. The objectives of the club were delineated: to observe the annual "Cannstadt folksfestival," to cultivate German culture, and to serve as an organ of charity. On May 7, 1878, when the first permanent quarters were established at "Klare's Hall" on 70 North Clark Street, the club numbered already 164 members. The "Schwabenverein's" first "Cannstadt folks festival," an old harvest festival transplanted from Germany, took place in Chicago in fall of 1878, and initiated a successful tradition of annual celebrations, which were observed for the 97th time on August 17 and 18, 1974 at the "Schwabencenter" in Buffalo Grove.

The "Schwabenverein" immediately initiated a drive to erect a monument to the Swabian poet Friedrich von Schiller. Soon after the club's inception, on November 18, 1879, it contributed $500 to start the Schiller fund, which was augmented on November 5, 1880 with a pledge to donate the proceeds of all the club's festivals until enough means would be available to erect a copy of a famous Schiller statue in Lincoln Park. By January 1, 1884 the fund amounted to $3,022, and it grew steadily, enabling the German element to lay the foundation stone for the Schiller monument on November 11, 1886. It was to be dedicated on May 9, 1886, the anniversary of the poet's death, but because of the disturbances in the wake of the Haymarket "Riot" of May 4, 1886, the dedicatory exercises were postponed for fear of anarchistic reprisals. When the Schiller statue was finally dedicated on May 15, 1886, it represented the first German monument in Chicago.

To the memory of the great German poet Johann Wolfgang von Goethe the "Schwabenverein" also wanted to erect a monument for which it contributed $500 already in 1890, but it took until 1914 before the Goethe monument could be dedicated in Lincoln Park on June 13 and 14. By the time of the dedication the "Schwabenverein" had donated a total of $15,000, a sum considerably larger than the total donations of all other German clubs. The other German clubs which contributed to the Goethe monument were as follows: "Germania Männerchor"—$500, "Chicago Turngemeinde"—$300, German Press Club—$250, "Braumeister Verein" (Brew Master Club)—$100, Germania Lodge, No. 182—$50, Chicago Bavarian Club—$50, "Schleswig-Holstein Verein"—$30; ten clubs gave each $25, two gave $15, twenty-one gave $10, and eight donated $5.

It is interesting to note that of individual donors, fifteen Chicagoans contributed each $1,000 to the Goethe monument, namely Horace Brand, F. J. Dewes, Fritz Glogauer, Charles Gunther, Thies Lefens, Augusta Lehmann, Levy Mayer, Hermann Paepcke, Julius Rosenwald, Harry Rubens, Dr. Otto L. Schmidt, Frau Conrad Seipp, W. C. Seipp, Edward G. Uihlein and Charles Wacker. Six donated $500, two gave $150 and eight others pledged $100 each. The "Schwabenverein" also contributed generously to other German Chicago monuments, such as the Fritz Reuter statue in Humboldt Park and to monuments abroad, such as the Bismark monument in Hamburg or the John Meyer statue in Wilster, Schleswig-Holstein.

Even though the "Schwabenverein" donated much to monuments, it gave for other purposes, most notably to charity. According to a report in the *Deutsch-Amerikanische Geschichtsblätter* of 1931, page 135, the "Schwabenverein" had spent, since its inception in 1878, $15,000 for the Goethe monument, $3,085 for the Schiller monument, $36,817 for other cultural expenditures, and $83,947 for charity.

Usually in October of every year, this club gave to various Chicago institutions specific amounts. For instance, the *Abendpost* of October 20, 1910 reported that the "Schwabenverein" had donated during the past year $3,325 to twenty-five organizations sums ranging between $50 and $300, as to the Alexian Brothers Hospital $300, the German Hospital $150, the South Chicago Hospital $100, the "Protective Angel Orphanage" $175, the Chicago Home for Incurables $150, and the Children's Home and Aid Society $100. The *Abendpost* of February 28, 1975 had a report of the "Schwabenverein's" donations for 1974. It gave $1,825 to some thirty Chicago and national organizations, such as the American Red Cross or the German Old Peoples Home in Forest Park and $450 to fifteen institutions in Germany, such as the City Orphanage of Berlin. The "Schwabenverein" contributed as much as it could to charity causes abroad, giving for instance $250 to the Chicago Committee for the Starving German Children in 1921.

Usually parallel with economic ups and downs, the club's membership figures fluctuated considerably, as some representative statistics will show. In its first year of existence it had 164 members, by 1880 only 143, but in 1883 again 211, then 191 in 1888, 252 in 1893, 704 in 1903, 1,004 in 1908, 1,361 in 1918, 1,277 in 1927, and 1,053 in 1935. At the present time perhaps the only

Chicago German organization that comes numerically close to its membership figure is the "Donauschwaben Verein" which was organized in 1953.

Though some of the "Schwabenverein" members have been prominent Chicagoans, such as its first president Ernst Hummel, who was city and county treasurer, E. L. Gauss, poet and librarian, the Eitel brothers, famous hotel proprietors, the packer Oscar Mayer, and Dr. Otto L. Schmidt, historian and humanitarian, but it has not been an elite club, such as the Germania Club, which on the whole was very likely the most important club of Chicago's German element. On December 10, 1975, the *Daily News* had an article on the club's 110th birthday.

The Germania Club likes to point out, as for instance in its *Centennial Book* of 1965, that it had its origin at the bier of Abraham Lincoln. Soon the "Germania Männerchor" was active, presenting on May 31, 1865 a concert by sixty singers at Crosby Opera House for the benefit of wounded Civil War soldiers. On January 24, 1866, the *Staatszeitung* reported that in spite of cold weather it had good attendance at a well performed concert. The club gradually grew and in 1888 decided to erect its own clubhouse.

After moving into its new clubhouse on April 6, 1889, the Germania Club had a roller coaster existence, fluctuating between a low of 63 members in 1937 (when yearly membership dues were $60 and, due to an indebtedness of $230,960.97, bankruptcy was declared) and a high of over 1,100 members in 1940 (when yearly membership dues were reduced to twenty-four dollars). In 1970 the club still numbered some 400, but now it has only some 270 members, whose main effort seems to be directed at the problem of what to do about the future of their clubhouse.

The recent sharp decline in the number of members is perhaps attributable to the uncertain fate of the club building. Since 1955 it faced demolition, because it stood in the path of urban renewal. In the 1960's the Carl Sandburg Village, a towering apartment complex, was built in its immediate vicinity, which caused the loss of about 200 club members. In 1968 and 1969 Chicago papers reported on the uncertain fate of the endangered Germania Club, and when on February 14, 1970 the "Red Star Inn" was sold by William Gallauer for $110,000 to make room for urban renewal, the *Tribune* predicted a short future for the adjacent Germania Club. Shortly thereafter, at a general meeting of the club, only 100 of 400 members were present to decide whether to sell the club house. Since they were evenly divided on whether to sell or not to sell, on February 20, 1970 Harry Semrow, the club's president sent letters to all members, stating that the department of urban renewal had offered over $500,000 for the club's property and asking that they indicate their opinion about the club building's future. At the present time, under its president John Meiszner, the club is still undecided about selling its clubhouse. Some members want to relocate at a less congested area, others intend to obtain landmark status for the building, thus assuring it a secure future.

Often the Germania Club's membership lists read like a *Who's Who* of Chicago's German element. The club's long list of some fifty presidents contains outstanding leaders from all walks of life. The charter president for 1865, John Gindele, a forty-eighter, who was forced to emigrate from Germany because he had supported the cause of the revolution by supplying a company of 500 armed men, was president of the Chicago Public Works and deserves a large part of the credit for the LaSalle Street and Washington Street tunnels, and was also County clerk from 1869 until his death in 1872. The next Germania Club president from 1865 to 1867, Heinrich Claussenius, was a highly respected banker and agent for the North German Lloyd, as well as German Consul from 1864 to 1894.

The remaining roster of the Germania Club presidents contains prominent Chicagoans. E. G. Halle and Otto Schneider, Germania presidents in 1887-1890 and 1897-1899 respectively, served as schoolboard presidents. Ernest Kruetgen, president in 1915-1916 and 1917-1923, not only operated his lithographing business, but also occupied many public offices which were crowned with his appointment as long-time postmaster in 1933. William DeVry, the founder of the DeVry Institute of Technology, elevated the Germania Club's reputation to unsurpassed heights when he was its president in 1961-1963.

After the Germania Club building had been erected in 1889, it became the focal point of Chicago's German element, much like the "Deutsches Haus" had been before the Great Fire of 1871. Many of the cultural, civic and charitable activities of Chicago's German element were planned there and initiated by members of the Germania Club. For instance, on March 2, 1900 a group of Germania members, consisting of Max Eberhardt, F. P. Kenkel, Emil Mannhardt, Dr. Philip Mathei, Levy Mayer, Leon Mandel, Hermann Petersen, Dr. Otto L. Schmidt, Professor Louis Schutt, William Vocke and Dr. G. E. Zimmermann, convened at the clubhouse to found the German-American Historical Society. It published the *Deutsch-Amerikanische Geschichtsblätter*, a successful historical journal from 1900-1937, which supplies much information about the role of the German element in America.

Another one of the Germania Club's functions was to welcome in their quarters renowned visitors from Germany to Chicago. Of the long lists of famous visitors, only a few representative examples must suffice. In 1900 Baron von Holleben, ambassador to the United States, was their guest and in 1902 Prince Heinrich of Prussia was the guest of honor at a $100 a plate banquet in the lavishly decorated ballroom at which expenditures amounted to about $20,000. Dr. Robert Koch, the famous bacteriologist, was received at the club in 1908. In 1921 Albert Einstein, who had been invited to present a lecture at the University of Chicago to coincide with the opening of the Field Museum, enjoyed the Germania Club's hospitality, as well as Richard Strauss, who had been received already in 1904. The famous "Dresden Cross Chorus" accepted the club's invitation in 1938, and in 1940 a visit by the Duke of Saxe-Coburg caused the club to stage a banquet tantamount to the splendor of Prince Henry's gala banquet in 1902. In 1952 Prince Louis Ferdinand and Princess Cecilia of Prussia were the club's distinguished visitors, and a year later the German Chancellor, Dr. Konrad Adenauer, was the club's guest of honor at several gala affairs. During the month of its 90th anniversary, October of 1955, the Germania Club hosted Heinz Krekeler, German ambassador to the United States, and other distinguished guests. Marina Orschel, the reigning Miss German, and Max Schmeling, former world heavyweight boxing champion, graced the Germania Club with their presence in 1958. The chairman of the "German Free Democratic Party," Dr. Erich Mende, enjoyed the club's hospitality in 1962. In 1964 Germania was host to Heinrich Knappstein, German ambassador to the United States, and to several members of the German Parliament, as well as to the cadets of the German training ship *Weser*.

The foremost of the German ladies' clubs in Chicago's history is undoubtedly the still extant Chicago Columbia Club which was founded on April 4, 1893 as "Columbia Damen Klub." When it was incorporated on February 26, 1896, it listed some 140 members under the presidency of Mrs. T. Bluthardt. Like the Germania Club, it is a prestigious club, listing among its past and present members many prominent Chicagoans, such as Mrs. Emil Eitel, Mrs. W. A. Wieboldt, and Mrs. Wm. F. Petersen. Under the present presidency of Mrs. Philip Kemper the club continues to actively pursue the goals of furthering the German language, literature, music, science, and good fellowship, as well as engaging in philanthropic interests. For instance, it donated in 1975 a substantial fellowship to worthy undergraduates majoring in German at the University of Illinois at Chicago Circle.

Only a few of the non-cultural German clubs in Chicago's history can be mentioned. A great number of them, amounting to over 150 in 1935, have been protective organizations against persecution or unforeseen financial calamities through sickness or death of the provider. As examples of such clubs may be mentioned mutual support clubs or lodges of Hermann's Sons, of which the first lodge was founded in Chicago on October 6, 1852. Together with the decrease of German immigration and improved social security provisions as well as better health and life insurance programs such mutual protection organizations of the German element have been decimated.

However, some of them still exist, such as the "Schwäbischer Unterstützungs-Verein" (Swabian Support Club), which was founded in 1883 and still welcomes "healthy German-speaking males between ages of eighteen and forty-five to its monthly meetings," according to an advertisement in the 1974 program of the "Cannstad Volksfest." Since a large portion of the German element, especially in the second half of the nineteenth and early part of the twentieth century, has been organized under these protective clubs, they must be dealt with.

By far the most numerous constituents of these protective clubs have been German workers who wanted to find financial security in the face of sudden, unexpected adversity. One of the most popular of these was the "Gegenseitiger Unterstützungsverein von Chicago" (Mutual Support Club of Chicago), a society which had its origin in the "Chicagoer Kranken Unterstützungsgesellschaft" (Chicago Sick Support Society), which was founded in 1865 by a group of Germans with the purpose of supporting its members in case of sickness, payments ranging between five and twenty-five dollars per week. A report of August 22, 1870 in the *Staatszeitung* supplies an interesting glimpse into the activities of this organization, which had as president C. Knobelsdorf and as secretary W. Katerbau. Between August 1, 1869 and August 1, 1870 the total receipts were $14,119.31. There was an extremely large turnover in membership, even though the number did not change much, amounting to 1,026 on August 1, 1869 and to 1,060 on August 1, 1870. 531 new members were received into the society while 497 memberships were cancelled. 265 persons, of whom twenty-one were women, received a total of $8,311.13 of sick pay, averaging $12.55 per week.

On May 13, 1871 this organization, which in the meantime also paid death benefits, was reorganized under the name of "Bismarck Bund" (Bismarck Association) in several sections which caused a drop in membership. By the time of the Great Fire in October of 1871 it had 897 active members in forty-five sections, of which seventeen were located in Chicago, and the other twenty-eight in various states of the Union. It is interesting to note that at several meetings in February of 1872 it was decided, after many vigorous debates, that women would be barred from the organization.

Between 1871 and 1923 the members paid between twelve and eighteen dollars per year which entitled them to payments of ten dollars per week up to twenty-six weeks per illness. In case of death their survivors were paid $500. After the reorganizations in 1871 until 1875, the society's membership list steadily climbed, but then various factors caused a drastic decline in membership. For instance, in May of 1875 the treasurer C. Neumann absconded with $1,100, and troubles with two life insurance companies caused many dissatisfied members to join other transient mutual support societies. Because of this and various other reasons, the organization was reorganized in April of 1877 under the name of "Gegenseitiger Unterstützungsverein von Chicago" (Mutual Support Club of Chicago), and membership was limited to residents of Chicago and immediate surroundings.

Slowly the club grew, numbering again 637 members in 1890, and from then until 1930 there was a drop in membership only in two instances. It was reduced from 1,021 in 1894 to 943 in 1895 presumably because the club's treasurer, Hugo Peters, absconded with an undisclosed, but obviously substantial, amount of the society's money, and during the World War I days the membership declined from 3,995 in 1916 to 3,987 and 3,784 for 1917 and 1918 respectively, because of rampant anti-German sentiments. The following figures available for the time between 1890 and 1930 demonstrate the society's successful operation. These statistics are adapted from page 155 of the 1931 *Deutsch-Amerikanische Geschichtsblätter*:

Year	Sick benefits paid	Death benefits paid	Assets of the society	Membership of the society
1890	$ 5,753	$ 4,900	$ 8,643	637
1895	9,753	6,600	9,692	943
1900	9,220	6,700	15,197	1,295
1905	11,393	10,225	26,841	1,885

(Table continued)

Year	Sick bene-fits paid	Death bene-fits paid	Assets of the society	Membership of the society
1910	15,002	15,400	41,416	2,641
1915	25,523	20,500	66,644	3,696
1920	21,163	23,650	91,933	3,969
1925	45,622	23,000	172,086	4,897
1930	56,374	32,250	203,991	5,666

All of the approximately 200 members of the Mutual Support Club who were drafted during the war lost their membership, but they were reinstated after the war if they applied for readmission. The club did not engage in any political or religious activities, but it did cultivate social amentities in numerous festivals, balls and other get-togethers. Being a mutual support organization, it provided relief during the depression in the 1930's to its most indigent members who suffered because of unemployment. Even though the society received most groceries gratuitously from sympathetic merchants and could rely on free labor, it still had monthly expenses of over $1,000 after November of 1930. It provided not only meals to its many single unemployed members, but also gave every second week about thirty-five pounds of groceries to married members out of work.

Though the "Gegenseitiger Unterstützungsverein" was one of the most successful protective clubs of Chicago's German element, there were others that were even more popular. As an example may be mentioned the "Gross-Stamm Verein" (Great Tribe Club) founded in 1870, which by 1894 already had close to 2,000 members, as many as the "Gegenseitiger Unterstützungsverein" had in 1906. The *Abendpost* of August 4, 1894 printed the "Gross-Stamm Verein's" annual report which shows that it paid $10,277 in sick benefits and $15,000 in death benefits to its approximately 2,000 members.

Because of decreased immigration, the number of German clubs in Chicago has dwindled from their heyday in the past. The *Abendpost* of May 30, 1910 reported that Chicago's German element again was represented with the largest number of clubs among the various ethnic groups at the fifth annual meeting of the United Association at the large "Bohemian Turnhalle" near 18th and Ashland streets. The paper's statistics reveal that 363 German clubs with 539 delegates were present, compared to 189 Bohemian clubs with 302 delegates, and eighty-one Polish clubs with 106 delegates. The decline in the number of German clubs in Chicago can clearly be shown by giving a survey of the continuous drop in the number of German singing clubs in Chicago's history. Their number steadily increased until 1900, when well over 200 of them were organized under three central Chicago organizations, but then this number declined because of decreased immigration and widespread anti-German sentiment generated during World War I.

Even though at first, when hostilities were confined to Europe, the war brought about the formation of a few patriotic or militant German clubs, such and Young Teuton-American Patriots' Association or Teutonic Americans, on the whole, the hectic period of World War I constituted the most devastating single factor in the decline of Chicago's German clubs. The *Staatszeitung* of June 25, 1917, reported that "nearly every day we are informed that another German-American society has given up its usual activities, that festivals, many of which serve charitable purposes, have been postponed, that meetings and conventions will not be held while the war lasts." Hardly any German club could conduct near normal activities. Even such an unobtrusive, disinterested organization as the German-American Historical Society had to suspend its activities for over two years, causing a corresponding delay in their publications. Name changing, to which many clubs resorted, such as "Germania Männerchor" changing to Chicago Lincoln Club on May 9, 1918, helped little to stem the tide of anti-German sentiment, but instead accelerated the decline of many clubs, for many Germans were reluctant to support or join a club which in their opinion had denied its German background in the face of adversity.

In the case of singing clubs, it took a long time after the war before German songs were popular again, which certainly did not help to stimulate interest in joining these clubs. On May 29, 1936 the *Chicago Herald and Examiner* stated that German song again drew a large crowd, adding wistfully that once there were some 250 German choruses, but now scarcely 100. More precisely the number was 92, according to the *Abendpost* of July 6, 1935. But this was still a much larger number than Chicago's element can muster at the present time, for the *Sonntagspost* of March 24, 1974 lists only ten active German singing clubs for the Chicago area.

The difficulty which some German clubs experienced in getting established may be seen in the example of the German Press Club. On September 12, 1890 the *Abendpost* reported on the first meeting of the German Press Club, which by August 6, 1891 listed in its first general assembly report 58 "ordinary" and 81 "extraordinary" members. However, this club must have passed out of existence almost immediately, because by November 17, 1893 the *Abendpost* announced that a new German Press Club had been organized in the last few days as part of the Schiller Club. Again this German Press Club disintegrated and on October 28, 1908 the *Abendpost* stated that "a 'German Press Club' has been started and organized yesterday." This club suffered a decline during World War I just like all other German clubs, but it recuperated sufficiently to be rather active in 1933. It appears to have become inactive before World War II started. The fate of the abortive German Press Club was shared by most of the German element's literary clubs.

Chicago's German element has produced several literary clubs, but only one of them, the "Literarische Gesellschaft" (Literary Society), continues to present monthly lectures at the present time. This society presumably evolved from a similar society, which was active as early as 1890, was reorganized in 1931, and again was resuscitated in 1943. On March 5, 1890 the *Abendpost* reported on a lecture on Persia presented at the "German Literary Society" at Northwestern University. Soon after the Chicago German newspapers contained regular announcements of its periodic lectures, such as the one on Annette von Droste-Hülshoff by Amalie von Ende on November 13, 1894 or on Gerhard Hauptmann's *Versunkene Glocke* (Sunken Bell) by Sigmund Zeisler on May 18, 1900.

In addition to this literary club, another one, the "Kunst und Literatur-Verein" (Society for Art and Literature) seems to have blossomed for a short time in the 1890's, for the *Abendpost* of October 29, 1895 mentioned that more than 300 of its members were entertained at a Goethe evening and that the librarian E. F. Gauss would present a Schiller lecture on the following Monday. Early in 1896 this club organized special evenings devoted to particular German poets. On January 5, 1896 Emil Hirsch lectured on Lessing's literary values, and appealed to all for a Lessing memorial in the form of a German library at the University of Chicago. On March 17 and 31, 1896 followed Fritz Reuter and Johann Ludwig Uhland evenings. Apparently this literary club did not survive World War I, sharing thus the fate of another German literary society, the Germanistic Society, which was founded around 1914 to present lectures by Chicago's German professors, such as Martin Schütze, Julius Goebel and James Hatfield.

An ambitious undertaking after the war, the German Federation of Chicago did not become as effective as envisioned by its founders. Founded early in 1922, after German culture in America had received an almost irreparable blow through the war, it was intended to preserve and to cultivate German literature as well as German art and science in America. Its charter board members were Dr. Otto L. Schmidt as president, Michael F. Girten and Wilhelm Arens as vice presidents, F. Matenaers as secretary and Otto Doederlein as treasurer.

The German Federation of Chicago organized a grand scale May Festival on May 28, 1922 to show "that the German Oak still stands" and to raise money for its cultural activities. Even though all work and much merchandise were donated, when the festival report was distributed on August 24, 1922, it became clear that in spite of receipts amounting to $8,610.48, the total deficit was $2,622.89. Presumably because of possible harassment people had been reluctant to attend the festival. According to the report, "in certain quarters efforts were made to discourage people from coming to the picnic and buying tickets." Moreover, advertising in the program was expected to exceed $5,000, but actually only $516 were realized.

Undaunted by these inauspicious beginnings, the German Federation of Chicago continued its activities, which were directed primarily at saving Chicago's floundering German theater from financial ruin, and instilling pride in its cultural heritage into the German element by offering lectures on a broad range of topics by renowned German speakers. Between October 1923 and July 1924 professors from America and Germany presented six lectures, such as Professor Harms from Kiel on "The Development of Sea Travel" or Professor Rohrbach from the University of Chicago on "The Social Development and the Activities of Working Students," but in every instance expenditures were considerably more than the income from admission tickets. The club's president, Dr. Otto L. Schmidt, paid the deficit amounting to over $1,000 from his own pocket, but when his generosity was sneered upon and interest in the German Federation's activities did not appreciably improve, Dr. Schmidt withdrew his support, which caused the club's demise before 1930.

Chapter 7

hopes, skills, attitudes

The Chicago Germans' Role in Industry and in the Work Force

Trying to do justice to the role of the German element in Chicago's industry, trade, and general work force in a single chapter seems like a futile undertaking, for it could scarcely be dealt with adequately in a monograph. But since the object is to convey an inkling of the Chicago Germans' importance in commerce rather than a complete, detailed appreciation, it should be sufficient to deal here with representative examples. An inquiry directed to Chicago's German-American Chamber of Commerce on June 6, 1974 revealed that at least twenty-seven German-owned plants or factories are now located in the Chicago area. They include such corporations as the Nixdorf Computer Inc. on 5725 East River Road in Chicago, producing computer systems, and the Robert Bosch Corporation in Broadview, which manufactures car radios, industrial tools, and various automatic equipment.

However, these twenty-seven German corporations represent only a meager remnant of a once powerful commerce. Many of the German immigrants who came to Chicago, depleted of financial resources but full of hope and an eagerness to work dilligently in their various skills to gain economic independence, reached their goals in building up reputable and profitable businesses. At times Chicagoans became aware of the success of some of them. On February 19, 1889 the *Staatszeitung* listed German businessmen of Chicago whose assets were worth between one and five million dollars. They included Michael Brand, Henry A. Cohn, Conrad Fürst, Ernst J. Lehmann, Jacob Rehm, Jacob Rosenberg, Georg Schneider, Peter Schoenhofen, Conrad Seipp, and Otto Young.

Most likely there were at that time several other German millionaires in Chicago, such as the banker Edward S. Dreyer or the "wagon king" Peter Schuettler, but for some reason they were not included. Periodically the German newspapers reported on the estates of prominent Chicago Germans, as on August 27, 1907 when the German packer Nelson Morris died and left an estate estimated between twenty and thirty million dollars, or on May 17, 1918 when the will of the recently deceased Joseph Schaffner disposed of over three million dollars. Julius Rosenwald, born of parents who emigrated from Germany in 1854, and president of Sears and Roebuck, often made headlines, as on April 1, 1914, when he was listed as paying the largest income tax in Chicago, for his 1913 income was a record sum of $1,320,000. In March of 1918 he was listed with three other Chicagoans, J. Ogden Armour, Cyrus H. McCormick, and Louis F. Swift in *Forbes Magazine* among the thirty richest Americans.

Many of the Chicago Germans who established large businesses provided employment for innumerable Chicagoans, as a few examples will show. Before the Great Fire of 1871 Peter Schuettler employed several hundred Chicagoans in his wagon shop. Peter Schuettler had been born in 1812 near Darmstadt and emigrated to America in 1834, after he had completed his apprenticeship and the journeyman's examination for the wheelwright's trade. Coming to Chicago in 1843, he started an unsuccessful brewery before he went into the wagon manufacturing business. His solidly-built wagons and the "prairie schooner," nicknamed the "old Reliable," won him lucrative special contracts with the westward-moving Mormons and later with the Union Army. The innumerable wagons which left his rapidly expanding business premises could soon be found all over the United States and played an important part in the winning of the West. It should be mentioned that he commissioned the architect van Osdel to design for him one of the most magnificent ante-fire residences in Chicago. When he died in 1865, his son Peter, the first of at least three succeeding generations, took over the largest wagon manufacturing business in the United States. Another mass employer, Jacob Beiersdorf, born in 1832 at Pirmasens, came to Chicago in 1854 as a master cabinetmaker. He established a furniture factory which by 1871 was the largest in Chicago and employed some 500 workers. But after it was totally destroyed in the 1871 Fire and the insurance company failed to pay for the loss, it was not rebuilt.

The main upsurge of the Germans' commerce came from after the 1871 Fire up to about World War I. J. Currey's three volume work on the *Manufacturing and Wholesale Industries of Chicago* of 1918 provides ample evidence of the German element's prominent role in Chicago's commerce. At about the turn of the century the following are some of an indeterminable number of businesses or factories owned by Chicago Germans who employed between about 300 and 4,500 persons: the one-time world's largest ready-made clothing factory of Hart, Schaffner and Marx; the Ludwig Wolff plumbing goods factory; the Bunte Brothers' candy factory; the Mandel Brothers' store; Moritz Lassig's Bridge Manufacturing Corporation; Spiegel's third largest mail order house in the United States; Paul Werner's Publishing House; Nelson Morris', the Arnold Brothers' and Oscar Mayer's packing houses; the Roos Furniture Company; Stephan Schneider's ball bearing factory; Simon Florsheim's pneumatic tool company; America's largest baking company owned by Paul Schulze; Frederick Bode's ladies' accessory factory; Joseph Alexander's Garden City Embroidery Works; Frank Diesel's American Can Company; Henry Fürst's and William Kerber's stone yard; the chocolate and candy factory of Fred W. Rueckheim, who invented the popular "Cracker Jacks;" Emil Eiger's millinery shop; and Christoph Baum's ornament factory.

The largest of these employers was most likely the still flourishing Hart, Schaffner and Marx Corporation, whose personnel fluctuated considerably with economic ups and downs, having at times close to 5,000 people on their payrolls. Harry Hart (1850-1929), the founder of the world famous ready-to-wear clothing establishment, was born at Eppelsheim in Rhenish Hesse and came in 1858 with his family to Chicago where in 1872 he opened a small clothing store at 436 South State Street. This business grew considerably, especially when his partners Joseph Schaffner and Marcus Marx joined forces. In 1909 they erected the still used twelve-story factory at Monroe and Franklin streets.

The Mandel brothers employed by about 1890 well over 800 Chicagoans. Leon Mandel, perhaps the most outstanding of the three brothers, was born at Kerzenheim, Bavaria in 1841 and emigrated with his family in 1852 directly to Chicago. He received little formal education, since already in 1853 he had become a "cash boy" for the dry good store of Ross and Foster, at that time the largest store west of New York. Two years later he and his two brothers opened a store at Clark and Van Buren streets. Their business increased successfully and in 1871 they erected their own store building at State and Harrison streets, but it was promptly destroyed in the 1871 Fire. However, their initiative was not destroyed and their business continued to grow in various quarters, forcing them to erect in 1901 a large store on State and Madison streets which periodically had to be enlarged.

Leon Mandel's financial success enabled him to be active as a philanthropist. He generously supported the University of Chicago, which gratefully honored him by naming one of the campus buildings "Mandel Hall." He also was a generous patron of the Art Institute and the Chicago Grand Opera. His interest extended to affairs of the German element. For example, he was one of the founders of the German American Historical Society of Illinois in 1900. In sundry charity work his name usually appeared with the directors in the letterhead, founding, for instance, the Jewish Manual Training School. When he died in 1911 he not only willed $50,000 to various charity organizations, but he also provided an equal sum to the general fund for his employees.

Of the above mentioned list of employers, Christoph Baum perhaps employed the smallest work force, amounting to some 300 people. He was born in 1853 at Eschwege, about 100 miles northeast of Frankfurt. After he passed the journeyman's exam as a weaver, he emigrated directly to Chicago in 1872 over the vigorous protests of his parents who did not want to have the only surviving of eight children go to the New World. After many different jobs, which included working as a door-to-door salesman, he formed a partnership with Emil Ernst in 1881 to establish at 150 Fifth Avenue the Baum and Ernst firm, engaged in manufacturing trimmings for clothes. After several changes of partners and business premises, in 1903 he, as sole owner, erected a six-story factory building at Frontier Avenue and Blackhawk Street.

Parallel with the German element's role in Chicago's commerce is the development of "The Fair," founded in 1875 by Ernst J. Lehmann. He was born at Schwerin, about sixty miles east of Hamburg, in 1849 and emigrated with his family to America in 1858. In 1860 he came to Chicago, where he worked as a salesman before he established a small department store on State and Adams streets in 1875. Good business practices, and buying at auctions the stocks of bankrupt stores, such as the once phenomenally successful Stein's Dollar Store, enabled him to enlarge his business steadily until he possessed the largest department store in Chicago, known as The Fair, at which, after the remodeling of 1897, some 3,000 people found employment.

Before Lehmann died in 1900, he founded the Arlington race track and the Shubert Theatre. His widow, Augusta, attempted to gain complete control of the business by buying in 1905 Otto

Young's interest in the store for an estimated ten million dollars. The Fair did not remain in the family, for in 1965 it was remodeled and became the downtown store of Montgomery Ward and Company. But descendants of Lehmann are still around, for in June of 1970 his grandson "Skip" Lehman was featured in the *Chicago Magazine* as one of Chicago's "ten best catches."

In the same article one could also read about "one of the legendary beauties of Chicago," Elizabeth Paepcke, nee Nitze, also of German extraction. Her late husband, Walter Paepcke, a second generation German, born in 1896 at Chicago, provided employment for many Chicagoans as president of the Container Corporation of America and the Chicago Mill and Lumber Corporation, one of the world's largest producers of hardwood lumber, wood boxes, crates, veneer, and plywood. Walter and Elizabeth Paepcke developed Aspen in Colorado and began the Aspen Institute for Humanistic Studies.

Even today Chicago business enterprises owned by citizens of German extraction still provide work for a large portion of Chicagoans. This becomes evident when such employers are mentioned as the Wieboldt Corporation, the Goldblatt and Kresge's K-mart stores, the Robert Bosch Corporation, and the Oscar Mayer packing house.

Chicago's German element was represented in all branches of industry and commerce, even dominating certain areas at particular times. Undoubtedly Chicago's brewing industry was monopolized by the Germans. Two Germans, William Haas and Konrad Sulzer, founded Chicago's first brewery in 1836, when they arrived from Watertown, New York with 150 barrels of ale and the proper requisites for brewing. In the small structure which they initially erected about 600 barrels of beer were produced per year. Haas was born somewhere in Germany in 1800 and emigrated at an undetermined time to Watertown. In Chicago he established in 1839 a partnership with William Ogden to found a brewery on Chicago Avenue and Pine Street which was sold in 1843 to William Lill and Michael Diversey, a German who had come to Chicago in 1836 to become an exceedingly prominent citizen. Haas died in 1861 at his estate in Boonville, Missouri.

Konrad Sulzer was born in 1807 at a bordertown between Germany and Switzerland. He received a good education which enabled him to work as a druggist between 1825 and 1827 at Zofingen. In 1833 he emigrated to Watertown, New York, where he met Haas. After coming to Chicago, he bought property in Lake View in the vicinity of Montrose Boulevard, which used to be named after him Sulzer Road. An interesting letter of May 15, 1851, from Sulzer to the druggist Friedrich Schultheiss of Winterthur, is reprinted in the October 1901 issue of *Deutsch-Amerikanische Geschichtsblätter*, of which the most interesting parts are given in the following translation:

> Chicago was a totally insignificant place at our arrival [in 1836]; its surrounding was a wilderness. There existed no Protestant community, but a Catholic one had just been organized so that one of my children, because of the absence of a Protestant minister, could not be baptized until three years old. Now, of course, things are quite different. Chicago is a large city with a harbor which constantly teems with ships and steamers, and is destined to become the most significant inland trading center because of its location. Through the Great Lakes it is connected with the East and through a canal with the Mississippi. In a short time four or five railroads will connect Chicago with all parts of the Union. Approximately a third of Chicago and its vicinity consists of Germans. It has a Catholic bishopry; and three German Protestant and four Catholic churches are established. Altogether Chicago has over thirty churches of every confession. One can see almost everywhere pretty towns and fertile farms. So much can be done to a wilderness in America within fifteen years . . . My farm of 100 acres lies five miles from the center or three miles from the border of the city. I am busy with a considerable number of livestock and with vegetable growing, an occupation which is most congenial to my disposition and which affords me satisfaction and independence, if not great riches. You can imagine that, because of the proximity of Chicago, I am lacking neither company nor reading material to fill my leisure time most pleasantly. Thus, I have reason to be satisfied with my situation, especially so, since my healthy children are growing up in an area where political disturbances, so common with you in Europe, cannot disturb them.

From this letter and other indications it appears that Sulzer sold his part of the brewery soon after 1836 and led a contented life as a farmer until he died in 1873.

Besides Haas, Sulzer and Diversey, other early Germans were active in Chicago's brewing industry before 1850. Mattias Best, who immigrated in 1841 from Bavaria, brewed beer in a small structure on Indiana Avenue and 14th Street. In 1849 Adolph P. Mueller produced beer at the corner of State and Randolph streets. At about the same time, John A. Huck (1819-78), who had come to Chicago in 1846 from Baden, started a brewery on Chicago Avenue and Superior Street. But in spite of these rudimentary attempts at brewing, Chicago's beer industry had a slow start, for by 1856 the first volume of Andreas's *History* lists on page 565 only the following brewers as plying their trade in Chicago:

Name of firm	Capital invested	Value of products in 1856	Number of employees	Barrels of beer produced in 1856
Conrad Seipp	$18,000	$ 8,960	6	1,120
Georg Metz	15,000	19,200	6	2,400
Braham & Co.	8,000	8,000	2	1,000
V. Busch	6,000	25,600	4	3,200
J. F. Rodermeyer	8,000	40,000	6	5,000
Bucher & Co.	5,000	11,200	2	1,400
Blattner & Co.	1,000	2,000	2	250
S. Irwin	3,000	8,000	2	1,000
Spriggs Co.	3,000	7,200	3	900
Total	67,000	130,160	33	16,270

The total output of Chicago's breweries in 1856, amounting to some 16,000 barrels a year, is diminishingly small compared to the 120,000 barrels produced in 1879 by the Conrad Seipp brewery or the 180,000 barrels by the Peter Schoenhofen brewery in 1893.

The main reason for the slow start in Chicago's brewing industry was that, generally speaking, there existed little demand for beer and similar products. The only consumers were at first the Germans. They often complained bitterly about discrimination because of their beer drinking habits. Chicago's Germans insisted that the so-called "Beer Riot" of 1855 should more adequately be called the battle between beer and whiskey, for the prohibitory city ordinances were strictly enforced with German innkeepers, but their whiskey serving American colleagues were able to circumvent the oppressive statutes.

With time, however, the brewing industry triumphed for several reasons. Gradually the Americans developed a taste for the weaker Teutonic drink. Their appreciation of beer, as well as the steady influx of Germans made the brewery business profitable so that a sharp increase in the number of Chicago breweries could be noticed, amounting in 1870 to twenty-three, of which most were German. A long article in the *Staatszeitung* of June 18, 1880 tells of Chicago's breweries, amounting at that time to nineteen. They provided work for over 1,000 employees and produced in the year ending May 1, 1880 450,000 barrels, which were sold for eight dollars each.

The largest brewery of Chicago and of the Midwest at that time was that of Conrad Seipp, which had produced 119,753 barrels within the previous year. The second largest was that of Michael Brand with 50,206 barrels per annum. According to page 149 of the third volume of Pierce's *History*, by 1890 (when Chicago's per capita consumption of beer, though below that of St. Louis and Milwaukee, amounted to forty-nine gallons a year, twice that of

Germany) all but two of Chicago's leading breweries were German. Some of the more prominent ones were those of Michael Brand, Valentin Busch, Francis J. Dewes, A. Gottfried, John Huck, Paul Pohl, Wilhelm Schmidt, William Ruehl, Peter Schoenhofen, Conrad Seipp, and Frederick Wacker. Several breweries conglomerated and gave up their individual firm names. For instance, Michael Brand's and William Ruehl's breweries became part of the United Breweries Company, which in 1893 consisted of thirteen breweries and had as president Valentin Blatz, vice president Leo Ernst, treasurer Rudolph Brand, and secretary M. E. Pavy.

For obvious reasons, Chicago's German brewers waged a vigorous campaign to render ineffective the efforts of the temperance advocates, who wanted to turn Chicago into a dry city. This had loomed ever since the teetotaler Levi Boone had been elected mayor of Chicago in 1855. The brewers were successful in their struggle against the temperance movement until the national prohibition amendment became law immediately after World War I. Then some breweries tried to stay within the law by either closing down or by concocting and selling a brew with a permissible alcohol content, but others continued their business, brewing contraband products. For instance, on May 19, 1924 Chicago newspapers reported that federal agents in a raid at the Michael Sieben Brewery at 1470 North Larrabee Street confiscated nine trucks being loaded with contraband. During the raid not only Chicago police officers who had been aiding the bootleggers were arrested, but also the notorious gangsters Dion O'Bannion and Johnny Torrio. After the repeal of the prohibition amendment, the Sieben brewery, like other German breweries, engaged again in legitimate activities, which consisted primarily of providing the numerous customers of the extremely popular "Sieben Bierstube" with beer until it closed in 1967, the year which also was the end of the Sieben Brewery. Practically all of the breweries founded by Chicago Germans have either vanished or have been sold to large corporations. It seems as though the decline of Chicago's brewing industry coincided with the numerical decline of the city's German element.

In their heyday the breweries of Chicago Germans not only provided employment for many people, but they also footed a large portion of the internal revenue collected in Chicago. In 1905 the total revenue collected was $6,937,232.35, of which the highest amount by far, namely $4,231,254 came from beer, ale, and the like. In comparison, only $651,331.35 was collected for smoking products and no more than $162,245.83 for distilled spirits.

A fair share of the German brewers of Chicago became known as patrons of the arts and for their philanthropic or charitable work. Francis J. Dewes paid for the Alexander von Humboldt monument, which was dedicated in Humboldt Park on October 16, 1892. Dewes was born in 1845 at Losheim, Rhenish Prussia and came to Chicago in 1868 where he founded in 1882 the Dewes brewery, later the Standard brewery. In 1893 $60,000 were paid by the Schoenhofen family to fourteen charitable organizations in Chicago. Peter Schoenhofen was born in 1827 at Wittbach, Bavaria, and when he came to Chicago in 1849 he was penniless, but by the time of his death in 1893 his estate was appraised at well over two million dollars.

The owners of the Seipp brewery have an outstanding record for charity. The founder of the brewery, Conrad Seipp, and his wife usually led the lists of contributions to worthy causes, but in addition to that they gave large sums to various projects. In 1910 Mrs. Conrad Seipp gave $150,000 to make possible the erection of new quarters for the German Hospital, now Grant Hospital, and an additional large sum was donated earlier to help erect the German Old People's Home in Forest Park. In 1890 the Seipp family donated $135,000 to sixteen charitable organizations and in 1912 $60,000 to eight institutions, including $5,000 to the Art Institute. The Seipp family had always taken an interest in cultural affairs. For instance, in 1904 Mrs. Catharina Seipp, upon the advice of Dr. O. L. Schmidt and the German consul Dr. Walther Wever, offered three prizes amounting to $6,000 to three monographs dealing with the German element in America. From this resulted the monumental work, *The German Element in the United States*, New York, 1909 by Albert Faust.

A surprisingly large number of German brewers have occupied public offices. The position of city treasurer was practically dominated by German brewers between 1879 and 1906. W. C. Seipp held the office from 1879 to 1881; then followed Rudolph Brand from 1881 to 1883. After a pause of four years, Hermann Plautz served between 1887 and 1889, followed by Bernhard Roesing 1889-91 and Peter Kiolbassa from 1891 to 1893. The next German city treasurer was the brewer Ernst Hummel, who occupied the office from 1897 to 1899 and again from 1903 to 1904. Adam Ortseifen, president of the McAvoy Brewing Company, served in 1899 and 1900 and Frederick Blocki from 1905 to 1906. The only other German city treasurers during these years were Adam Wolf, a dry goods merchant, who served from 1895 to 1897; and from 1901 to 1902 served Charles F. Gunther, the famous "Candy

Man," who erected the Coliseum and whose enormous collection of historical objects induced the Chicago Historical Society to move to larger quarters in Lincoln Park.

Several of the German brewers who served as city treasurers also occupied other public offices. Ernst Hummel, who was born in 1842 near Stuttgart and came in 1856 to Chicago where he established in 1880 a brewery in partnership with Rudolph Brand, was also elected collector of the North Side in 1876, besides being city treasurer. Moreover, he occupied simultaneously the office of legislator and school board member from 1885 to 1887, and was alderman of the 33rd Ward from 1889 to 1892. Hermann Plautz (1844-1904) came in 1862 to Chicago from his native Pomerania and was at first president of the Chicago Drug and Chemical Company before he became owner of the Northwestern Brewery. Before he served as city treasurer from 1887 to 1889, he became city clerk on the Republican ticket when it was shown that his opponent's initial victory was the result of a blatant election fraud. As Chicago's ambassador of goodwill he was received in 1890 by the German emperor and by the Russian czar.

Though it seemed like Chicago's German brewers held a monopoly on the office of city treasurer, they also occupied other public offices. For instance, Louis C. Huck, who was born in 1842 at Steinbach, Baden, and among other businesses owned the Huck Brewery, was elected county treasurer in 1875. Jacob Rehm, who came in 1841 to Chicago from Germany and owned the National Brewery after 1896, started his controversial public career rather modestly as a policeman in 1851. After that he served as street commissioner in 1855; as city marshal in 1857 and 1858; as county treasurer in 1863; as superintendent of police in 1862 and from 1866 to 1868; and, finally, as Chicago's chief of police from 1873 to 1875. Then in 1876 his career as public servant came to a scandalous halt, when he was indicted as one of the main conspirators in the infamous "Whiskey Ring." In spite of the fact that he turned state's witness, he still had to pay a $10,000 fine and was imprisoned for six months.

Even though no other branch of Chicago's industry was dominated by the German element like that of brewing, some areas had a disproportionately large number of German undertakings. This is the case in the manufacture of musical instruments. In the 1880's the piano factory of the Chicago German Julius Bauer was the largest in the Midwest. John Gerts, who was born in Westphalia in 1845 and came to Chicago in 1870, founded in 1880 the piano-manufacturing concern of Bush and Gerts which by 1917 had an annual output of 4,000 pianos and gave employment to some 250 workers. The still flourishing Harmony Company established in 1892 by William F. Schultz, who was born at Hamburg in 1857 and came to Chicago in 1882, employed in the 1920's about 125 people to produce violins, guitars, drums and the like. Other German names in the manufacturing of musical instruments are Charles Geib, Fred Gretsch, the Ludwig Industries, the Mittenwald Company, and the Schilke Music Products. The German element also established large numbers of businesses in the production of clothing and shoes, furniture, bakery goods, chemical products, tools, and building materials, which will not be listed here.

Chicago's German element not only provided employment in the business undertakings mentioned above, but it also supplied a large part of Chicago's general work force. According to the 1870 federal census, the birthplace of Chicago's workers was Germany for 25,778, Ireland for 22,337, and America for 39,755. Since these figures list only first generation Germans, it is obvious that among the 39,755 American-born many must have been second generation Germans. Various factors, such as the building of canals, the expansion of the city, and rebuilding it after the 1871 Fire, establishing Chicago as a railroad center, and the mushrooming of all branches of industry, attracted thousands of German immigrants in quest of a comfortable livelihood.

It is not possible to ascertain the exact figures of German workers in Chicago for the city's entire history, but the few statistics which are available afford glimpses at interesting situations. Most of the German workers who did not have friends or relatives to help them find work in Chicago, relied on the German Aid Society's employment office to find a livelihood. This society periodically published reports which told how many Germans had availed themselves of the society's services and how many were actually placed. At times these reports even classified them according to their various skills.

On October 8, 1881, the *Staatszeitung* contained a detailed monthly report of the German Aid Society, which stated that in the month of September 1,482 persons called at their office, of whom 253 were women and girls and 1,229 men and boys. The males were subcategorized as follows:

Laborers	785	Gardeners	9	Goldsmiths	4
Clerks	88	Blacksmiths	7	Wheelwrights	4
Shoemakers	55	Bricklayers	7	Miners	3
Locksmiths	52	Bookbinders	6	Stone cutters	3

(Table continued on following page)

Machinists	43	Brewery workers	6	Tailors	3
Bakers	33	Coopers	6	Potters	2
Carpenters	25	Druggists	6	Printers	2
Cabinetmakers	24	Painters	6	Saddlers	2
Typesetters	11	Dyers	5	Waiters	2
Millers	10	Butchers	5	Hatters	1
Teachers	9	Engineers	4	Paper hangers	1
				Total	1,229

These statistics for one month are interesting, but not representative. While B. Pierce asserted on page 152 in volume two of her *History of Chicago* that only thirty percent of the German workers were unskilled, the percentage of the unskilled workers listed here for September 1881 amounted to 64 percent.

More representative statistics are available from the federal census reports of 1880 and 1890. In the following chart, the number and percentage of German workers in Chicago, constituting the greatest number of foreign-born workers, are compared to those of the second largest number of foreign-born, the Irish:

		German		Irish	
Occupations	Year	Number	Percent	Number	Percent
Manufacturing	1880	24,154	26.30	12,585	13.70
& Mechanical	1890	46,866	22.51	19,532	9.33
Trade	1880	6,677	18.43	2,531	6.99
	1890	11,508	18.27	3,547	5.63
Domestic &	1880	2,781	15.16	3,383	18.45
Personal Service	1890	7,615	16.07	7,132	15.05
Transportation &	1880	2,166	12.46	2,959	17.02
Communication	1890	5,334	15.32	4,516	12.97
Professional	1880	599	11.74	232	4.55
Services	1890	1,089	8.83	368	2.98
Public	1880	264	13.35	403	20.38
Services	1890	720	11.88	1,446	23.87
Agriculture	1880	448	33.26	161	11.95
	1890	505	37.69	72	5.37
Clerical	1880	57	5.09	33	2.95
Services	1890	2,772	6.76	1,778	4.34
Unclassified	1880	3,701	20.11	1,631	8.86
& Unknown	1890	9,020	20.41	2,945	6.67
Total	1880	40,847	21.30	23,918	12.47
	1890	85,429	18.64	41,336	9.02

German workers continued to pour into Chicago until about 1914, when Germany became embroiled in the first World War. After a pause of some eight years, extremely adverse economic conditions in the homeland again induced innumerable workers to emigrate to Chicago and other American cities in quest of a livelihood. But the depression in the late twenties and thirties, as well as the simultaneous high unemployment rate again acted as deterrents. On February 13, 1927 the *Abendpost* reported that "only once in the last 74 years, in 1922, has unemployment among the Germans in Chicago been so serious as at present, according to the latest reports of the German Aid Society. Over 3,000 people have applied for work at the office of the society, but only seventy-two were given employment. Wages are reduced considerably, and many employers only supply food and shelter, but no wages at all."

With the rise of Naziism and the apparent prospering of the Germans, few German workers came to Chicago, even though a veritable exodus from Germany was evident for the intelligentsia. After World War II a new influx of German workers occurred which, of course, never attained the proportions of the peak years during the pre-quota period, and which steadily declined as prosperity returned to Germany. It is interesting to compare statistics of the major occupational groups of German naturalized citizens in the year ending June 30, 1973 and those of German immigrants admitted during the same time span. These figures are taken from the 1973 *Annual Report* of the Immigration and Naturalization Service:

Occupations	Naturalized in 1972/73	Immigrated in 1972/73
Service workers except private households	568	197
Craftsmen, foremen and kindred workers	550	204
Professional, technical and kindred workers	528	583
Clerical and kindred workers	521	346
Operatives and kindred workers	337	130
Managers, officials, and proprietors	242	216
Sales workers	171	94
Laborers, except farm and mine	147	28
Private household workers	31	25
Farmers and farm managers	11	2
Farm laborers and foremen	9	5
Housewives, children, and others with no occupation, or occupation not reported	3,555	4,770
Total	6,670	6.600

These national statistics indicate that more German workers came in the past than in the year 1972/73. Comparable detailed figures for Chicago are not available. The 1973 *Annual Report* of the Immigration and Naturalization Service merely states that in 1972/73,

562 German-born became naturalized American citizens in Chicago, and 109 German immigrants were admitted to this city. If the national statistics may serve as an index, at least half of the newly arriving Germans fit the category "housewives, children or no occupation" and cannot be properly considered part of Chicago's general work force. The rest, which for 1972/73 most likely did not exceed fifty, can scarcely be considered a numerically important part of Chicago's work force.

In the past, however, the collective strength of the German workers was considerable. According to the 1886 *Fourth Biennial Report* of the Illinois Bureau of Labor, there were a total of 18,355 Knights of Labor in Cook County, of whom 3,804 German-born members represented the largest group of the foreign-born constituents. The 1886 statistics for the trade union members in Illinois, 88 percent of whom lived in Cook County, are even more startling. Of a total of 23,712 members, the 9,839 German members by far outnumbered all other groups, including the 2,977 American-born members. The following statistics for the individual unions, taken from page 537 of volume three of Pierce's *History of Chicago*, contrast the three largest groups, the Germans, the Scandinavians, and the Irish, and disregard other ethnic groups, such as the Poles who were represented only with 366 members in the Lumbermen's Laborers Union.

Organization	Total	German	Scandinavian	Irish
Bricklayers & Stonemasons	4,000	1,015	740	1,270
Hod Carriers	3,500	1,200	700	1,000
Metal Workers	3,023	1,815	500	21
Seamen	2,500		1,666	278
Furniture Workers	2,429	1,458	396	25
Lumbermen's Laborers	1,921	1,545		
Carpenters and Joiners	1,868	1,259	45	101
Cigarmakers	1,674	489	17	53
Typographers	1,597	358	87	225
Butchers	1,200	700	50	300
Total	23,712	9,839	4,201	3,273

During the heyday of German immigration in the second half of the nineteenth century German workers became exceedingly important in the movement to ameliorate the lot of the working class. More than any other group in Chicago's work force, they seem to have endorsed the idea that in order to bring about changes they needed to organize societies or unions. Already in the 1850's the "Chicago Arbeiterverein" was organized for the benefit of workers; and it was so popular that by 1865 it numbered over 1,000 members. Some of their reports, reprinted in still extant issues of the *Staatszeitung*, convey an idea of their activities. This society not only attempted to enlighten the workers by establishing a library, which in 1865 amounted to over 3,000 volumes, by managing a night school, and by arranging periodic lectures on relevant topics, but it also tried to improve their economic situation in various ways.

During the Civil War it financially supported the families of the killed, wounded or impoverished workers who had signed up for military service. The *Staatszeitung* of May 26, 1862 reprinted a quarterly report of the "Arbeiterverein," which shows that $305 had been paid to worker-soldiers or their families. In this same report the president of the club, Theodor Hielscher, proposed that the club buy coal wholesale and sell it at a profit to members, but still cheaper than retail suppliers. To be sure, these efforts which helped to improve the day-to-day living conditions of the workers were relatively insignificant compared to the efforts which aimed at insuring their human rights and bringing about acceptable working conditions.

Much of the German workers' collective efforts were directed toward instituting the eight-hour workday. On various occasions, such as the Fourth of July 1879, they demonstrated for improved working conditions and a shorter workday, which usually precipitated hateful harangues by the "capitalist-controlled" English and German language press. A standard argument of the innumerable editorials in the *Staatszeitung* against the eight-hour day was that workers, not knowing how to spend their additional leisure time wisely, would actually deteriorate because of the lighter work load, for they would spend additional hours carousing in bars.

Collective action was the only effective means for the workers to attain some rights in a system which heavily favored the employers at the expense of the employed. Henry David tersely summarized the prevailing conditions in his book, *The History of the Haymarket Affair*, stating on page forty seven that

> the law was so fashioned that it placed as little hindrance as possible in the way of money-making activities of the employer. Labor, on the other hand, was seriously hampered by the limitations upon its collective activities. Sometimes they were restrictive enough to outlaw completely all collective efforts to improve conditions. The employer was relatively free in his dealings with those who sold him their labor. Generally speaking, he could discharge them without

> cause; he could lock them out; he could force them to sign ironclad oaths; he could blacklist them without fear of suffering punishment. He could combine with other manufacturers to form associations injurious to a 'third party,' and remain untouched by the law . . . Furthermore, the employer could expect State and municipal authorities to place at his disposal the police, militia and other coercive instruments in times of serious industrial disputes.

The German workers often bore the brunt of unprovoked, violent attacks by Chicago police and Pinkerton's Protective Patrol, which numbered by 1887 some 1,600 men. The *Staatszeitung* of April 26, 1879 reported on one such instance, the trial of "Harmonia vs. Hilkey," which resulted from a police raid of the "Vorwärts Turnhalle" on July 26, 1877, at which at least one worker, the cabinetmaker Karl Tessmann, was killed. Ex-Sergeant Brenan, who had been given no particular orders, led the raid with thirty men into the hall at which some 300 workers were holding a peaceful meeting. The report continued, "many witnesses agreed that police stormed the 'Turnhalle' and started swinging their clubs and firing their pistols indiscriminately. William Remien, a cabinetmaker, saw a man in a dark suit lying in the center of the hall and a policeman standing about twenty feet away, shooting at his body. Remien was so severely beaten that he almost fainted from loss of blood. Jacob Schnoepfel said that he was severely hurt. At least six policemen trounced on him and six or eight shots were fired at him. He suffered three broken ribs and a lung injury."

Later in 1877 a veritable battle between police and what newspapers called a "mob" at the Halsted viaduct resulted in a heavy toll on life. Since the press supported the police activities, no matter how indefensible their attacks on the workers were, and since the courts provided no protection, several workers' organizations instituted armed sections. For instance, the "Lehr und Wehrverein" or the "Jägerverein" started to drill and parade with their weapons openly, which added to the tense situation and divided the workers, but did little to improve the lot of the workers. In fact, it even worsened the workers' situation, for their activities were suppressed even more ruthlessly.

Gradually, the Socialists, consisting primarily of Germans, were gaining a strong foothold in Chicago's work force, and they were trying to elect some of their candidates to effect improvements for the workers. Though not strikingly successful, they nevertheless brought about some improvements. Dr. Ernst Schmidt, mayoral candidate of the Socialist Labor party in 1879, described one of the victories of the Socialists, reprinted here from Frederick Schmidt's *He Chose*, page 122:

> Because of Harrison's understanding and sympathy for the worker's plight, I consented in 1879 to become candidate for mayor on the Socialist Labor party's ticket. Two years earlier Frank Stauber had been elected on this ticket as alderman of the Fourteenth Ward, due to the efforts of politically minded workingmen acting through their trade organizations. However, it required a whole year to seat him because of the brazen attempts of the Republicans to defraud him of his rightful victory at the polls.
>
> With me, a rank outsider, running for mayor on the Socialist Labor party's ticket, Chicago was faced with a three-way-mayoralty battle. The Republican candidate, Abner Wright, had the support of some 450 businessmen and the press, especially *The Tribune*, which was backing Wright's anti-labor policy and labeling Harrison and me 'advocates of communism.' This was not as bad as some of the choice epithets other local papers hurled at me—'lout,' 'ex-convict,' 'brigand' and 'anarchist.'
>
> Democrat Harrison was not conceded a chance against Wright because of the latter's Republican backers from Prairie Avenue, among whom were Marshall Field, Chauncey Blair, Henry King and Joseph Ryerson.
>
> But we of the Socialist Labor party hoped to get enough votes away from Wright to enable Harrison to win, and this we did. To my great surprise and the consternation of Society's 'Five Hundred,' almost 12,000 citizens voted the Socialist Labor party's ticket, thereby according Democrat Harrison a 5,000-vote victory over Republican Wright.

Frank Stauber's arduous seating as alderman, which Dr. Schmidt mentioned, destroyed the faith of many Socialists in the efficiency of the electoral process. Stauber had been fraudulently deprived of his seat by venal election judges and only after costly, drawn out litigations could he assume his office, but the election judges who had stuffed a ballot box and forged documents in an effort to defeat him were found "not guilty" in an ensuing trial. The more radical element of the Socialist party insisted that the entrenched parties could deprive successful Socialist candidates of their rightful office with impunity and that the Socialists could attain their rights only through force.

It is, therefore, not surprising to find in the newspapers controlled by the workers, namely the German *Arbeiterzeitung*, *Der Vorbote*, and *Die Fackel*, as well as in the English *Alarm*, incendiary articles advocating the use of force to bring about an improvement of the workman's lot. They preached in no uncertain terms the destruction of the prevailing order before a new, better system could be initiated, which helped to give them the epithet of "the anarchists." Though many Chicagoans were irked by the content of these radical papers, their threats were not taken seriously.

Meanwhile, at an ever increasing pace, clashes occurred between the police and workers, which were especially notorious while Captain John Bonfield led the police. According to page five of Ernest Zeisler's, *The Haymarket Riot*, on July 6, 1885 a petition bearing well over 1,000 signatures was presented to the chief of police, Austin Doyle, in which uninvolved eyewitnesses gave testimony of "the brutal and inhuman treatment inflicted upon a number of our fellow citizens by the hand of Captain Bonfield." It continued that his acts "were more like the acts of a man who intended to incite riot than of one paid to preserve the peace."

The strikes which Chicago workers held in 1886 to bring about the eight-hour workday and higher pay provided many opportunities for Bonfield to even exceed the brutalities against the workers of previous years. Bloodshed was an almost daily occurrence. On Saturday, May 1, 1886, workingmen's organizations called for strikes and demonstrations, which were viewed with apprehension from many quarters. In spite of the fact that 30,000 workers struck, demanding "ten-hour pay for eight-hour work," no serious incident happened until May 3, 1886. On that day several fatalities occurred at the McCormick factory because of a clash between police and strikers who had attacked strike breakers. August Spies, the editor of the *Arbeiterzeitung*, who had come upon the battle scene immediately after he had addressed a peaceful meeting some three or four blocks away, saw how workers were felled by the clubs and bullets of the police and, apparently without obtaining facts, rushed to his office to write an indignant appeal, which became known as the "Revenge circular."

An English translation of the German version is reprinted here from page 199 in John H. Mackay's *The Anarchists:*

> Revenge! Revenge! Workingmen! To Arms!
>
> Working people, this afternoon the bloodhounds, your exploiters, murdered six of your brothers at McCormick's. Why did they murder them? Because they dared to be dissatisfied with the lot which your exploiters made for them. They asked for bread, and were answered with lead, mindful of the fact that the people thus can be most effectively brought to silence. For many, many years you have submitted to all humiliations without a murmur, have slaved from early morning till late in the evening, have suffered privations of every kind, have sacrificed even your children,—all in order to fill

> the coffers of your masters, all for them! And now, when you go before them and ask them to lessen your burden, they send their bloodhounds, the police, against you, in gratitude for your services, to cure you of your discontent by means of leaden balls. Slaves, we ask and entreat you, in the name of all that is dear and sacred to you to avenge this horrible murder that was perpetrated against your brothers, and that may be perpetrated against you tomorrow. Working people, Hercules, you are at the parting of the ways! Which is your choice? Slavery and hunger, or liberty and bread? If you choose the latter, and do not delay a moment; then, people, to arms! Destruction upon the human beasts who call themselves your masters! Reckless destruction,—that must be your watchword. Think of the heroes whose blood has enriched the path of progress, of liberty, and of humanity—and strive to prove yourselves worthy of them.

On the next day, Tuesday, May 4, 1886 there were many clashes between workers and police. A circular printed by the *Arbeiterzeitung* invited readers to a mass meeting at the Haymarket on Randolph Street between Des Plaines and Halsted streets. Several hundred of the some 20,000 printed contained the line "Workingmen arm yourselves and appear in full force!" Since an exceedingly large, trouble-bound crowd was anticipated, authorities held 180 policemen ready to bring order to the meeting. But according to the testimony of eyewitnesses, including Mayor Carter Harrison, the meeting was neither well attended nor were there any indications that the assembled workers would cause trouble serious enough for police intervention.

After August Spies and Albert Parsons, editor of *The Alarm*, had addressed the meeting, Samuel Fielden talked to the steadily diminishing crowd, which at the most amounted to 1,000, when after about twenty minutes of Fielden's speech, 180 policemen, led by Inspector John Bonfield and Captain Ward, marched up to the speakers. The startled crowd heard Captain Ward's words: "In the name of the people of the state of Illinois I command you to disperse!" Fielden had barely time to utter: "Why, Captain, this is a peaceable meeting!" when a dynamite bomb landed amidst the police, exploding immediately. One officer, Matthias J. Degan, was killed instantly and six others died later, the seventh being Nels Hansen, who expired forty-four days later. In addition, about sixty policemen were more or less seriously wounded. Of the workers, at least one was killed and an undetermined number were wounded when the police fired upon them after the explosion of the bomb.

Chicago was stunned and America was shocked. Up until the bomb explosion the incendiary speeches and writings of the radical Socialists had been shrugged off as the rantings of impotent rabble-rousers. But after this fateful May 4, 1886 there was unmistakable proof that the anarchists constituted a grave danger to the established order. Society moved swiftly to eliminate this threat. The newspapers invariably asserted that the speakers at the meeting, as well as labor agitators, were the perpetrators of the heinous crime and that one ought to "hang them first and try them afterwards." Innumerable rumors fanned the fire of hatred.

The police and special Pinkerton agents in dragnet operations arrested anyone who could possibly be termed a radical Socialist. Three days after the bomb explosion, on May 7, 1886, Chicago newspapers reported that the principal police stations were filled with anarchists, usually German, that at the Des Plaines Street station alone there were over fifty, at the Armory nearly seventy-five, and at the Twelfth Street station about twenty-five. Arrests of "notorious anarchists" were described triumphantly in the newspapers in tedious details. The most spectacular capture was that of Louis Lingg on May 14, 1886 by the second generation German, Captain Hermann Schuettler (1861-1918), who ended his illustrious career as Chicago's chief of police. He was termed the "Greatest policeman in the world" not only during his thirty-five years of service, but also in an article about him in the *Tribune* of March 1, 1936.

Another police officer of German extraction, Captain Michael Schaack, must be mentioned for his important role in the dragnet operation, which induced him to write a book, *Anarchy and Anarchists.* A perusal of this book clearly shows that he suffered from megalomania, portraying himself as a dashing master detective who singlehandedly saved Chicago from a takeover by the anarchists. He also calumniated his superior, Frederick Ebersold, Chicago's second German chief of police, who said the following of Schaack in a declaration reprinted from page 223 of David's *The History of the Haymarket Affair:*

> It was my policy to quiet matters down as soon as possible after the 4th of May. The general unsettled state of things was an injury to Chicago.
>
> On the other hand, Captain Schaack wanted to keep things stirring. He wanted bombs to be found here, there, all around, everywhere. I thought people would lie down to sleep better if they were not afraid their homes would be blown to pieces any minute. But this man, Schaack, . . . wanted none of that policy. Now, here is

> something the public does not know. After we got the anarchist societies broken up, Schaack wanted to send out men to organize new societies right away. You see what this would do. He wanted to keep the thing boiling, keep himself prominent before the public. Well, I sat down on that . . . and, of course, Schaack didn't like it.
>
> After I heard that, I began to think there was perhaps not so much to all this anarchist business as they claimed, and I believe I was right.

While Chicago Germans played an important part on the side of the law in connection with the Haymarket "Riot," many of them were on the side of the transgressors. By far most of the people apprehended were Germans. When the grand jury convened after May 17, 1886, it indicted thirty-one persons on 69 counts, but of those indicted only ten were accused of murder. Of the ten accused, the German Rudolph Schnaubelt, who was believed to have thrown the bomb, was never apprehended, and the German William Seliger avoided trial by becoming a state's witness. The other eight were Georg Engel, Samuel Fielden, Adolph Fischer, Louis Lingg, Oscar Neebe, Albert Parsons, Michael Schwab, and August Spies; all but Fielden and Parsons were of German extraction.

The biographies of most Haymarket "conspirators" were similar in that they had emigrated from Germany to find a better livelihood, but that they also had become dissatisfied with the working conditions in America. Georg Engel was born at Kassel in 1836 and learned the printer's trade before he came to Chicago in 1874. He and Adolph Fischer, who came to America as a fifteen-year-old boy from Bremen in 1873 and learned the printer's trade before coming to Chicago in 1881, were pictured as the most radical of the group. Engel's last words before his execution allegedly were: "This is the happiest moment of my life!" and Fischer died after having uttered: "Hurrah for anarchy." Louis Lingg, the youngest of the "conspirators," was born in 1864 in Mannheim and came as a carpenter to Chicago in 1885. Oscar Neebe was born of German parents in New York City, but spent his childhood in Kassel, Germany, and came to Chicago in 1877 to work as a tinsmith. Michael Schwab was born in 1853 near Mannheim and learned the bookbinder's trade before coming to Chicago in 1879 to work on the staff of the *Arbeiterzeitung*.

The most articulate of all "conspirators," August Spies, was born in Landeck, Hesse in 1855. He came to Chicago in 1873, where he worked for several years as an upholsterer. After 1880 he was associated with the *Arbeiterzeitung*, succeeding Paul Grottkau as editor in chief in 1884. His long speech, "Reasons Why Sentence Should Not Be Pronounced," before the jury on October 7, 1887, was perhaps the most eloquent speech of the entire trial. Even the *Tribune* deigned to refute his arguments.

Though exceedingly interesting, the sensational trial cannot be retold here. The anarchists, on the explicit instructions of the presiding judge, Joseph E. Gary, were tried not for throwing the bomb, but for causing someone to throw the bomb. They were doomed from the beginning because of a packed jury and various other adverse factors, as Governor John P. Altgeld pointed out in his *Reasons for Pardoning Fielden, Neebe and Schwab* of 1893. After the jury returned a verdict of guilty on August 20, 1886, it was only a matter of time before the death sentence, imposed on all but Neebe, was executed.

It certainly appears as if a few labor leaders were made scapegoats. Especially enlightening is the case of Oscar Neebe, who was found guilty of murder and was sentenced to fifteen years imprisonment in the penitentiary at Joliet. According to page 280 of Henry David's *The History of the Haymarket Affair*,

> the evidence presented by the prosecution to prove him guilty of that crime consists in: (1) he held stock to the value of two dollars in the organization which owned the *Arbeiterzeitung*; (2) on the evening of May 3, he was in Franz Heun's saloon, showed the latter the 'Revenge Circular,' conversed with him about the McCormick disturbance, and remarked, 'It's a shame that the police act that way, but maybe the time comes when it gives the other way—that they [the workers] get a chance too;' (3) he was in the *Arbeiterzeitung* office in the absence of Spies and Schwab on May 5; (4) he was a member of the I.W.P.A.; (5) when his home was searched without a warrant on May 7, a pistol, a sword, a breech-loading gun and a red flag were found . . . Even at that time Neebe's arrest and indictment caused amazement. 'It seems hardly credible,' it was said shortly afterwards, 'yet it is true that all the testimony against Neebe would not justify a five dollar fine.'

It should be mentioned that when Neebe's wife died upon hearing of his fifteen-year sentence, according the the *Staatszeitung* of March 14, 1887, several thousand attended her funeral, and sympathy demonstrations were organized.

On November 10, 1887 Governor Richard J. Oglesby commuted Fielden's and Schwab's sentence to life imprisonment, and on November 11, 1887 Spies, Parsons, Fischer and Engel were hanged, a day after Lingg mysteriously died in his cell when an object exploded in his face.

On June 26, 1893 Governor J. P. Altgeld issued an absolute pardon for Fielden, Neebe and Schwab, and called the execution of the other Haymarket "conspirators" "judicial murder." Chicago citizens erected a monument at the Haymarket to commemorate those police officers who died or were injured in the bomb blast, but there was also a group of Chicagoans who commissioned the sculptor Adolph Weinert to create the so-called "Anarchist Monument" for the final resting place of the Haymarket "conspirators." On June 26, 1893, the day of Altgeld's pardoning, the monument was dedicated at Waldheim Cemetery in the presence of a large mass of people, mainly of the working class. Two female figures, symbolizing Revolution and Liberty, rise form a granite pedestal which contains August Spies's last words before his execution, "There will come a time when our silence will be more powerful than the voices you strangle today." From all appearances, every year on November 11, there seem to have been memorial services at Waldheim Cemetery for the executed German labor leaders.

Chapter 8

Chicago's German Newspapers and Journalists

The German language press of Chicago must be dealt with, for it often reflected or shaped the role of the city's German element. If one considers that Benjamin Franklin had published the German *Philadelphische Zeitung* on May 6, 1732 and that in 1840 the *Freiheitsbote für Illinois* was issued in Belleville, Illinois, it might seem that Chicago's first German newspaper, the *Chicago Volksfreund* of 1845 appeared relatively late. Nevertheless, the *Chicago Volksfreund* was the city's first foreign language newspaper, appearing twelve years after Chicago's very first paper, John Calhoun's *Chicago Democrat* of November 26, 1833, and seven years before the first newspaper in another foreign language, which was the Norwegian *Frihed's Banneret*, published for the first time in 1852.

The *Chicago Volksfreund* was edited by Robert Hoeffgen for the first time in September of 1845 as a weekly paper with an initial subscription list of about forty. Francis Hoffmann, a pastor at Dunkley's Grove, wrote the editorials, while the type was set by a certain Schneider, who went to California in 1848 to try his luck at gold mining. Hoeffgen, who, depending on need, occupied all positions from publisher to carrier, sold his paper in 1848 to a cleric, named Waldburger or Waldenburger, for 700 dollars.

In the same year, on April 7, 1848 Robert Hoeffgen started the weekly *Illinois Staatszeitung* with the aid of the apprentice John Simon, whose weekly salary was 75 cents. Later in 1848 the physician Dr. Karl Helmuth became the first editor of the *Staatszeitung*, followed by Arno Voss and Hermann Kriege, who died in 1850 in New York. Then Dr. Helmuth again became editor and changed it to a bi-weekly.

In the meantime Hoeffgen also became the first printer in Chicago to publish pamphlets and books in a foreign language. According to McMurtrie's *Bibliography of Chicago Imprints*, at least two job printings were done by him in 1849, namely "Dritter Synodal-Bericht der deutschen Evangelisch-Lutherischen Synode von Missouri, Ohio und anderen Staaten vom Jahre 1849" and "Constitution und Nebengesetze des Christlichen Hilfsvereins in Chicago, Gegruendet am 1. Februar 1849." But Hoeffgen was not the only press owner who printed German works in Chicago before 1850, for a second edition of "Republik oder Monarchie? Geantwortet durch Thomas Paine's 'Gesunder Menschenverstand' und 'Menschenrechte'" was printed by Charles Petersen on Clybourne Avenue in 1849.

On April 8, 1873 the *Staatszeitung* reviewed its own history, giving an interesting account of its early publishing practices. Not much printing paper, which was bartered for with rags, was necessary for the 150 copies of the four page paper, which contained two pages of advertisements. For ten cents a week the paper was delivered to the homes of 150 subscribers on a certain day of the week, to be retrieved on the following day by the carriers and delivered to the rest of the readers. Thus, 150 copies served between 200 and 300 subscribers. The lot of the *Staatszeitung* and its readers improved considerably when the forty-eighter, Georg Schneider, came on August 25, 1851 from St. Louis to assume the editorship, immediately transforming the paper into a daily. The newspaper was then read by some 700 subscribers, who were no longer obliged to return their copy after they had read it. The *Staatszeitung* steadily increased its size, its number of subscribers, and its sphere of influence while its ownership passed from Robert Hoeffgen to Georg Schneider to Lorenz Brentano and in 1867 to A. C. Hesing, who owned and controlled it until his death in 1895. In 1854 this paper became the first one in Chicago's history to issue a Sunday paper, entitled *Der Westen*.

Eminently able journalists on its staff, such as Georg Hillgaertner, Wilhelm Rapp, and Hermann Raster transformed this humbly conceived paper into an enormously powerful political tool within a short time. It was the first newspaper to call on January 29, 1854 for a meeting to oppose the Nebraska Bill and its concomitant extension of slavery. The *Staatszeitung* converted the Germans almost to a man to the Republican party and was instrumental in helping to elect Lincoln in 1860. Its outspoken abolitionist stand inflamed many Chicagoan, some of whom mobbed the offices of the newspaper in 1854 but were repelled by the armed resistance of Georg Schneider and his staff.

The *Staatszeitung* was not the only German newspaper in Chicago before the Great Fire of 1871. According to F. Scott's bibliography, *Newspapers and Periodicals of Illinois*, the following daily, weekly, or monthly newspapers and journals were started with varying success in ante-fire Chicago. The dates indicated represent the papers' first appearances:

Chicago Volksfreund—1845
Illinois Staatszeitung—1848
Atlantis—1854
Der Deutsch-Amerikaner—1854
Der Beobachter von Michigan—1855
Der National-Demokrat—1855
Chicago Union—1855
Die Abendzeitung—1856
Der Demokrat—1856
Der Zeitgeist—1857
Das Heimatland—1860
Das Katholische Wochenblatt—1860
Die Stimme des Volkes—1860
Der Telegraph—1862
Die Blätter—1863
Der Hausfreund—1863
Deutsch-Amerikanische Monatshefte—1864
Der Deutschamerikaner—1864
Der Wahrheitsbote—1864
Die Belletristische Zeitung—1866
Westliche Unterhaltungsblätter—1866
Der Anzeiger—1867
Der Juxbruder—1867
Der Amerikanische Botschafter—1868
Der Fortschrittsfreund—1869
Die Laterne—1869
Der Lutherische Kirchenfreund—1869
Zeichen der Zeit—1869
Der deutsche Arbeiter—1870
Illinois Volkszeitung—1870
Landwirt und Hausfreund—1870
Der Leedle Vanderer—1870
Der Westliche Odd Fellow—1870
Der Amerikanische Farmer—1871
Daheim—1871
Die Freie Presse—1871
Chicago Neue Freie Presse—1871

The Great Fire of 1871 did not destroy Chicago's German press, for at least thirty-two new German newspapers or journals appeared from 1872 to 1879. Nevertheless, it wiped out some foundering publications and it inflicted much damage to the *Staatszeitung.* The offices of the *Staatszeitung* were gutted by the fire, which consumed most of the newspaper's back issues. Pre-1871 copies of the paper are indeed a rarity. In addition, all of its eleven printing presses were destroyed. However, according to the *Staatszeitung* of April 8, 1873, only a single number of the paper, that of Tuesday, October 10, 1871, failed to appear.

Immediately after the fire, late on October 10, 1871, three staff members met by chance in a restaurant on the corner of Clinton and Madison streets where they wrote the first post-fire issue, which was printed in Milwaukee. On October 11, 1871 a single sheet printed on one side was issued, giving fire-related news, such as estimates of damages incurred and persons missing or saved. On October 12, 1871 there were already two pages with five columns. The printing of the newspaper, which steadily increased in size, was done in Milwaukee, while the editorial staff occupied temporary quarters in Chicago. On November 29, 1871, the *Staatszeitung* proudly announced that its present thirty-six columns matched its former size and asserted that it was equal to the *Tribune*, but far outdistanced the *Times*, *Republican*, *Evening Journal*, *Evening Post*, *Union*, and *Mail.* In the anniversary copy of October 9, 1872, the paper asserted that it was the biggest German newspaper ever published in the United States. Disregarding thirty-five columns of advertisements, its forty-five columns of articles would amount to a 200 page book.

The *Staatszeitung* continued to have a highly successful recovery. The *Tribune* of April 6, 1877 gave it credit for its role in the last city election as follows: "Among the agencies that contributed most powerfully to the enormous success of the Republicans in the last city election was the *Illinois Staatszeitung.*" Indications are that it was the most important foreign newspaper in the Midwest. *Der Westen* of March 16, 1879 listed the postage for subscribers of the most prominent German newspapers in the Midwest for the last six months as follows:

Newspaper	Daily postage	Weekly postage	Total
Illinois Staatszeitung	$469.02	$915.72	$1,384.74
Anzeiger des Westens	$353.60	$603.62	$957.22
Cincinnati Volksfreund			$836.80
Die Westliche Post	$303.88	$505.70	$809.58
Chicago Freie Presse			$139.58
Chicago Volksfreund			$21.52

By July 18, 1888 the *Staatszeitung* called itself the greatest German newspaper in the Midwest, supporting its assertion by citing subscription statistics. It had regular subscribers in thirty-seven states and eight territories of the United States and sent close to 1,000 copies regularly to Germany.

In spite of the apparent prominence of the *Staatszeitung* in the 1880's, it was on a gradual downhill slide from its high level of journalistic and financial success during the 1860's and 1870's. When its world famous editor Hermann Raster died in 1891, its collapse was stayed only for a few years.

Raster was born at Zerbst, some seventy miles southwest of Berlin in 1827 and was educated as a journalist at the universities of Leipzig and Berlin. On account of his journalistic fight for the liberal movement during the 1848 Revolution, German authorities compelled him to emigrate from the fatherland by threatening him with the alternative of public trial. As editor of the *Staatszeitung* from 1867 to 1891, he enjoyed international fame as a top journalist who was able to sway the readers of his lucid editorials on many public issues. The Republican party platforms of 1860 and 1872 were written partly by him. Of the numerous public offices that he held, it should be mentioned that he was tax collector in 1871 and 1872, a member of the first board of directors of Chicago's Public Library, and served on the Cook County school board. His name is perpetuated in an elementary school on South Hermitage and in a plaque in Chicago's Public Library.

Reeling under the heavy blow of Raster's death in 1891, the *Staatszeitung* was kept alive primarily through the vigorous efforts of its owner, Anton C. Hesing, a highly controversial public figure, who had complete control of the newspaper from 1867 until his death in 1895. Anton Hesing probably had more impact on the German element and its standing within the community than any other German in Chicago's history. Born on January 6, 1823 in Vechta, halfway between Bremen and Osnabrück, he emigrated in 1839 to Cincinnati, where he was occupied as a merchant and hotel proprietor, besides being active in the Whig party.

In 1854 he moved with his family to Chicago, was a brick manufacturer until 1857, became deputy sheriff of Cook County in 1858, and two years later sheriff. While he himself did not serve in the Civil War, he was very active in recruiting soldiers among the Germans. He organized and funded company B, the "Hesing sharpshooters," of the 82nd Illinois infantry regiment. He bought an interest in the *Staatszeitung* in 1862 while he was sheriff, becoming its sole owner in 1867.

For several years Hesing was able to enjoy his popularity and ever increasing wealth, but the Great Fire of 1871 proved to be his downfall. While he was on an extended vacation in Europe not only was his newspaper temporarily destroyed, but he also incurred devastating losses in other business enterprises. Alone in the Garden City Manufacturing Company he lost approximately $375,000. Immediately after the conflagration, Hesing returned to Chicago from Germany, being eagerly awaited. Even the *Chicago Union*, which before 1871 had waged a virulent anti-Hesing campaign, expressed admiration of Hesing, in spite of political animosity, in an editorial of November 5, 1871: "Today we, and thousands of German fellow citizens with us, expect a man back who at the present time is more impatiently awaited than anybody else . . . Therefore, we heartily bid Mr. Hesing welcome!"

The financial crash of 1873 seems to have plunged Hesing into an even more desperate position, for his newspaper obviously sank to venality, and he became involved in several questionable deals. On April 25, 1874, he found it necessary to make an open declaration with regard to his involvement in the Germania Fire Insurance Company, a scheme headed by the Greenebaum House which bilked innumerable German workers of over $650,000. In an obvious appeal to the sympathy of his readers, he told of his enormous losses: that during the 1871 Fire three of his businesses and four rental houses became prey of the flames, and that during the recent financial crash he had lost $225,000 in promissory notes because of the machinations of certain unscrupulous people.

Hesing could not quiet the suspicions of those who had trusted him earlier with his obfuscating rhetoric. Rumors and allegations were flying fast and furious, which caused Hesing to have the following printed in a somewhat megalomaniacal editorial in the *Staatszeitung* of April 29, 1874: "No man in the United States, President Grant not excepted, has been written about so much in the newspapers of both languages as has Anton C. Hesing."

Sometimes expressions of sympathies were extended to Hesing by political enemies which were promptly published in his newspaper, as on June 13, 1874, when Joseph Medill, Chicago's mayor from 1871 to 1873 and editor of the fiercely hostile *Tribune* sent him a benign letter from Milan, Italy. Medill consoled him about his enormous financial losses and expressed hope that their future interaction would be a return to the amicable relationship they had had between 1854 and 1872. More frequently, however, Hesing was attacked by both the German and the English press, driving him into a corner from which he lashed out against his detractors with unrestrained fury.

To mention one example, in July and August of 1874 he repeatedly was charged by the *Times* with dishonest manipulations in the land buy for the Cook County Hospital. As an example, on August 9, 1874, the *Times* printed a hearsay headline: "A. C. Hesing Shown to Be a Bribed Scoundrel." Hesing vigorously denied any wrongdoing, while at the same time leveling countercharges of licentiousness against W. F. Storey, the editor of the *Times.* He apparently did not stop there, for early in August of 1874 he was fined for allegedly beating the reporter McCleuthen from the *Times.* On August 10, 1874 Hesing climaxed his unrestrained attack against the *Times'* editor by stating, in a "Declaration to the Public," in the *Staatszeitung:* "And if I say that if someone should shoot W. F. Storey down on the open street as one would a mad dog, no jury of twelve men could be found in this city which would consider this man guilty of murder." This almost landed him in jail, for Judge Hinsdale's warrant to arrest Hesing had already been given to Constable Laimbeer, when an order from "higher up" rescinded the arrest warrant, giving the undaunted Hesing cause to describe Storey on August 12, 1874 as a "quivering coward fearing for his life."

Hesing did not become conciliatory, for on August 14, 1874, his paper printed the vituperative editorial, "Chicago's Curse," describing Wilbur F. Storey as, "a hoary old criminal, in comparison with whom every culprit sentenced to life imprisonment in the penitentiary at Joliet is an innocent angel." Finally, on August 15, 1874 he topped his rage against the *Times'* editor in the venomous editorial, "Old Fagin," by asserting, "whatever vilifications 'Old Fagin' prints in the *Times* about Mr. A. C. Hesing or the *Illinois Staatszeitung,* we shall henceforth consider it the harmless raving of a caged wild beast." This was the end of the feud on Hesing's part, to the regret of Chicagoans who were betting on the form of future outgrowths of the "warfare" between the editors of the two newspapers.

Again and again Hesing was accused of bilking the people of Chicago in various questionable deals, but he countered by saying that the alleged bribes and payoffs were "gifts." Only later did any definite statements appear which showed how substantial these gifts were. In 1873 there was a strong temperance movement in Chicago which appeared to become successful in closing all taverns on Sundays. But through Hesing's efforts the so-called "Hesing ordinance" was adopted which permitted the innkeepers to keep their pubs open on Sundays, provided that they did not disturb the peace. On April 2, 1882, the *Staatszeitung* claimed credit for the victory, stating at the same time that the German innkeepers were so grateful to Hesing that they gave him $30,000 as a "gift."

In November of 1875 Hesing was defeated in his bid for the office of county treasurer, for which he ran in order to "pay for his debts," as he himself stated. In the *Staatszeitung* of November 3, 1875 a bitter editorial blamed the ungrateful German element for his defeat: "Lies have fulfilled their aim. Knavery has won. A. C. Hesing has been beaten. The man who always took the part of his fellow countrymen has been forsaken by them, at least by a great number of them." Only a few weeks later did Chicagoans find out that Hesing's candidacy for county treasurer was a desperate last-ditch effort to avert an enormous impending scandal, known as the "Whiskey Ring Conspiracy."

On January 27, 1876 the *Tribune* reported the explosive story that the Germans A. C. Hesing and Jacob Rehm, superintendent of police, former County Treasurer Miller, and a few others had been indicted. They were charged with distilling and selling hard liquor illegally. Hesing and Rehm each had to post a $50,000 bail. Subsequent reports alleged that the conspirators cheated the government of taxes on well over 1,000,000 gallons of brandy and whiskey.

It is interesting to look at the following excerpts of an editorial, entitled "The Whiskey Tax Swindle," which appeared in the *Staatszeitung* on December 27, 1867, at a time when Hesing already had sole control of the paper: "20,000,000 gallons per year is a conservative estimate of the local production. But the statistics for the last fiscal year show that the receipts in whiskey taxes amounted to only $400,000. That means that taxes were paid for only one out of every 100 gallons . . . This state of affairs is certainly revolting in the extreme . . . Thus every inhabitant of the United States has a right to look upon these thievish distillers and their partners in crime, the bribed Federal officers, as mean, low thieves, who have taken money from his pocket . . . It is deplorable that these offenders are not ostracized, but hold prominent places for a crime worthy for penetentiary . . . "

In the course of the trial, "Jake" Rehm turned state's witness. During cross-examination he stated that he was drawn into the Whiskey Ring in 1872 by Hesing, and he estimated that he had received between $110,000 and $120,000 for his part in the conspiracy. Keeping this in mind, it is enlightening to read in the *Staatszeitung* of December 28, 1871 that the police commissioner Jacob Rehm was highly praised as an exemplary citizen for having proposed that the city, in order to save money, reduce the annual salary of the three police commissioners from $3,000 to $500.

It is interesting to note that during the trial the Hesing-controlled *Staatszeitung* became fiercely hostile to Rehm, trying to picture him as the ringleader who exploited the good-natured, only passively involved Hesing. However, during cross-examination on May 19, 1876 Hesing admitted that he actively collected money for contraband whiskey from County Treasurer Miller. In addition to that, he confessed having received $500-$600 a month from the county money's interest for supporting Miller in his newspaper when he was a candidate for county treasurer in 1873. When the trial ended early in July of 1876, Hesing was punished with a six month prison term and a fine of $10,000. This judgment was followed by an insolent editorial in the *Staatszeitung* of July 8, 1876, branding "the scoundrel Rehm" as the "mastermind of Chicago's whiskey conspiracy" and haranguing the judicial process as follows: "as we do not want to make ourselves liable to contempt of court, we are not going to say that the decision of Judge Blodgett is insolently unjust, that it is a mockery of justice, that it offends the sensibilities of people more than any fraud of the whiskey ring . . . " And so it went on and on, insulting the judge, the jury, and the intelligence of the reader, after having stated that it would not comment on the situation.

Through the incessant efforts of the *Staatszeitung*, Hesing was pardoned and released from prison on September 23, 1876, which precipitated an immediate campaign by the paper to whitewash him. Hesing continued to use his paper in an effort to enrich himself in other questionable business enterprises. As an example, late in 1878 and early in 1879, he printed innumerable ads for the Chicago Mining and Milling Corporation. Almost every day in January of 1879 he attempted to induce 10,000 people to obtain $100 shares in the business, stretching the facts at times. For example, on January 2, 1879 he stated that the Arizonian Carl Soyer had given him $2,000 as investment. But on January 22, 1879 he asserted that all directors and stockholders lived in Chicago or immediate vicinity; and he had to convince the Chicago readers that it was not a California corporation as had been mentioned earlier. Since Chicagoans did not forget Hesing's past escapades, his name gradually disappeared from the *Staatszeitung*.

The *Staatszeitung*, which tried to obscure the fact that Hesing was its owner, was involved in many feuds with individuals or newspapers of the German element, usually because it had sold its support to certain political candidates and was intended to minimize the popularity of the opposing candidates. When the German Civil War fighter General Hermann Lieb was a successful candidate for clerk of Cook County in 1872, 1874, and 1876, the *Staatszeitung* actively supported him, but then their relationship somehow went awry, as may be seen in an editorial of July 11, 1881, in which party hatred was discussed with regard to President Garfield's assassination: "The worst offender in this respect is one of C. Harrison's appointees, the infamous General Lieb, a man devoid of character and of conscience, a mercenary turncoat and adventurer, whose moral standards are on the same level as Giuteau's [Garfield's assassin]."

The strife among Chicago's German newspapers prevented a consolidation of forces by the city's German element for decisive, forceful actions in vital issues. This factor undoubtedly was largely responsible for the minimal role which Chicago's German element played in public affairs. There was much rivalry among the *Staatszeitung* and the lesser Chicago German papers for printing contracts, especially the profitable municipal announcements. The German newspapers frequently tried to minimize the effect of competitors while at the same time claiming a much larger number of subscribers than their rivals. Nor did they shrink back from personal attacks. For instance, on April 8, 1881 Hesing lashed out in the *Staatszeitung* at the *Inter-Ocean* and its German editor, Ernst Pruessing, who had attacked him before. While he even admitted to bribery, he accused Pruessing of various questionable past actions, such as having cruelly evicted from his land poor laborers who had failed to keep up payments.

The *Staatszeitung* was always attacking fledgling publications of the working class, such as the *Chicago Arbeiterzeitung.* High-minded Chicagoans of German descent tried to give the exploited workers an organ with which they could exert some political pressures to ameliorate their conditions, but these papers suffered ruthless suppression by the industrialists. For instance, Dr. Ernst Schmidt founded the workingmen's papers *Der Telegraph* in 1862 and *Der Vorbote* in 1874, but they did not last long in the severely adverse milieu.

The *Staatszeitung* was hardly ever *sympathetic* to the workers' cause. In learned essays it demonstrated, on such days as July 17 and July 25 of 1879, and April 10, 1889, that the workers were much better off with a ten-hour day than with an eight-hour day, for they would not know what to do with their additional spare time. At a time when Hesing received a "gift" of $30,000 from the German innkeepers for his effortless support of their demands to keep taverns open on Sundays, his paper indignantly inquired why the German workers were unhappy with their lot, stating in an editorial of August 8, 1878, that they were so much better off than their colleagues in Germany: "There is, today, in Germany in scarcely any trade a workingman who earns half the $1.75 per day offered by the employers here . . ."

The *Arbeiterzeitung* and the *Staatszeitung* waged a continuous feud, which reached its climax in 1886 during the Haymarket tragedy, when the *Staatszeitung* screeched loudly for the summary execution of their compatriotic "conspirators." Ernest Zeisler accused in his book, *The Haymarket Riot*, the *Tribune* of suggesting that the Haymarket defendants be lynched. Certainly the same charge could be leveled at the *Staatszeitung*, for on May 4, 1887 it stated in an editorial: "If the twelve instigators responsible for this tragedy had been taken from their cells and hanged, as they would have deserved, the public mind would not have raised any objections . . . " Then again in September of 1887, two months before the execution of the labor leaders, the *Staatszeitung*, in especially virulent editorials, called for a speedy dispatchment of the conspirators, which caused the *Arbeiterzeitung* of September 27, 1887 to declare the editor Hermann Raster mentally deranged and to demand a boycott of the *Staatszeitung.*

These two German newspapers continued to antagonize each other for a long time. On August 2, 1888 the *Arbeiterzeitung* stated that Hermann Raster of the *Staatszeitung* was offered $22,500 for his support in the presidential campaign, but would refrain from giving his support until offered $50,000. The *Staatszeitung's* attack at the "criminal socialist" newspaper and at the "rabble that is not satisfied with perfect working conditions" was countered with editorials such as the following in the *Arbeiterzeitung* of April 12, 1889: "There exists only one person who, against the demands of the social economists, the doctors, and humanitarians, declares that the achievement of the eight-hour working day would be nonsense—nay would constitute a crime. Who is this criminal? His name is Hermann Raster, and he is the chief editor of the *Illinois Staatszeitung*, a paper which is still being read by people who claim to be intelligent and humanitarian . . . We declare everybody publicly as criminal, who fights the eight-hour day movement in the same way as Raster did yesterday."

The *Arbeiterzeitung*, however, was not only on the war path with the *Staatszeitung*, but also with the *Chicago Freie Presse*, likewise a capitalist-controlled German newspaper. It frequently exposed both newspapers in caustic editorials for supporting and whitewashing corrupt political candidates running for public offices. In April of 1889 the *Freie Presse* often became the butt of the *Arbeiterzeitung*, which not only called it "a second hand cheese paper" in an editorial of April 22, but also stated that "there exists in Chicago a so-called German (?) paper, better known as the 'reptile' (the real name is *Freie Presse*), which led several attacks on our 'Verein's' treasurer." On April 26, 1889, it told of allegedly crooked deals by Richard Michaelis with politicians, for which he was rewarded with the lucrative commission of printing municipal announcements in his paper, *Freie Presse*, even though the number of subscribers was minimal compared to other German papers.

The *Arbeiterzeitung* did not mince words, for it called him "the Prussian-American Judas Iscariot, whose paper was a disgrace to all Germans of Chicago." Three days later, on April 29, it derided the *Staatszeitung's* endorsement of a German political candidate of questionable integrity who would "naturally be honest" as follows: "Mr. Raster finds it 'natural' that Germans, whether Democrats or Republicans, always execute honestly and fairly the public office which they accept. Does Mr. Raster, perhaps, remember the names Hesing, Rehm, Ochs and Wassermann, or does he want us to increase this list by a few dozens more names in the history of Chicago?" All of the names mentioned were notorious Chicago Germans who had violated the public trust in various elected offices.

The *Staatszeitung's* most crucial moment, and at the same time the final flash before its first demise, came when its editor Washington Hesing, postmaster of Chicago and son of Anton Hesing, ran as an independent candidate for mayor in 1897. The paper's vigorous campaign generated an illusionary widespread popularity of Hesing, but when the votes were counted, he had received only five percent of the total cast. Neither he nor his paper survived this crushing defeat.

After Washington Hesing died late in 1897, the *Staatszeitung* filed for bankruptcy and was eventually bought by Richard Michaelis, who then owned both the *Staatszeitung* and the *Freie Presse*, founded in 1871 and formerly a fiercely antagonistic paper to the *Staatszeitung*. Both of these papers continued to appear daily, the *Staatszeitung* in the morning and the *Freie Presse* as an evening paper. Neither attained a highly significant status, and since they were troubled with financial difficulties, with the advent of World War I and sharply reduced incomes for advertisements, their days were numbered. Horace Brand controlled the *Staatszeitung* when war engulfed the European nations and he wrote bellicose, pro-German editorials, which hastened the paper's demise.

When the United States became an enemy of Germany in April of 1917, Chicago's German newspapers were censored and pressured to comply with America's war efforts against Germany. The *Abendpost*, under persuasion of the censors, printed editorials critical of Germany's role in the war. On September 20, 1918 it had to defend itself against the assertions by readers that it had been bought to criticize Germany in the war.

But the *Staatszeitung* was not as tractable as the authorities and Chicagoans would have liked. It became dangerous to advertise in the paper, for those whose name appeared in it were harassed by people who thought they were being patriotic. Though the paper survived the war through various maneuvers, it was in serious financial shape. As a consequence, it became a weekly paper in 1918. Its board of directors even had to suspend its publication a few times, as in April of 1920. The newspaper's shareholders were further alienated by a feud between its editor, Arthur Lorenz, and Horace Brand, the dominant shareholder, who was determined to obtain complete control of the paper, for which he was willing to pay $50,000, as he expressed in a confidential letter of August 27, 1920 to Dr. Otto L. Schmidt. In the same letter he also asserted that the paper had cleared $24,000 a year when he had run it. But Brand did not obtain the paper's ownership, for through the intricate machinations of different feuding factions, it passed into the hands of the "Beobachter Publishing Company."

Before this happened, though, the old fighting spirit returned once more to the paper. According to the *Abendpost* of February 4, 1926, the *Staatszeitung* printed an editorial sometime in 1922, calling members of the American Legion bums and tramps, for which its editor Arthur Lorenz had to start a six months' jail sentence for criminal libel early in 1926. When the *Staatszeitung* appeared for the last time in 1925, hardly anybody was shocked, for many German newspapers of Chicago had failed before. The *Abendpost* of November 9, 1892 reported that several German newspapers of Chicago had failed between 1889 and 1892.

The first World War eliminated several fledgling German papers in Chicago, but one of them, the *Abendpost*, survived this trying period for the German element, mainly because it did not express blatantly pro-German sentiments, and in general followed a course of moderate non-committment to most issues. This paper was founded in 1888/89 by Fritz Glogauer and Wilhelm Kaufmann. Soon it was the most widely read German newspaper of Chicago due to its outstanding editor Paul Mueller, who served the paper from 1894 until his death in 1931.

Still extant today, the *Abendpost* passed through difficult times, most notably the two world wars. For example, on February 12, 1940, in an urgent appeal for support it stated that only World War I days were more devastating to the newspaper than the current ominous times. In January of 1940 the paper received $1,500 less for advertisements than in January of 1939, and in order to survive, it had to announce an increase in price from two to three cents. Nevertheless, it still appears under the editorship of Ludwig Gehrken from Tuesday through Friday as the only German daily in North America, and has a weekend edition entitled *Sonntagspost.* But lacking the enormous number of subscribers of its heyday around 1900, it no longer aims to be a determining factor in Chicago's development, but rather intends to be a newspaper which serves the dwindling German element of Chicago as an instrument of communication in its accustomed mother tongue.

Just as the number of Germans in the United States has dwindled drastically, the number of German newspapers has also been reduced considerably. A few statistics will give an inkling of the enormous change. According to page 371 of the second volume of Albert Faust's *The German Element in the United States*, the number of German publications was 641 in 1880, 727 in 1890, and 613 in 1900. They far outdistanced the number of newspapers in any other foreign language, the Scandinavian being second with 49 in 1880, 112 in 1890, and 115 in 1900. However, by 1972 the situation had changed drastically, as the following statistics from Lubomyr Wynar's book, *Directory of Ethnic Newspapers* indicate:

Ethnic group	Number of publications	Circulation
Jewish	170	3,694,419
Spanish	39	1,142,630
Polish	58	626,014
German	66	449,666
Italian	50	437,801
Greek	27	184,184

Undoubtedly some of the newspapers which now are Jewish would have listed themselves as German before the Nazi period. Of the present 66 German publications in the United States, the breakdown is as follows: one daily, two semi-weeklies, twenty-nine weeklies, two semi-monthlies, twenty-five monthlies, three quarterlies, and three appearing irregularly.

For Chicago an enormous drop in the number of German newspapers within the last 60 years can also be seen. In a letter of December 11, 1917 to Dr. Otto L. Schmidt, the press agent Dr.

Walter Briggs supplied the following publication statistics for Chicago's foreign language press:

Ethnic group	Daily	Other	Circulation
German	7	36	255,645
Polish	3	8	251,342
Swedish	-	14	288,468
French	-	1	5,000

The fact that America had entered the war against Germany by the time these statistics were supplied must also be taken into consideration.

Of the German publications which now appear in Chicago, one is a daily and at least eight others appear less frequently. The following is a list of them. Their first appearances are indicated by the dates.

Abendpost/Sonntagspost—daily—1889
Amerika-Woche—weekly—1973
Der Deutschamerikaner—monthly—1959
Eintracht—weekly—1923
Die Hausfrau—monthly—1904
Der Katholische Jugenfreund—monthly—1877
Milwaukee Deutsche Zeitung—1889
Nachrichten der Donauschwaben—monthly—1955
Der Sendbote—monthly—1853 (?)
Kolping Banner—monthly—1929

It should also be mentioned that the German element played a role in American journalism not only in German newspapers, but also in American ones. The industrialist Hermann Kohlsaat, a second generation German, is perhaps the most important example, for he controlled several important Chicago papers, beginning with the Republican *Inter-Ocean* in the 1880's. Later he bought the *Times* and the *Herald* to publish them as the *Chicago Times-Herald* until 1901 when he bought Victor Lawson's *Chicago Record* and called his newspaper the *Chicago Record-Herald.* It was known under that title until 1918, when William R. Hearst bought and combined it with the *Chicago Examiner* under the title *Herald Examiner.* Paul Carus, editor of *The Open Court* and *The Monist,* was born in Ilsenburg, Germany. At the present time, the owner of the *Chicago Daily Defender*, John H. Sengstacke, the editor of the *Chicago Daily News*, Daryle M. Feldmeir, as well as the managing editor of *Ebony*, Hans J. Massaquoi, are outstanding examples of journalists from Chicago's German element.

It would be impossible to mention all the photographers, reporters, editors, and other newspaper men of German background employed by American newspapers. An example of the importance of Chicago's German element in American journalism is W. H. Schmedtgen, pioneer in newspaper illustrating on the staff of the *Chicago Record-Herald*, or Herbert Block, whose editorial cartoons appeared in innumerable newspapers with the characteristic Herblock trade name signature.

Some of the printing and publishing houses in Chicago have been founded by men who came from Germany. The Regensteiner Publishing House was founded by a wood carver, named Regensteiner, from Bavaria. An ancestor of the Regnery Company came from the vicinity of Trier, Germany.

Chapter 9

The Chicago Germans in the Fields of Learning and Education

Chicago's German element has taken a prominent position in the fields of learning and education. Its impact on the public schools system may be seen in the many German names which Chicago schools still bear despite vigorous attempts to eradicate the Teutonic imprint during two world wars. Following is a partial list of Chicago public schools named after Germans: Altgeld, Baum, Beethoven, Beidler, Brennemann, Brentano, Eberhart, Ebinger, Einstein, Felsenthal, Foreman, Froebel, Goethe, Gunsaulus, Herzl, Hirsch, Horner, Jahn, Jungmann, Keller, Mayer, Nettelhorst, Pruessing, Raster, Reinberg, Roentgen, Rosenwald, Schiller, Schley, Schmid, Schneider, Schurz, Steinmetz, Stock, Humboldt, von Steuben, and Wacker. As can be seen, these names represent Germans from all walks of life, politicians, philanthropists, bankers, and poets among them. Several of these schools, such as Pruessing, Eberhart, Brentano, Nettelhorst, and Raster, were named after Chicago Germans prominent in public education.

From the beginning of Chicago's public school system Germans have taken an active part in teaching and policy making. Elias Greenebaum became school agent in 1856, and John F. Eberhart served as Cook County superintendent of schools in 1859. Probably the first school board member from the German element was Frederick Baumann in 1857, and its first school board president was Lorenz Brentano, in 1867 and 1868. He had been on the board since 1863. Since then many Chicago Germans have served on the school board, sometimes even comprising a majority. The fact that Chicago's German element was accustomed to good representation on the school board may be seen in an editorial in the *Staatszeitung* of April 3, 1881, which dealt with Mayor Harrison, regarding representation of Germans on the school board: "As candidate for mayor two years ago, Carter H. Harrison emphasized his friendship for the German people, and especially his great interest in German instruction in public schools. But he reduced the number of German members of the school board from four to three and appointed two of the worst enemies of the Germans, General Stiles and John Curran."

Most of the German representatives appointed to the school board fulfilled their duties in a monotonous routine which encompassed the gamut from ineptitude to excellence. But there was at least one German member, Otto C. Schneider, president of the board from 1907 to 1909, who should receive more than fleeting attention. Because of his flamboyantly controversial nature, he has become the object of at least one study, in the 1961 summer issue of *Chicago History*, which served as a basis for the following sketch.

Schneider was born in Kusel, a small town about seventy miles southwest of Frankfurt on the Main, in 1856. At the age of fourteen he emigrated alone to Chicago, where he completed his education. After graduating from high school, he first managed a drugstore until 1883; then he went into the tobacco business in the August Beck Company, becoming its sole owner after a few years. In 1899 he sold his establishment to retire from business life. He had been appointed by Mayor Swift to the board of education in 1895 and served until 1897. Then he became president of the Germania Club from 1897 to 1899 while he also occupied a few public offices, such as Lincoln Park commissioner. In 1907 he was appointed to the board of education by Mayor Fred Busse, being immediately elected its president.

For the next two years he was often the focal point of controversies. Undauntedly he pursued what he considered to be a common sense approach to education, but often sharply grated the nerves of many Chicagoans. He had some strong convictions about public education and did not mince words in expressing his opinion. Being a "Turner" himself and embracing the dictum "a healthy mind needs a healthy body," all-around physical exercises were important to him, but he rejected the spectator sports. In the *Tribune* of November 5, 1907, he called football "the most brutal game that ever was invented," which ought to be eliminated from high school. In his own words,

> Our system of 'sports' in the high schools is anything but education. Indeed, football and baseball, as they are played, have reached a point where they have become a disease in our schools. The games make heroes out of a dozen boys and leave the rest of the school to occupy the seats in the amphitheater. The younsters that do the playing are taught that they are better men than their fellows, and if they manage to beat a team from another school, as they are urged to do by hook or crook, they are exalted like demigods . . . Sport does not educate. It overdevelops certain muscles at the expense of others, overtrains men, and frequently results in untimely death. Rational physical culture aims at the development of the weak; not the giving of advantage to the strong.

To Schneider the American educational system stressed wrong priorities. In his 1908-09 report as president of the school board he asserted that competition ought to be stressed in scholarship rather than in sports, and he criticized those who eliminated prizes for scholarship: "A certain class of well-meaning people has succeeded in banishing from the schools prizes in the shape of medals and diplomas which had formerly been offered to those who excelled in their school work. The reason advanced was that one child should not be upheld as superior to the others. Apparently they should be considered to be either all mud or all diamond. Why competition in mental accomplishments should be ruled out of the schools and hero worship of physical superiority be cultivated remains a question hard to answer." He had a conservative approach to education, ridiculing "progressive education which, instead of stressing conscientious hard work, aims to accomplish as much by play and by humoring children into tasks."

Schneider maintained that "the three R's must be mastered, must become the intellectual property of every child, and serve as the foundation upon which it may build up its future career, whatever it may be . . . We are accustomed in America to humoring our children into an education instead of drilling and training them in that stern sense of duty which teaches men to confront life's difficulties with an earnest mien. As a result they cultivate the 'I don't care' smile of indifference."

In general, Schneider expressed a distrust of professional educators who, in his opinion, became so enthralled in their theories that they often failed to heed common sense: "The science of pedagogy is not so abstruse or complex that it cannot be comprehended by an ordinary person of common sense. In fact, it takes plain common sense to turn back to reason some of the so-called educational experts who become dangerous zealots for some pet theories that work incalculable harm to the cause of education. Some of the best measures come direct from the laymen of the Board of Education, and not from the superintendent's office."

Schneider was especially irked by arbitrary requirements for teachers imposed by the superintendent's office, which eliminated superior candidates while favoring mediocre ones: "The argument of the Superintendent's office was that no one should be employed as a teacher who did not possess the same culture as the average school teacher. On this basis it may be impossible for a Paderewski to get a position as music teacher or for an expert German scholar who does not happen to be as highly cultivated in English to obtain a position as teacher of German."

Schneider saw many faults in the public school system which he unhesitatingly set out to improve. He felt that superior teachers needed to be attracted and, noting that a public school teacher earned an average of only about $550, compared to over $3,000 for full professors at the University of Chicago, he announced a substantial across-the-board pay raise for public school teachers on February 8, 1908. On the other hand, he tried to make the work easier for the teachers by curtailing some of the students' accustomed privileges.

In the school report for 1907-08 he lashed out at the high school fraternities and sororities. He wanted to suppress them, because the members of these societies stood academically below average, while their "snobbishness and pretentious society affectation" were detrimental to "the brotherhood of an unripe intellect." On September 8, 1908 Schneider ordered high school principals to expel any student who retained his or her fraternity or sorority membership. From Hyde Park High School alone fifty-one boys were expelled. Because of intercessions by important people, and various other factors, the board of education consented to grant the suspended students a hearing on September 14, 1908. On the following day an interview with Schneider appeared in the *Tribune*, in which subscribers could read about the impudent and ill-mannered conduct of the students at the conference. According to Schneider, the "frat evil" could be disposed of in minutes, "if the boys could be taken out behind the school building and given a good old fashioned spanking which would do more good than all the rules the board can pass."

While Schneider readily criticized public education himself, he reacted violently when someone else took it upon himself to pass judgment on any aspect of the public school system. On March 3, 1909 the Oak Park physician, J. W. van Derslice, stated before the

Chicago Medical Society that, on the basis of personal inspection of the physical and sanitary conditions in the Chicago public schools, he must conclude that they were "dirty, unpainted, poorly ventilated, and poorly lighted." He planned to present his findings at an international congress at Budapest and this, perhaps, explains Schneider's caustic public rebuttal in the *Tribune* of March 4, 1909, which started off with the following "poem:"

It takes a mind that's rare and wise
To better matters as we pass;
The privilege to criticize
Belongs to every blooming ass.

Further on the paper continued to give testimony of Schneider's wrath against the physician: "If Dr. van Derslice made these statements, he is an unmitigated liar. When such a blatherskite as this breaks loose he must not be taken seriously. If he makes these charges at Budapest, he will be a malicious falsifier . . . I know his statements are all lies because I made a personal and thorough inspection trip through every school in Chicago last year."

School Board President Schneider was also accused of making profits in school textbooks, to which he angrily retorted in the *Tribune* of June 12, 1909 that he would resign if "certain newspapers" did not stop criticizing him, adding that he would return to Germany, "where there are some gentlemen left." It was inconceivable to Schneider that he would not be reelected as president, but for most school board members he was too outspoken and they refused to endorse him as president when his first term terminated, which again caused him to threaten that he would return to Europe. While Schneider seemed to have been a devoted public servant, in scorning diplomacy he made many enemies which caused him to become an embittered, lonely man who resigned from most clubs well before he died in 1924.

The foremost concern expressed by the German board of education members was the instruction of German in the public schools. Mainly through the efforts of Lorenz Brentano, president of the school board from 1865 to 1867, German was first introduced on a trial basis at Washington School in October of 1865. Mrs. Pauline Reed, a native German, was the first teacher of German for 165 pupils. Since the public response was gratifying, German was introduced the following year in Wells, Franklin, Moseley, and Newberry schools; and by the end of 1866 some 700 pupils were registered in German. More and more schools introduced German so that the *Staatszeitung* of January 2, 1871 could report that of

20,000 pupils in the public schools 3,654 in grades three through twelve were taking German. But in later reports of the same year the number of pupils registered for German was revised to 4,297 and later to 4,533.

The fluctuation in the German enrollment for the Chicago public school system was considerable, for German, more so than any other subject, had a tenuous hold in the curriculum and was the primary object of attack whenever a scapegoat was needed. Already on July 21, 1871 the *Chicago Times* attacked German instruction in public schools. After the Great Fire in October of 1871, German instruction was in fact curtailed. The *Staatszeitung* of October 31, 1871 reported that, "the school board of Chicago has used the Great Fire as a welcome chance to play an especially mean and infamous trick. Because 'instruction is to be limited to the barest essentials,' the school board has fired most German teachers, including Miss Ahlefeld at Skinner, Miss Horn at Carpenter, Mrs. Forster at Wells, and Mrs. McAffree at Washington schools."

German was not completely eliminated from public schools and despite later periodic motions to do away with it, such as in March of 1876 and February of 1879, it gradually climbed until 1880, when twenty-eight German teachers instructed 3,981 pupils in thirty primary and three high schools. From 1880 to 1892 the enrollment in German spiralled. The *Abendpost* of August 5, 1892 reprinted statistics from the school report for 1890-91, which showed that a total of 36,133 pupils studied German, of whom the nationalities were: 16,527 German, 10,132 Anglo-American, and 9,474 other. By 1892 some 44,270 were taught by 242 teachers.

Despite the popularity of German as as academic subject, attempts to abolish it continued to abound. In May of 1883 the *Tribune* launched a campaign to eliminate German from the schools by stressing that only about 40,000 Chicagoans spoke German and that their offspring became Americanized so quickly that they preferred to be taught in English. But the *Arbeiterzeitung* of May 12, 1883 showed, on the basis of the 1880 federal census, that over 150,000 Chicagoans spoke German, and it asserted that they had a right to be taught in their mother tongue.

By February 18, 1893 the *Tribune* tried a different tune: "Everybody who understands the subject and who is honest and candid knows that the attempt to teach German in the primary grades is absurd, that it is a waste of time and a nuisance." In 1893 it so happened that the school board decided that there was no money to offer German in third and fourth grade, and that other German classes would have to be curtailed as well. The result was that over a hundred German teachers lost their jobs, despite the vigorous protests of the board members Halle, Bluthardt, Boldenweck and Goetz, and a petition with 36,000 signatures asking for the retention of German. It is interesting to note that in the next year, according to the *Abendpost* of April 10, 1894, C. F. Adams, former Professor at the University of Kentucky, opened a "school specializing in German for Negroes."

The ups and downs of German as a academic subject continued, depending largely on how well the German element was represented on the school board. When the German E. G. Halle became president of the board of education in 1896, the enrollment in German climbed to 40,003 in 1899. However, in 1900 a proposal to eliminate German, actively supported by the *Times Herald*, was again cause for a public outcry among the Chicago Germans. Their protests were of no avail, because School Board President Cooley actively discouraged instruction in German. And so, the *Staatszeitung* of January 27, 1901 reported that the Citizens' Committee on Education had decided to eliminate German and algebra from the curriculum of the elementary schools. Thus, in 1902 only 19,284 pupils took German, but in 1903 the figure was up to 41,932, according to A. G. Zimmermann, superintendent of German instruction in Chicago's public schools. Of this number, 15,826 were German, 13,129 Anglo-American, and 12,977 belonged to other nationalities. This peak of enrollment in German was not held very long. By 1911 only about 7,000 pupils studied German in Chicago's public schools, which again constituted an ebb after which enrollment increased. The *Staatszeitung* of June 17, 1915 contained the following statistics for enrollment in German in the public schools for the preceding years, taken from a report by the superintendent of German instruction, Martin Schmidhofer:

Year	Number of schools offering German	Number of students enrolled in German
1912	53	7,806
1913	83	13,507
1914	103	17,001
1915	112	18,140

In the 1910's Chicago's German newspapers, in an all-out effort to boost the interest in German, wrote innumerable editorital exhorting its readers to cultivate interest in their mother tongue. For instance, the *Abendpost* of September 9, 1914 urged its readers to have their children instructed in German beginning with the fifth grade. The paper asserted in an editorial that German was going to be the world language. Soon, the suppression of German became more and more oppressive. As the reports of German "atrocities" in the newspapers increasingly antagonized Americans, the fate of German instruction was sealed. The *Abendpost* of February 9, 1916 reported that many teachers and principals were hostile to teaching German. One school after another dropped German entirely as "patriotic" citizens filed petition after petition to eliminate from the curriculum the language of the hated "Hun enemies."

In the midst of the general anti-German sentiments during the World War I era, German instruction in Chicago's public schools came to a virtual halt. The *Abendpost* of September 5, 1919 reported that Mr. E. G. Willner, a prominent businessman, wanted his daughter to study German at Tuley High School, but was told by the Principal, Franklin Fisk, that only French was offered. Mr. Willner wrote a letter of protest to the school board, saying that French was not abolished in Germany during the Franco-Prussian War. The school board replied that German was abolished in the elementary curriculum because of the Samuel Insull Act, but that any high school would offer it if at least twenty-five students requested it, which hardly ever happened.

While the World War I era constituted the nadir of German instruction in Chicago's history, later times, even the World War II days, were more propitious to German as an academic subject. For instance, by 1919 the German enrollment in Crane Tech had dropped to forty-five from the previous low of 200 in 1918, but on April 5, 1929 the *Abendpost* reported that Crane Tech again had a peak enrollment in German, amounting to 852 students. With the decrease of German speaking immigrants to Chicago the demand for German in the public schools also decreased so that it stood on a level with all other foreign languages offered, and it shared their fate of ups and downs determined by the fluctuating interest for learning a different tongue.

Besides the teaching of their own language, the German element has supported and energetically furthered some other subjects in public education, such as music. The Germans were instrumental in introducing it in Chicago, furnishing some of the first music teachers, such as Christoph Plagge, who was hired in 1853. But they must be given credit for introducing physical education in Chicago's public school system. The forty-eighters, who came from Germany to Chicago as political exiles for their involvement in the 1848 Revolution, vigorously emphasized the development of the body in a systematic manner which they thought could best be accomplished in an educational setting.

In stressing physical education the forty-eighters practiced the precepts of their admired compatriot, Friedrich L. Jahn (1778-1852), the "Father of Gymnastics." Jahn was a renowned patriot and pedagogue who conceived the idea that Germany's morale, which had received a staggering blow under Napoleon's yoke, could be restored by building up physical and moral powers through the practice of gymnastics. In 1804 he became a teacher at Berlin, where he opened the first "Turnplatz," an open-air gymnasium, in 1811, stressing the idea that his pupils were to become the elite core for the emancipation of the fatherland. Patriotic student fraternities enthusiastically accepted him as their leader, especially when he became a martyr figure after his Turnplatz was closed and he was thrown into prison. His ideas, which are summarized in the motto "a sound mind in a sound body," spread like wildfire, being propagated in his own writings and those of his disciples.

When his admirers were forced to flee from their fatherland, they founded "Turnvereine" wherever they went, so that kindred spirits could practice Jahn's teachings. In 1852 Chicago had its first "Turnverein," the "Chicago Turngemeinde," which attempted to popularize gymnastics in a variety of ways, most notably in the public schools. The *Staatszeitung* of September 6, 1866 reported that, "in the meeting which the school board held last evening, President Lorenz Brentano read a proposal of the 'Chicago Turngemeinde,' requesting that gymnastics be included in the regular schedule of all public high schools. The proposal was unanimously adopted, and the Executive Board was instructed to take all necessary measures for its implementation." In spite of this favorable attitude by the school board, apparently not much came of physical education in public schools for a number of years.

Probably the first Chicago public school to introduce gymnastics in its curriculum was the West Side German High School, which started it early in 1871, according to a report in the *Staatszeitung* of March 21, 1871. But despite their initial failures to have gymnastics introduced in the high school curriculum, the "Turnvereine," supported by the "Sokol movement," waged a continuous campaign for its acceptance and, finally, in 1884 they were successful in their attempts. In 1886 eight German-American "Turners" were hired by the school board to introduce gymnastics in selected high schools on a trial basis. All of these eight instructors were graduates from the German-American Gymnastic School of Milwaukee. They were Henry Suder, the first director of physical education in Chicago, Alfred Benefeldt, Joseph Grundhofer, Hermann Hein, William Kopp, Moritz Schmidt, Oskar Weinebrodt, and August Zapp. Since physical education was favorably received, soon additional German "Turners" were hired as instructors. On April 25, 1936, the *Daily News* reported on a celebration, honoring three of the eight surviving pioneer instructors, Henry Suder, William Kopp, and Hermann Hein.

Physical education, like German, frequently being the target of criticism, had a precarious existence. On March 8, 1901, for example, the *Evening Post* reprinted a criticism by Mr. Hanecy, mayoral candidate of the Republican party, who in analyzing the school budget had quipped, "Here is another outrageous appropriation of $10,400 for salaries of teachers of physical culture." But the Germans were not deterred in their enthusiasm for physical education and always were staunch supporters when its abolition from the curriculum loomed. In 1907 they held a big celebration when through their efforts a new school at Lincoln Avenue and Belmont Street was named the Frederick Jahn School. According to the *Abendpost* of December 29, 1907, an original sculpture by Hermann Gensch and an original oil painting of Jahn by Hermann Rascher were dedicated at the new school in impressive ceremonies.

When in 1909 the Chicago school board proposed to build schools without gymnasiums because, "the money could be used for a better purpose," the German board member Karl Greifenhagen, spurred on by the German element, vigorously objected and finally convinced the board that gymnasiums were to be installed for the best interest of the children. The German element proudly pointed out that a grandson of "Turnvater Jahn," namely Frederick L. Jahn (d. 1932), had given many years of service to Chicago's school children first at the Jahn School and the last fifteen years at Crane Tech.

While the German element advocated the teaching of such subjects as German, music, and physical education as being beneficial to the child's educational process, it strongly opposed the teaching of religion in the public schools as a deterrent to a good education. When in 1875 the school board adopted a resolution to forbid the use of the Bible as a textbook, it was enthusiastically lauded in editorials and letters to the editor in several issues of the *Staatszeitung.*

The average German's stand against religious issues in the public school system was pointed out in the *Staatszeitung* of May 8, 1879, in a report on Theodor Weber's testament, drawn up in June of 1876. Mr. Weber decreed that, "the sum of $10,000 be set aside for a German high school to be built between Chicago Avenue and Fullerton Avenue provided that other parties raise an additional $90,000 and that the German language, German history, and German literature be always taught in the institution, and that Bible reading, praying and religious instruction be permanently excluded from the curriculum."

Chicago Germans always were wary when religious matters tended to become so important that they overshadowed public education. Early in 1896 a movement was started to introduce in Chicago's schools a reader of about 200 pages containing selections of Biblical sayings and stories, the result of several years of work by the Universalist C. C. Bonney, the Presbyterian J. H. Barrows, and the Catholic W. T. Onahan. The German element was up in arms, organizing innumerable meetings to combat the adoption of the reader. On July 1, 1896, the *Abendpost* reported on a mass meeting in Koch's Hall at 104 Randolph Street at which 200 German societies sent representatives to pool their efforts in the fight against the reader. Over 18,000 signatures had been collected for a petition to bar the reader, and the collecting of signatures was still in progress. Again in 1907, when Otto Schneider was president of the school board, a committee studied the advisability of introducing a Biblical reader, but because of Schneider's persuasion voiced unanimous opposition to the reader for public instruction.

The German element stressed the value of a good education, but it was sometimes accused of opposing compulsory education, as in an article in the *Tribune* of October 23, 1890, which criticized the Germans' opposition to the nativistic Edward's Law. In many rebuttals the German newspapers, such as the *Staatszeitung* of April 22 and October 25, 1890, stressed the point that the Germans were in favor of compulsory attendance, but they were also against the elimination of parochial schools. The *Staatszeitung* of November 16, 1892 reported on Reverend Herzberger's fight against nativists, such as the Patriotic Sons of America, and his protest against the persecution of Catholics. The paper reprinted part of his statement, "that neither the Lutherans nor the Germans in general are against compulsory school attendance or against instruction in English, or against our public school system. They maintain parochial schools because their children receive more efficient instructions in English and German . . . "

Most of the German children in Chicago, of course, went to public schools where they soon became Americanized, but there were some special schools founded by Germans in which the old tradition was longer emphasized. At the latest by 1842 the Germans erected a school of their own, for on March 10, 1842 the school inspectors voted that a school be established in the "Dutch Settlement," also known as "New Buffalo," on the North Side, provided that the Germans furnish their own building. A later order modified this, in that $211.02 was granted from the general school fund for building material if the North Siders would consent to erecting the building themselves. This was agreeable to the Germans, who were eager to have a school, and within a short time a building stood on Green Bay Road between Chicago and North avenues which housed school number three of District Four until 1846. It is interesting to note that in 1845 all school rooms in District Four were declared to be, "wholly inadequate and unfit for the uses to which they were put, with the exception of that in the 'Dutch Settlement,'" as Andreas documented on page 212 of his first volume of *History*. When a big two-story school building was erected at the corner of Ohio and La Salle streets, the little school in the "Dutch Settlement" was discontinued. Then a group of Germans, headed by Michael Diversey and Peter Gabel, asked permission to buy it and to run their own German school at their expense, which was granted them on January 30, 1846 after they had signed a promissory note amounting to $110. This was probably Chicago's first school in which the language of instruction was exclusively German, but soon others followed. By 1848 a certain A. Unterherr taught about sixty pupils only in German at 134 Wells Street. By 1859 there were at least two other German schools, one between Indiana and Ohio streets at which Georg Fischer instructed some seventy-five pupils. Another one was the former public school at Ohio and La Salle streets which in the meantime had become a purely German school, a C. P. Weber being its principal.

After 1860 German schools mushroomed in Chicago. Until 1871 Andreas lists on page 116 in volume two of his *History*, forty-one schools which are clearly designated as German private or parochial schools. By 1870 the Germans had founded several high schools, such as the German High School on the West Side and Dyhrenfurth's Educational and High School. As the influx of Germans increased, more and more schools were established to accommodate them, some of them being Sunday schools and evening schools. As an example of a Sunday school the school managed by the "Chicago Turngemeinde" at 257-59 North Clark Street in the 1870's may be mentioned. According to the *Staatszeitung* of May 12, 1871, children paid two dollars to the society and adults four dollars to be instructed in drawing, penmanship, arithmetic, geometry, rhetoric and stylistics, and fundamentals of music. The same paper of September 19, 1875 announced the opening of an evening school at "North Side Turnhall" for which, "tuition charges are so low that even the most impecunious can afford it." The proposed schedule was, "Monday: German and Latin; Tuesday: English literature, French, drawing, and stenography; Wednesday: elocution, penmanship, and English grammar; Friday: vocal instruction and English for Germans."

It would be tedious if not impossible to list the various schools founded by German individuals or groups in the Chicago area, but it ought to be mentioned that even today numerous weekend German schools are managed by such organizations as the "Donauschwaben" and the German American National Congress; and also by individuals independent of any society. In February and March of 1974 the *Sonntagspost* has a series of reports on various German weekend schools in the Chicago area. On February 10, 1974 it reported on the "Donauschwaben School" which was established in 1955 with an enrollment fluctuating between about 270 and 360 pupils in the last six years. On February 17, 1974 it reported on the German American National Congress School in the St. Alphonsus Church, founded in 1964, where some 240 children are instructed in nine classes. The November 1974 issue of *Der Deutschamerikaner*, the official newspaper of the German American National Congress, gives an account of their eighteen schools in Chicago, where almost 1,000 pupils are taught by fifty-three teachers.

The German element's role in Chicago's higher education is rather elusive. The German educators at the college and university level tended to be more mobile than those from the elementary and secondary levels. They usually did not remain long enough in Chicago to become instrumental in the city's development and, if they did, normally preferred to stay aloof from German affairs, so that it is often rather difficult to ascertain their nationality and their impact, which was generally directed at other than local targets. Nevertheless, Germans have occupied a prominent place in various aspects of higher education.

There is hardly a campus in the Chicago area at which not at least one lecture hall, classroom building, or library perpetuates the name of a liberal donor of German extraction. A stroll through the Concordia College campus shows that many buildings are named after Germans. At the University of Chicago the physical imprint of the Germans is also evident. The Affiliated Germanic

Group, which was formed in 1925 by some 200 prominent Chicagoans of German descent, headed by the chairman Dr. Otto L. Schmidt, raised well over a million dollars for the university. Some of the group's more salient results were the erection of Wieboldt Hall, made possible through a $500,000 grant from the Wieboldt Foundation. It was the first university building in America specifically designated for the study of modern languages. The Affiliated Germanic Group also provided funds for professorial chairs which enabled the University of Chicago to offer research positions to outstanding scholars, such as Archer Taylor, perhaps the most renowned folklorist in America.

The German element was also responsible for establishing institutions of higher learning and specialized fields. Already in 1861 Bishop John Esher (1823-1901) of the Evangelical church, who had come as a seven-year-old boy from Alsace, helped to found Northwestern College, later known as North Central College of Naperville. In 1867 Florenz Ziegfeld founded the Chicago Academy of Music and in 1879 Hans Balatka the Balatka Musical College, two conservatories which soon became world famous. In 1870 German Jesuits established St. Ignatius College, which was known after 1909 as Loyola University. A year later Germans, foremost among them Reverend Joseph Hartmann (1823-87), founded the College of the Evangelical Synod of North America at Elmhurst now known as Elmhurst College. Another institute which still exists, the Siebel Institute of Technology, was founded in 1872 by the German scholar Dr. J. E. Siebel, who was known as the author of the *Siebel Manual for Bakers and Millers* and as editor of the *Siebel Technical Review.* It was at first especially oriented to brewing and baking, but became more diversified in 1893 when it assumed its present name.

As the years progressed and the number of Germans steadily increased, more and more German-founded schools of higher learning and specialized fields appeared. Between 1890 and 1900 Germans founded at least eight successful schools which either became the nucleus of larger institutes known under different names, or still exist under the same name in more or less altered form. They were the German Gynecological College at Laflin and 13th streets in 1890, the German Homeopathic College at Noble and Milwaukee streets in 1891, the German College for Medicine and Maternity at 512-14 Noble Street in 1891, the Northwest Business College by Professor Georg Jenssen in 1892, St. John's Lutheran College which was endowed with $50,000 by J. P. Badem in 1893, the Nissen Commercial College at Carpenter and

Milwaukee streets in 1895, the German-American Dental College at 758-62 North Park Avenue in 1898, and the German School of Obstetrics at 191 North Avenue in 1900. However, at times there was little substance behind newly founded schools, as the *Abendpost* of November 3, 1897 alerted its readers. It printed an extremely negative account of the so-called "Chicago German-American University," which had mailed a prospectus announcing its opening in January of 1898. The pamphlet, which "reads like a carnival joke," announced as rector and treasurer a person who apparently had failed in previous similar enterprises. Some of the more important recent institutions of higher learning in the founding of which Germans have been instrumental are Mundelein College in 1930, named after the second generation German Cardinal Mundelein, the Chicago Institute for Psychoanalysis in 1932, and the DeVry Institute of Technology founded by William DeVry, president of the Germania Club from 1958-60 and 1961-63.

Chicago's German element furnished a large share of propagators of knowledge. An inkling of this is given when one surveys the list of Nobel laureates affiliated with the University of Chicago, published by Muriel Beadle in the 1967 winter issue of *Chicago Magazine.* At least six scholars of German descent were awarded the coveted Nobel prize, perhaps the most obvious expression of scholarly recognition. The German-born Albert Michelson, who had been at the university since 1892, was the first American to receive the Nobel prize in science when he was awarded the coveted honor in 1907 for inventing several ingenious instruments to measure light waves. The physicist Werner Heisenberg, who received the prize in 1932, was only a short-term professor at the university in 1929, when he lectured on quantum mechanics. It is interesting to note that while Enrico Fermi conducted his pioneer work on the atomic bomb at the University of Chicago, Heisenberg worked on atomic fission for the Nazis.

Two Nobel laureates, James Franck and Maria Goeppert-Mayer had strangely interwoven fates, according to Muriel Beadle. James Franck, who won the Nobel prize in physics in 1925, had been a professor at the University of Göttingen before he fled from Nazi Germany in 1938 to eventually head the Institute for the Study of Metals at the University of Chicago. While at Göttingen, Franck at some time in the 1920's advised his post-graduate student Joseph Mayer from the University of California at Berkeley to rent a room from a Mrs. Goeppert, who accepted roomers since only she and her daughter Maria occupied a large house. Thus, Franck became their matchmaker and when Maria Goeppert-

Mayer came as a research associate to Chicago, she was James Franck's colleague from 1945 to 1960. When Franck died in 1964 at the age of 81, the University of Chicago formally honored his memory by renaming the Institute for the Study of Metals the James Franck Institute. In 1963 Maria Goeppert-Mayer became the only woman scientist after Marie Curie to receive the Nobel prize. Karl Ziegler was a visiting professor at the University of Chicago in 1936, and received the award in 1963 for basic discoveries essential for the production of high octane fuels, detergents, and plastics. Konrad Bloch did much of his work on the nature of cholesterol at the University of Chicago between 1946 and 1954, for which he received the prestigious award in 1964.

Though the number of Nobel laureates stemming from Chicago's German element is great, this alone does not serve as a reliable indicator of its impact on Chicago's role in higher education. There were many scholars or educators of German extraction who gained an enviable reputation. F.W. Gunsaulus (1855-1921), president of the Armour Institute of Technology and noted bibliophile, as an example. Laura Fermi points out in her book, *Illustrious Immigrants*, that, of the German scholars who had fled from the Nazi regime, many were attracted to the institutes of higher learning in the Chicago area. On January 14, 1936 the *Chicago Daily News* reported that on a single day two eminent art historians from Germany, Ludwig Bachhofer and Ulrich Middledorf, had joined the art department at the University of Chicago. But they were only two of many outstanding men of learning who came for more or less extended periods of time to Chicago. Other exiles from Germany were the political scientist Arnold Bergsträsser, who in 1947 founded the renowned cultural history journal, *Deutsche Beiträge zur geistigen Uberlieferung*, and Hans Morgenthau, director of the Center for the Study of American Foreign and Military Policy; the theologian Paul Tillich, who culminated his life's work at Chicago in writing the three volume *Systematic Theology*; the philosopher Leo Straus, author of *Natural Right and History*; and the highly influential architect Ludwig Mies van der Rohe, who headed the department of architecture at the Illinois Institute of Technology. The historian Hans Rothfels did his best to elevate Germany's reputation in writing the book, *The German Opposition to Hitler*, which demonstrated that not all Germans blindly followed Hitler.

Even though a higher proportion of German men of learning came to Chicago during the Nazi regime than during any other historical era, Chicago's German element has had its fair share of propagators of knowledge throughout its history. The political exiles of the 1848 era, like the political refugees of the Nazi regime, had come primarily because of ideological reasons and likewise consisted to a large part of highly educated men that served as disseminators of knowledge. One only needs to think of famous journalists like Georg Schneider, Wilhelm Rapp, and Hermann Raster, or of scientists like the doctors Carl Helmuth, Ernst Schmidt, and Theodor Bluthardt to see their high caliber.

Of course, many outstanding scholars of German extraction received their formal education in America where they had come with immigrant parents or where they were born to them. An example of this case is Maximilian Eberhardt, who was born in 1843 in Germersheim. King Maximilian II of Bavaria served as his godfather. When his father did not prove sufficiently loyal during the 1848 Revolution, he lost his patronage job as supervisor of the army bakeries and fell into general disgrace, which finally forced him to emigrate in 1853 to New York. Young Maximilian went to public schools there until 1859, when he went to Cincinnati, where he continued his education to become a lawyer in 1864. After having come to Chicago in 1867, he was appointed judge in 1875 by Governor Beveridge. Eberhardt not only published several volumes of poetry, but also scholarly articles and a book, *Woman's Rights in Marriage*, for which he received recognition in being invested with the honorary doctor's degree from the Chicago Law School and the Illinois College of Law.

A few other outstanding scholars of German descent active in Chicago ought to be mentioned. Andreas Bolter (1820-1900), born in Sigmaringen on the Danube and having come as an 1848 Revolutionary to Chicago, was an outstanding entomologist who discovered several insects which are now named after him. The eminent historian Hermann Eduard von Holst (1841-1904) came for the first time to America in 1867 and stayed until 1872, gathering material and doing research for his major work, *Constitutional and Political History of the United States.* After he came back to America, he served from 1892 to 1902 as head of the history department at the University of Chicago, where he frequently incurred the wrath of the populace with his outspoken opinions, especially when he criticized America's role in the Spanish American War. Other university professors of German background who attained international fame were the history professors Georg Scherger and Ferdinand Schevill; the professors in various literatures Phillip Allen, William Nitze, Robert Pietsch, and Martin Schütze; and the music professor Carl Bricken.

Perhaps Chicago's most important musicologist was the German Bernhard Ziehn, to whom volumes twenty-six and twenty-seven of the *Deutsch-Amerikanische Geschichtsblätter* were dedicated. Born in 1845 at Erfurt, where he received a solid education as an elementary teacher, he taught three years in Mühlhausen before he emigrated to Chicago in 1868, to teach until 1871 at a parochial school. After 1871 he dedicated himself exclusively to the study of music, giving private lessons to those who were fortunate enough to be accepted by him. Most of his works appeared in German, such as his best-known work, *Harmonie- und Modulationslehre* in 1887, but he also published some works in English, like *Canonical Studies, A New Technique in Composition* in 1912.

Ziehn was a harsh critic, but highly respected for his candid, unfailing appraisals. As an example may be mentioned a devastating criticism, which Ziehn published in the *Allgemeine Musikzeitung* in April 20, 1890, of performances in Chicago by Hans von Bülow (1830-94), a famous German pianist and conductor. In his criticism he accused von Bülow of having previously insulted the Chicago Germans in McCormick Hall on February 5, 1876 by calling them "Dutch who understand little about music." This time again, he asserted, von Bülow assumed his audience were, "Hottentots and played accordingly. He played Beethoven's grandest works in a style that he would not have excused in any of his pupils . . . Mr. von Bülow has sowed bad seed. It were much to be regretted if this seed should sprout." Von Bülow admitted his bad performance which had been analyzed minutely by Ziehn, and in a conciliatory move commissioned Eugen D'Albert (1869-1932), the Anglo-French composer, to assure Ziehn of his greatest respect. When Bernhard Ziehn died on September 8, 1912, from cancer of the larynx, he was mourned by the international music world.

Chicago's German element was not only prominent in the transmission of knowledge, but has also taken an important part in its preservation in libraries and museums. Though not keeping an ethnic museum of its own, it contributed much to these cultural temples in Chicago. Many of the administrators, experts, and curators at museums or the Art Institute have been of German background, such as the native of Cologne, Dr. Berthold Laufer, an outstanding anthropologist and ethnologist, who also was curator of the Field Museum from 1908 to 1934. He died in 1934 under mysterious circumstances at the Chicago Beach Hotel in a fall from an upper floor.

Dr. Otto Schmidt, one of Chicago's foremost historians, not only donated much historical evidence to the museum of the

Chicago Historical Society, of which he was president, but he was also instrumental in the purchase of the magnificent Gunther collection. This hoard of historical objects not only became the object of several articles and talks by the director of the Chicago Historical Society, Dr. Clement M. Silvestro, but also, because of its magnitude, made it necessary for the society to erect its present, more spacious quarters in Lincoln Park.

Charles F. Gunther (1837-1920) was known to most Chicagoans around the turn of the century as "The Candy Man" who, among other things, had invented caramel. He was born at the small town of Wildberg in the Black Forest and emigrated with his parents as a five-year-old boy to Pennsylvania. In 1850 the Gunther family moved to Peru, Illinois, where he completed his schooling and worked at various clerical jobs before he accepted a job in Memphis, Tennessee in 1860. Gunther served during the Civil War in the ranks of the Confederates as purser on the steamer *Rose Douglas.* It is interesting to note that the *Staatszeitung* of April 1, 1901 endorsed Theodor Bluthardt rather than Charles Gunther as candidate for state representative because Bluthardt had fought on the Union's side but Gunther on the Confederates'. For a short time Gunther became a prisoner of war, but then he returned to Illinois and eventually to Chicago, where he obtained positions as a traveling salesman for various pastry factories and, finally, in 1868 opened his own candy shop at 125 Clark Street.

While his business continued to prosper at different Chicago locations, Gunther not only was active as a public servant, occupying such offices as alderman and city treasurer, but he also became an avid collector who spared neither efforts nor money to attain one of the largest and most diversified collections of historical objects ever accumulated by a single individual. Sensation-seeking customers had the privilege of viewing such rarities as an Egyptian mummy, "said to be Pharoah's daughter who found Moses in the wicker basket," or the "skin of the serpent which seduced the first woman," but sedate scholars were also attracted by innumerable choice items, such as many autographs from the George Washington collection, or incunabula not preserved anywhere else.

Gunther always had problems in housing the enormous quantity of his treasures, and this may have been the primary reason why in 1889, over the vigorous protests of Chicago newspapers and businessmen fearing loss of southern trade, he brought the Civil War Libby Prison from Richmond, Virginia, to Chicago. He rebuilt it, complete with a secret tunnel at Wabash Avenue between 14th and 16th streets. Later it was named "The Coliseum" and became the scene of many grand events of all kinds as well as of national political conventions, such as the one in 1908 where William H. Taft received the presidential nomination.

When the four-story prison museum was opened in a gala affair late in 1889, crammed to capacity with various relics, it was an immediate success and people streamed to it. Within the first three months over 100,000 visitors had come to inspect it as one of the nation's top attractions, driving the value of stockholders' shares within one month from $110 to $150. This phenomenal success instantly propelled Gunther into the limelight as a collector of international fame, which in turn caused people to inundate Gunther with relics that defy description.

On September 28, 1899 fire destroyed his candy store at 212 State Street and also damaged part of his museum kept there, making him painfully aware of the vulnerability of his priceless collection to destruction. Consequently, according to the *Tribune* of February 16, 1900, he offered to give his immense collection of historical objects, paintings, and documents to the city if the authorities would erect a suitable fireproof building. This offer was rejected and likewise a similar one on March 4, 1908, when Gunther announced his retirement. Before the Chicago Historical Society could purchase the remnants of the collection from the Gunther heirs in 1920, priceless objects had been given to various repositories, such as the Field Museum or the Museum of Science and Industry.

The Museum of Science and Industry also owes much of its existence to the German element. Julius Rosenwald (1862-1932) (son of Samuel Rosenwald, who came from Germany about 1854 to establish himself as a leading clothing merchant in Springfield, Illinois) founded the Museum of Science and Industry in 1929. At one time Chicago's wealthiest man, Rosenwald established in 1917 the Rosenwald Fund, which amounted to $40,000,000 in 1928, and in addition donated over $22,000,000 to various causes, including some $6,600,000 to the Museum of Science and Industry. Rosenwald was impressed by the popularity of European technical museums and conceived the idea of establishing such a museum in Chicago. Already on November 8, 1925 the *Abendpost* reported that he and other Chicagoans had invited Dr. Oscar Miller from Munich to present plans for a technical museum in Chicago after the model of the "Deutsche Museum" in Munich. Finally, in 1929 Rosenwald presented to the South Park commissioners an offer to endow the proposed museum with an initial amount of three million dollars, provided that enough public support could be generated to erect a suitable edifice.

Germans have been responsible for capturing the past and preserving knowledge about pioneer days not only within the city, but also in the suburbs. In Bensenville, Johann Heinrich Franzen, who came from Germany in 1835, operated a linseed oil mill, part of which was dedicated as a monument in 1934. In Hinsdale a certain Frederick Graue, who had emigrated in 1833 from the small town Stolzenau, about thirty miles northwest of Hannover, founded a gristmill in 1852 which, after its restoration in 1950, has become a popular tourist attraction as well as the object of a recent television program, on October 12, 1974, when Channel Five at 9:30 P.M. reported on the museum as well as its milling process.

With regard to libraries, the Chicago Germans furnished a fair share of the means to extend the intellectual horizon. When the nine members of the first board of directors of the Chicago Public Library convened on April 11, 1872, one could find among them two representatives of the German element, the famous journalist Hermann Raster and the lawyer Julius Rosenthal, whose responsibility it was to make sure the library was provided with a good stock of foreign holdings. In addition to Raster and Rosenthal, the following representatives of the German element served as members of the library board until 1890: William Cadlec, William Caspar, Edward Dreyer, Dr. Emil Hirsch, Dr. F.C. Hotz, Bernhard Löwenthal, Emil Mannhardt, Bernhard Moos, Adolph Moses, Harry Rubens, and Dr. Ernst Schmidt. Of these Bernhard Moos and Dr. Hirsch were responsible for starting branch libraries in various parts of the city. Though the percentage rate of the German element in Chicago declined, citizens of German extraction continued to be on the library board. For instance, the *Abendpost* of December 16, 1930 reported that Mayor Thompson appointed the German-American attorney Leopold Saltiel to the library board to replace the departing German-American Frederick Seidenburg, dean of Loyola University.

For a long time Chicago Germans pressed for accessible libraries. Some of them possessed extensive private libraries, especially the forty-eighters, such as Caspar Butz (1825-85), whose priceless library was destroyed in the Great Fire of 1871. But since relatively few Germans could afford to buy all that they wanted to read, they severely felt the lack of a free public library. The *Staatszeitung* of December 6, 1871 attempted to goad the Germans into replacing Butz's destroyed library as a nucleus of a general German circulating library, to be part of a larger public library. This seems to have had its desired effect, for within the next few months many books were collected and entrusted to A.A. Dyhrenfurth and B. Kihlholz.

Soon, however, a controversy raged among factions of the German element concerning the fate of the collected reading material. One faction, made up mainly of German workers, advocated the erection of a separate German library, because they wanted to make sure the library would be open on Sundays, the only day they would have leisure to visit there. Another faction, represented by the *Staatszeitung*, insisted that such a library would have a wretched existence and that Chicago's Germans could be assured of an adequate reading repertory only if they allied themselves with the rest of Chicago to establish one common public library. In order to resolve the library issue, a committee was formed.

On February 1, 1872 the *Staatszeitung* reported that a German Library Association had been established, which was made up of the following board: President—Georg Schneider, Vice President—Consul Heinrich Claussenius, Treasurer—Hermann Eschenburg, Secretary—Max Eberhardt. This body finally reached a compromise, whereby the Germans surrendered all of their reading material to the public library under the condition that it remain open on Sundays. The *Staatszeitung* of November 18, 1873 asserted that the Germans were faithful visitors to the public library, supporting their claim with selected statistics. During the month of October 1873 the newspaper, *Wiener Neue Freie Presse*, was requested fifty-one times, the *Kölnische Zeitung* fifty-two times, and the periodical, *Gartenlaube*, eighty-five times.

When the Chicago Public Library received the coveted gold medal of excellence at the Paris World Exhibition in 1889, Chicago's German element was extremely proud, for it believed that it was due a great share of the honor. The *Staatszeitung* repeatedly stressed in 1889 that not only the head librarian, Frederick Hild, was of German background, but also his first assistant, E.F. Gauss, who was responsible for and exhibited the award winning display. Frederick Hild (1859-1914), whose name is perpetuated in a branch library at 4536 North Lincoln Avenue, was employed at the library since its inception in 1872, serving as head librarian from 1887-1909, when he was fired as a result of an extended feud with the library trustees. In January of 1902 he became the object of a controversy when he publicly asserted that he would not follow the recommendations of eastern librarians that fiction be held off the library shelves until a year after publication. Finally, on April

13, 1909 the Chicago papers reported that, despite the vigorous support of Hild by various individuals and groups, Carl B. Roden assumed Hild's duties.

E.F. Gauss was born at Stuttgart in 1842, and came to New York in 1859, teaching there before serving two years in the Civil War in Company K of the first New York infantry regiment. After the war he studied to become an Evangelical minister, serving first the community of Bunker Hill, Illinois, from 1870-74; then at a church in Zurich, Switzerland, until 1878; and, finally, in Galena, Illinois, from 1878 to 1880. In that year he came to Chicago to accept a government post, which he exchanged in 1887 for a position at the public library. Though recognized as a competent librarian, among the German element he was known more as a poet and forceful public speaker than as a librarian. Scarcely a German celebration passed at which he did not recite one of his many poems. His facility in both languages, evident in masterful translations of German literary works into English and vice versa, was generally applauded when he served as official translator at the Haymarket "Riot" trial.

In addition to the public library, the Germans were interested in other library projects. Perhaps the first "library" designed to lend books to Germans was managed by the "Chicago Leseverein," about which little is known except that it existed in 1848 and lent popular reading material to its members.

The next earliest library of which we know that it lent books to Germans was organized sometime in 1857 by the "Chicago Arbeiterverein," a club expressly formed to further the German worker socially as well as intellectually. A quarterly report in the *Staatszeitung* of May 26, 1862 by the "Arbeiterverein's" president, Theodor Hielscher, informs about the club and its 389 members' cultural activities. From November 1861 to May 1862 the expenditure for books amounted to $223 and for periodicals to $72, causing Hielscher to assert, "we can view our shelves with great satisfaction, since we have purchased the works of Dickens, Sir Walter Scott, Feuerbach, Hacklaender, Freiligrath, Cooper, Auerbach, Spindler, etc. . . . our members are making good use of this source of education." The library was but one means for improvement: the report continued that the club's night school had had maximum attendance throughout the winter and that lectures had been given. Here Hielscher, a full-time school master and part-time poet, could not refrain from criticizing those members who were bored with a recent lecture on the death of Elijah Lovejoy in 1837, "a martyr to the cause of liberty." Though this club lost its library in the Conflagration of 1871, it again possessed over 4,000 books by 1876, according to the *Staatszeitung* of February 22, 1876, which reported on the club's dedication of a new hall on Des Plaines Road.

Most likely, the library of the "Arbeiterverein" was available only to members, but there was at least one library managed by a German in pre-fire days at which Chicago's entire population could obtain books and periodicals. The *Staatszeitung* of September 30, 1867 contained a notice of perhaps the first rental library in Chicago by Edward Buehler of 111 Monroe Street, stating that he would rent, for a modest charge, illustrated periodicals and books on mechanics which were not to be had on the local market.

There continued to be separate German libraries. The most ambitious undertaking was the Germania Club's attempt to collect all the literary products of Germans published in America. In 1891 the club elected a board of its members, consisting of Joseph Brucker, Washington Hesing, Frederick Hild, Dr. Karl Pietsch, and Dr. A.G. Zimmermann under the presidency of the attorney Harry Rubens, in order to accomplish that goal. Their efforts culminated in a publication of a survey of German literature in America in 1893, but by now many of the books collected in the club's library have been scattered to various Chicago libraries.

Most of the other library projects were rather insignificant. The *Abendpost* of October 2, 1897 reported on the opening of a German library in Harlem, since that town was inhabited chiefly by Germans. The same paper had an article on December 25, 1932, concerning a German library at 13th and Homan streets and on October 28, 1934, reported on a German library in a "South Side Ballroom" where 1,500 volumes were ready for circulation among the area's German readers.

Only a few of many individuals of the German element can be mentioned for their meritorious activities with regard to Chicago's libraries. The *Staatszeitung* of December 5, 1887 proudly announced that the second generation German Hermann Kohlsaat, West Side Park commissioner and prominent publisher of various Chicago newspapers, had founded the Colored Men's Library Association with a working fund of $1,000 and a basic stock of over 300 books, at the corner of Dearborn and Harrison streets. In the 1920's the Julius Rosenwald Fund, primarily intended to better the conditions of Negroes through education, provided the means for numerous schools and libraries in many states. In addition to the above-mentioned librarians of German descent, the following outstanding ones ought to be mentioned as having been active for some time in Chicago: Karl Pietsch and Curt F. Buehler at the Newberry Library; and Henry Legler, head librarian at the Chicago Public Library. Even the present head librarian at the Chicago Public Library, David Reich, is of German extraction.

Chapter 10

Religious Institutions and the German Element

The ascent and the gradual decline in number of Chicago's German element is mirrored in the development of its churches in the Chicago area. Understandably, the earliest German settlers in Chicago did not have the opportunity to worship among their German compatriots. By 1833 only three regular congregations existed in Chicago, namely a Catholic, a Presbyterian, and a Baptist Church. Germans did in fact join these religious organizations until they started to erect their own churches in the 1840's. For instance, there were many German Catholics in Chicago who belonged to St. Mary's Church until they built their own Catholic churches in 1846. From the very beginning this first Catholic church in Chicago had German members. This is substantiated by the fact that when a group of Chicagoans petitioned the Catholic Bishop of the St. Louis Diocese early in April of 1833 to send a priest to Chicago, the Germans John Hondorf and Johann Mann affixed their signatures to the petition.

The first group of Germans who organized and built their own separate church in Chicago was the German Evangelical Association, a sect established in Pennsylvania by the German preacher Jacob Albrecht in 1790. Four members of this sect, Georg C. Gross, Daniel and Christoph Stanger, and Jacob Schnaebele came in 1835 from Pennsylvania to the Chicago area. After they had sent enthusiastic letters describing the fertile lands of Illinois, several of their fellow believers followed them in 1836 and 1837 to Chicago, among them Jacob and Martin Escher and their families, Adam Knopp, Jacob Ott and three sons, Johann Rehm, and

Georg Strubler. It is interesting to note that John J. Escher (1823-1901), Bishop of the Evangelical Church, author of the *Evangelical Church Catechism*, and founder of North Central College in Naperville in 1861, was the son of Jacob Escher, who had emigrated from Alsace to Pennsylvania in 1830.

The incipient German Evangelical communities in Chicago and Naperville were served for a few years in makeshift quarters or in the homes of members by several itinerant preachers. Their first one was the Reverend Jacob Boas, who came in August of 1837 from Pennsylvania. The Naperville community erected the first church building in 1842. The Chicago community did so in 1843, when Grant Goodrich donated a building site on Monroe Street and Wabash Avenue, and the preacher Frederick Wahl was successful in raising the necessary $500 for building a structure some thirty by forty feet in size. This small building served the ever increasing community until 1852, when the congregation split to erect their respective church buildings on Clark Street near Van Buren Street, and on the corner of Chicago Avenue and Wells Street. This sect continued to proliferate in Chicago, numbering eleven communities by 1900. From 1843 until 1852 the Chicago community was served by the preachers Frederick Wahl, C. Augenstein, Jacob Kopp, G. A. Blank, G. G. Platz, Christian Holl, Joseph Hallacher, J. P. Kramer, Israel Kuter and J. H. Raggatz.

In the meantime a German United Lutheran community blossomed in Dunkley's Grove, now Addison, which became the mother community of many later Lutheran communities in DuPage and Cook Counties. In June of 1834 the families of Frederick Graue and Bernhard Köhler, altogether ten people, of whom the youngest, August Köhler, was five years old, settled in Dunkley's Grove after having emigrated in 1833 from their small hometown of Stolzenau, some thirty miles northwest of Hannover. Apparently, their enthusiastic letters to friends and relatives in Germany induced many of their compatriots to come to the New World and settle in the vicinity of Chicago. Of the several Germans who came soon after Graue and Köhler, Friedrich Buchholz, apparently an articulate, well-educated man, led the community in worship for three years. Buchholz had come with his family from Stolzenau in 1835 and was killed in an accident on February 15, 1838, while helping to erect a home for the newly immigrated Wilhelm Plagge.

After the death of Buchholz the community was served for two years by its first professional minister, Ludwig Cachand-Ervendberg. Before he went in 1840 to Neu Braunfels, Texas, where he was killed in 1863 by marauding Indians, he had kept a detailed church record book for the years 1838 and 1839. On January 1, 1839, Ludwig Cachand-Ervendberg counted 221 souls in the church community which he named Teuto, and which included 67 persons in Chicago. Until 1842 no special church building existed, though the community had had a school building since 1840. It is also interesting to note that for most members of the Teuto community adhering to people of their own nationality was more important than worshiping with brethren of their own faith, for even in Chicago, where St. Mary's Church would have been available to German Catholics and several Protestant churches to German Protestants, the Reverend Cachand-Ervendberg indiscriminately served German members of every faith.

After Ludwig Cachand-Ervendberg went to Texas, Francis A. Hoffmann (1822-1903) became his successor. He had emigrated from his native town of Herford late in 1839, and came immediately to Chicago. He had worked at various odd jobs before he was called to Dunkley's Grove to teach at the German school for a yearly salary of fifty dollars and for the privilege of "boarding around," that is, living for set periods of time with the parents of his pupils. Hoffmann was asked by members of the community to lead them in their Sunday worship and finally was elected by them to serve as their minister. Under Hoffmann's pastorate the Teuto community erected a church building in 1842, which sufficed until 1861, when it was replaced by a larger structure. In 1847 Hoffmann accepted a call to the newly founded Lutheran Church in Schaumburg, several miles northwest of Dunkley's Grove.

While serving as minister, Francis A. Hoffmann also demonstrated interests in other pursuits. He was simultaneously schoolmaster, postmaster and township clerk of Dunkley's Grove, worked on the editorial boards of the *Chicago Democrat*, the *Staatszeitung*, and of *Der Missionsbote*, and functioned as a delegate of DuPage County to the Rivers and Harbors Convention at Chicago in 1847. When failing health made the pastorate in Schaumburg too onerous for him in 1851, he moved to Chicago, where he had a phenomenally successful career, described earlier. In the year of 1873 he assumed the pen name Hans Buschbauer and retired to his farm in Jefferson, Wisconsin, where he wrote a great number of articles and books for the benefit of recently immigrated German farmers who were not familiar with the American milieu.

Meanwhile, a group of Germans from the Teuto community met at Chicago in the summer of 1843 to make plans for the erection of their own church building within the city to be named St. Paul's Evangelical United Church. A committee was elected to procure a proper building site. It was successful in obtaining gratuitously from William Ogden and Walter Newberry a piece of land on the corner of Ohio and LaSalle streets. Later in 1843 a frame structure measuring about thirty by fifty feet was dedicated to serve St. Paul's Evangelical United community. The most active founders of the church were B. A. Beyer, Wilhelm Frank, Arnold Kröger, Jacob Letz, John Pfund, Hermann Rantze, G. Schairer, Karl Stein and K. Teschner. For three years the steadily growing congregation was served by itinerant preachers. When August Selle, its first settled minister, arrived in 1846, the community contained already seventy-six voting families, and in 1847 it was necessary to enlarge the church building. Early in 1848 a dispute over the form of confession precipitated an irreconcilable schism in the community. Consequently, on April 9, 1848 the Reverend August Selle and four members, R. Ohm, C. Michel, C. Blüss and W. Brockschmidt separated from St. Paul's Evangelical United Church to establish their own St. Paul's Lutheran community.

St. Paul's Evangelical United congregation soon recovered from the split. Gustav Fischer replaced August Selle as pastor, but he also had difficulties with the community and had to resign in 1851. Under his successor Joseph Hartmann (1823-87), who had to flee from Germany in 1849 for taking part in the revolution, this congregation grew immensely. Hartmann became in 1859 the founder of the "German Evangelical Synod of North America," founder in 1871 of the College of the Evangelical Synod of North America at Elmhurst, now known as Elmhurst College, and in 1867 induced Mr. and Mrs. Uhlich to provide the means to found an orphanage, still known as Uhlich Children's Home.

The newly founded St. Paul's Lutheran Church also flourished, consisting by the end of 1848, the year of separation, of forty-three heads of households. At first they worshipped in the Chicago Courthouse, but in 1849 erected their first church building on Indiana Street between Wells and Franklin streets. When Heinrich Wunder became pastor in 1851, the church grew so rapidly that a much larger building had to be erected on Superior and North Franklin streets, which was destroyed in the 1871 Fire but rebuilt exactly as the old one on the same spot.

Heinrich Wunder served as pastor of Chicago's St. Paul's Lutheran congregation so long that he was able to celebrate his fiftieth jubilee on September 23, 1901. He was born in 1830 at the small town of Muggendorf in Upper Frankonia, as the ninth child of a miller. When he was only nine years old, his father was killed in an accident. After he had attended a missionary school for two years, he sailed in 1846 on the *Carolina* from Bremen to New York, a trip which lasted 63 days. At various institutions in Illinois and Missouri he completed his education before he was called in 1849 as pastor to the German Lutheran community in Millstadt, Illinois. He remained there until accepting the position at St. Paul's Lutheran community in Chicago in September of 1851, where he gained a highly respected and influential position, serving for several years as district president of Illinois in the synod of Missouri, Ohio and other states. While Heinrich Wunder was pastor of St. Paul's Lutheran Church, many branch churches originated from it, amounting to at least thirty-one by 1896.

By 1845 the German element had established several churches in the Chicago metropolitan area. There were two German churches in the city of Chicago, namely the German Evangelical Association on Monroe Street and Wabash Avenue, under the Reverend Jacob Kopp, and St. Paul's Evangelical United Church on the corner of LaSalle and Ohio streets, under intinerant preachers. There were also German churches in various suburbs. One was the Evangelical United Church in Addison, serving several towns, under pastor Francis A. Hoffmann. There was also a German Methodist community in Bremen Township, which existed only briefly in 1843. A rudimentary Catholic community at New Strassburg in Bloom Township was founded in 1845 by Matthias Franz, H. Kalvelage, Josef Klein, Peter Kloss, Karl Reichert, Vincent and Charles Sauter, and Josef Wolf. In addition, there were several loosely organized congregations, such as the one in Proviso where, beginning in 1840, the Lutheran pastor Brandstätter held sporadic services in the home of Christian Langguth or in Rosehill, where services in the home of Peter Schmidt led to the establishment of St. Henry's community in 1851.

Many other German settlers in Chicago and vicinity had joined the most conveniently located congregation regardless of nationality. This was especially true for German Catholics, because, instead of organizing their own church, they joined St. Mary's community. As Emil Mannhardt pointed out on page twenty-eight of the October 1905 issue of *Deutsch-Amerikanische Geschichtsblätter*, there were many German Catholics present in Chicago before 1840, among them Adam Amberg, John Belz, A. Eberhardt, John Hondorf, Johann Mann and John Wode already in 1833. The Berg brothers and John Raber arrived at Chicago in 1834, and many other German Catholics joined St. Mary's community before 1840, among them the following: John and Franz Busch, Johann Blasen, Jacob Gross, Solomon Haas, A. Hettinger, Hubert Maas,

Josef Jaeger, Michael Kleinhaus, John Paul, Casper Pfeiffer, Nicholas and Peter Reis, Andreas Schall, A. Schaller and Joseph Schumacher.

Since the organization of Chicago's St. Mary's church in May of 1833, the German element has been active in it. On July 13, 1833 the German couple John and Katharina Wode, nee Kannenkoth, asked St. Mary's priest, Father John St. Cyr to baptize their twins, apparently the first children born in Chicago of German parents. The next baptisms of German children in St. Mary's Church were recorded for August 24, 1835 and June 19, 1836. The earliest marriages of Germans in St. Mary's community were solemnized by Father John St. Cyr between Jacob Müller and Catharine Baumgarten on April 4, 1836 and between John Betz and Veronika Periolat early in 1837. One of the first persons to suffer a violent death in Chicago was apparently a German buried by the priest of St. Mary's Church, for on July 17, 1836, Father John St. Cyr entered into the church book that he had interred in the presence of many Germans a man known only as "John" who had been stabbed to death. It is interesting to note that between October of 1836 and some time in 1840 St. Mary, the only Catholic community of Chicago, was served by a German priest, Father Leander Schaefer, who had accepted a call to St. Mary after its first priest, Father St. Cyr, had left the community.

By 1846 the number of German Catholics in Chicago had grown to such proportions that they decided to organize their own churches. On June 28, 1846, a general meeting of all German Catholics decreed that two church buildings be erected. One was to be built on the North Side and one on the South Side.

St. Peter's church was erected on the South Side after J. Y. Scammon had donated a building site on Washington Street between Wells and Franklin streets. For about $750 a forty-by-sixty-foot frame structure was erected, which was capable of seating some 700 people. Some of the most prominent founders, many of whom had been members of the St. Mary community, were Adam Amberg, the Berg brothers, John and Franz Busch, Michael Eule, Johann Glasen, Jacob Gross, F. Hahn, Joseph Jaeger, Michael Kleinhaus, Hubert Maas, John Paul, Casper Pfeiffer, Nicholas and Peter Reis, Andreas Schall, A. Schaller, and Joseph Schumacher. Already on August 2, 1846, this church was dedicated by Bishop Quarter under Father Johann Jung. It served a community which consisted in 1846 of about thirty families; and had some 160 families in 1853, when various factors forced the congregation to move their house of worship to the corner of Clark and Polk streets, where the first mass was celebrated on Christmas of 1853. Because of the enormous growth of the community it was necessary to erect in 1864 at a cost of $65,000 a much larger church building which by 1870 served 1,200 families. Until 1875, when Franciscan friars began to serve the by then highly mobile community, the congregation was served by the Fathers Johann Jung, O. G. Ostlangenberg, Anton Völker, Bernhard Westkamp, G. H. Plathe, C. Schilling, Hermann Liermann, John Mager, Peter Fischer and G. Fröhlich. From the St. Peter community originated the branch communities of St. Anton, St. Georg, and St. Martin.

In order to build the St. Joseph's church on the North Side, a group of Germans organized, among them Peter Annen, Lorenz Baer, Moritz Baumgarten, Peter Berens, Michael Diversey, Peter Gabel, August Gauer, Henry Gherken, Michael Hoffmann, Matthias Kreiser, M. Laux, Joseph Marbach, Jacob and Matthias Miller, Thomas Minwegen, Jacob Raskopf, Franz Spohr and Johann Vogt. A lot was acquired on the northeast corner of Chicago Avenue and Cass Street at a cost of about $700, and a frame building about thirty-six by sixty-five feet was erected which was capable of seating about 600 people. When it was dedicated on August 15, 1846 by Bishop Quarter, its minister was Father Johann Jung, who also served St. Peter's church on the South Side.

The community had problems in attracting a permanent pastor. Of the great number of preachers who served St. Joseph's Church, barely the names are recorded until the Benedictine friars were called in 1861 to serve the community. When the first Benedictine father, Ludwig Marie Fink, later Bishop of Leavenworth, Kansas, accepted the pastorate in 1861, he erected a magnificent church building at a cost of $60,000. At the time of its dedication on March 19, 1865, it was considered the most beautiful church in Chicago, capable of seating over 1,000 people. After it was destroyed in the 1871 conflagration, a new church was begun at the corner of Market and Hill streets to accommodate the shifting congregation. However, since the entire community had lost most of its possessions in the fire, a lack of funds delayed its completion until October of 1878. The St. Joseph church operated several highly popular parochial schools, of which St. Joseph's Academy in LaGrange still enjoys an enviable reputation.

Of the several branch churches which stemmed from St. Joseph, the most important one was St. Michael's church. When the St. Joseph congregation on the North Side became too crowded in 1852, the congregation called a meeting for January 20, 1852 at which it decided to found a new Catholic community. Its principal founders were Michael Diversey, Wilhelm Düsemann, Henry Gherken, Bernhardt Hansen, Christian and John Kuhn, Andreas and Matthias Miller, Heinrich Rohrbach and Florian Schmidt. Michael Diversey (1810-69), who had come to Chicago from Germany in 1838 to become one of the foremost Chicagoans in his time, donated the building site for the proposed church and a substantial amount of money. This caused the congregation to honor him by naming the new church after his patron saint. On October 17, 1852 the new church, measuring about forty by sixty feet, was dedicated at the corner of North Avenue and Church Street for a community which numbered over 800 people. For the next eight years it was served by the fathers August Kramer, Eusebius Kaiser, Joseph Zägel, Anton Sälger and Aloys Hatala. After 1860 it was served by the Redemptorist fathers.

The St. Michael community became the largest Catholic congregation in Illinois under the first Redemptorist father, Joseph Müller. Before coming to Chicago, he had demonstrated great organizational talents in his parishes at Baltimore, New York, and Pittsburg. In order to accommodate all the parishioners, a substantially larger church had to be built at an expenditure of close to $200,000. A stone structure measuring some 80 by 200 feet, erected at the corner of Hurlbut and Linden streets, was dedicated on September 29, 1869. It was partly destroyed in the Great Fire of 1871 and was rededicated in October of 1873 after the interior had been rebuilt. In 1900 the St. Michael community consisted of some 2,000 families and its parochial school accommodated 839 boys and 828 girls.

Chicago's first German Methodist Episcopal church was organized in August of 1847 by some twenty-five Germans, among them A. Biedermann, John Bink, Ernst Dickermann, F. Heinz, Charles Kessler, Andrew and Georg Krinbill, Friedrich Muchike, Christian Müller, John Stoetzel, and Anton Waller. During their first year of existence they were served by itinerant preachers in the homes of some of the members, but in 1848 they moved into their own church building on Indiana Street near Wells Street, and appointed the first resident minister, Philipp Barth. In 1857 they moved from their Indiana Street location to Clybourn Avenue in an effort to accommodate the shifting German population, erecting a thirty by fifty foot frame structure there at a cost of approximately $2,000. Their third church, a larger two-story brick building, measured forty by seventy feet and was erected in 1863 at the same spot as their second church at a cost of about $10,000. There it served the 190 families of the community until it was destroyed in the conflagration of 1871. The pre-fire ministers were Philipp Barth, A. Korfliage, J. J. Dreier, Louis Kuntz, Christian Wentz, J. H. Westerfeld, John L. Schaefer, Jacob Haas, Frederick Kluckhohn, William Pfaffle, Jacob Bletsch, G. F. Mulfinger, and Friedrich Rinder. After worshipping until May 1873 in a temporary building, the community erected a two-story structure forty-five by ninety foot at a cost of $17,000 which served 210 families.

Various German religious groups continued to organize churches in Chicago with increasing frequency and with a more or less predictably mushrooming development. According to page 544, volume two of Pierce's *History of Chicago*, the total number of foreign churches founded in Chicago prior to 1872 amounted to forty-one, of which the Germans had erected well over half. As the influx of German immigrants continued, more and more German churches were founded. Of the nine Catholic churches founded by ethnic groups before 1872, the Germans had erected seven, namely St. Peter on Washington Street between Franklin and Wells streets in 1846, St. Joseph on Chicago Avenue and Cass Street also in 1846, St. Henry at Rosehill in 1850, St. Michael on North Avenue and Church Street in 1852, St. Francis on Clinton and Miller streets in 1853, St. Mauritius on Hoyne Avenue and 36th Street in 1860 and St. Boniface at Cornell and Noble streets in 1865. Seventeen foreign Lutheran churches were erected in pre-fire days, of which ten stemmed from the German St. Paul's Lutheran Church alone.

Between 1872 and 1892 the various ethnic groups of Chicago founded 110 churches of the leading denominations, according to page 544 of the second volume of Pierce's *History of Chicago*. Of these 110 churches, the Germans had erected forty-eight, the Scandinavians thirty-five, the Bohemians ten, the Poles had built nine, the French and the Italians each three, and the Lithuanians as well as the Welsh each one. Of the forty-eight German churches, there were twenty Lutheran, fifteen Catholic, six Methodist, three Baptist, three Congregational, and one Presbyterian.

Most German churches in Chicago were founded from 1881, when the tide of German immigration crested, to about 1900. A report in the *Staatszeitung* of November 9, 1891, is symptomatic for the proliferation of German churches, because the paper announced the dedication of two new German churches, namely the German Lutheran Zion Church at Winston Avenue and 99th Street and the German Methodist Church at Dobbins and 99th streets. *Chicago und sein Deutschthum* lists for 1900 a total of 122 German churches within Chicago and fifteen German churches in the suburbs. The subtotals for the various denominations of the 122 German churches within Chicago were seventy-four Protestant and Lutheran, twenty-four Catholic, thirteen Methodist, four Baptist, three Congregational, two Reformed and two Adventist churches.

Most of the German churches in the suburbs were Catholic churches. They were St. Peter and Paul in South Chicago, Immaculate Conception in Riverdale, St. Francis-Haver in Avondale, St. Dionysius in Hawthorn, St. Benedict in Blue Island, St. Joseph in Wilmette, St. Peter in Niles Center, St. Nicholas in Evanston, St. Alphonsus in Lemont, Immaculate Conception in Buffalo Grove and St. Ann in Richton. However, there were also four suburban German Protestant churches, namely a Zion Church in both Auburn Park and Washington Heights, the Trinity Church in Hansen Park and St. Nicholas in Avondale.

The decline in number of Chicago's German element is reflected in the reduced number of German churches in Chicago at the present time. A list of Chicago area churches which offer German services, most of them once a week, is printed every week in the local *Sonntagspost*. Their total number amounts to thirty-six in the city and five in the suburbs. The five suburban churches are all Protestant, namely the Evangelical Fellowship Chapel in Elk Grove Village, Zion's Church in Bellwood, St. John's Church in Forest Park, the Trinity Church in Glencoe and St. Paul's Church in Melrose Park.

Within the city German services are at the present time offered at thirty-one Protestant-Lutheran churches, and one each at Catholic, Baptist, Adventist, Pentecost, and Free German Christian Community churches. It is interesting to note that the most precipitous decline in all German denominations is that of the Catholic, for whereas the ratio of the number of churches in 1975 to number of churches in 1900 is thirty-six to seventy-eight for German Lutheran-Protestant churches, that of German Catholic churches is one to thirty-five. It seems that the *Staatszeitung* was indeed prophetic when on August 19, 1887 it printed the editorial, "The German Language Jeopardized." In that editorial the paper expressed the opinion that German Catholics were much less interested in perpetuating a priceless cultural legacy, their mother tongue, than were other German denominations.

Of the great number of churchmen active among Chicago's German element, there have been many outstanding individuals. There were prominent men like Henry Wunder, pastor of St. Paul's Lutheran Church for over fifty years and Illinois president of the

Missouri Synod; Bishop John Escher, founder of North Central College in Naperville; or Joseph Hartmann, founder of the German Evangelical Synod of North America and of Elmhurst College. However, perhaps the most universally recognized churchman of Chicago's German element was the second generation German, George William Mundelein.

George William Mundelein was born of German immigrants on July 2, 1872 in the German settlement of the lower East Side of New York City. He had an extraordinarily successful career. After studying at the Manhattan College and at St. Vincent Seminary in Beatty, Pennsylvania, he went to Rome, Italy, in order to connclude his training in theology. At Rome he was ordained a priest in 1895. In the same year he became secretary to Bishop McDonnell of Brooklyn, New York. At more or less regular intervals he was promoted to chancellor of the diocese in 1897, to auxiliary bishop of Brooklyn in 1909, and finally in 1915 he was appointed to succeed James E. Quigley as archbishop of Chicago. In 1924 Mundelein was named cardinal by Pope Pius XI. Two years later Cardinal Mundelein organized the Eucharistic Congress at Chicago, in June of 1926, which helped to establish him as the most powerful leader of the Roman Catholic church in America. Before he died in 1939, he founded in the town of Mundelein, named in his honor, the St. Mary of the Lake Seminary. It should also be mentioned that in the northern part of the city on Lake Michigan Mundelein College, a former women's college which only recently became coed, also perpetuates the cardinal's name.

Chapter 11

Chicago's German Element in the Field of Healing

Chicago's German element contributed its fair share to the medical field from the incorporation of the city to the present time. The first practicing German physician in Chicago seems to have been a certain P. Bomino, who offered his services in the *Chicago American* of March 16, 1837 as follows:

TO THE AFFLICTED

GERMAN DOCTOR

The undersigned, from Hanover, in Germany, proffers his services in the practice of

MEDICINE, SURGERY, ETC.

His system in practice is principally Botanical. He graduated in Europe, served as Surgeon in Bonaparte's army, and was elected shipdoctor on his voyage to America for 300 passengers. His office is opposite the Lake House in the second story of Kinzie's Warehouse, Chicago, Ill.

Since he came to this country he has cured Cholera, Hardness of Hearing, Tetter, Ring Worm, Scorbutic Eruptions, Leprosy, Mercurial Diseases, Scrofula or King's Evil, Diseases of the Liver, Dispepsia, Piles, Gravel, Dropsy, Pthisis, Cancer, Weak Eyes, Asthma, Catarrh, Foul Gleers, Sore Legs, Venereal Diseases, Gonorrhoea, White Flood, Rheumatism, Pains in the Joints from cold, etc.

Dr. Bomino has been practicing in Cinncinnati, Columbus, Janesville, Cleveland, etc. for the last six years.

Chicago, June 21st. P. Bomino.

It is not known how long Dr. Bomino plied his trade in Chicago, but since he seems to have been an itinerant physician, it is unlikely that he stayed for an extended period of time in this city.

The next German physician in Chicago about whom we know anything was Heinrich Lemcke, who had his office on Clark Street north of the Presbyterian Church, according to an advertisement in the *Chicago American* of August 23, 1843. Other German medical doctors that seem to have been in Chicago by 1845 were M. L. Knapp, Johann Rauch, and C. A. Helmuth, who became editor of the newly founded *Illinois Staatszeitung* in 1848 and was also known as an ornithologist. The *Staatszeitung* of *April* 22, 1892 reported that Dr. Helmuth had completed an exhaustive index of birds comparable to Audubon's, but since its printing would cost $40,000 the project had not been published.

After Rush Medical College was established in 1843, German doctors could always be found on its staff beginning with M. L. Knapp, professor of obstetrics, who was one of the first four faculty members. In September of 1857 there were enough Chicago physicians of German descent to formally organize the first German Medical Society. William Wagner was elected president, Ernst Schmidt assumed the office of vice president and Georg Schloetzer served as secretary.

The doctors Wagner and Schmidt were both graduates from the University of Würzburg, were political exiles because of their involvement in the 1848 Revolution, and fought on the Union's side in the Civil War. Dr. Wagner served as Chief Surgeon of the Twenty-fourth Illinois Infantry Regiment and in General Starkweather's brigade. After the return to Chicago, he was elected coroner of Cook County from 1864 to 1870, was one of the organizers of Cook County Hospital in 1866, and gave outstanding service to the city not only on the staff of several hospitals, but also in general public affairs. An early death in 1870 left his family impecunious. His friend and colleague, Dr. Ernst Schmidt, not only delivered a moving eulogy in English, German and Latin at his funeral, but also untiringly interceded in behalf of the widow so that the deceased's three sons were able to obtain good educations.

The life of "the red doctor" Ernst Schmidt (1830-1900), thus named because of his red hair and his sympathies for the Haymarket "conspirators," was exceedingly beneficial to many people, as his biography, *He Chose*, by Frederick R. Schmidt, demonstrates. Even though pardoned for his political agitation during the 1848 Revolution, Dr. Schmidt had to suffer discrimination in his social and professional life at Würzburg and in 1857 decided to come to Chicago, where he met many friends from the revolutionary era. Almost immediately he became a leader in the abolitionist movement, jeopardizing his material existence in actively supporting the "Underground Railroad." His commemoratory oration during a memorial service for John Brown finally caused his ostracism from Chicago. Dr. Schmidt later wrote about the happenings which forced him to leave Chicago as follows, taken from page 98 of F. R. Schmidt's *He Chose*:

> The campaign of defamation carried out against me by the proslavery partisans—and who wasn't one at that time—soon reduced the number of my paying patients by 50 per cent. When these, too, began to leave me during the year 1859, I was left with 'free patients' only. Not being able to feed my little family on this patronage, I began to look around for a teaching position in another city.
>
> To make matters worse, I made a speech before a handful of John Brown's followers at Kinzie Hall on the evening of December 2, 1859, the day of his execution. A proslavery mob had gathered outside and, after my talk, followed me down the street, shouting, 'Lynch the red-haired Dutch bastard!' Mayor Milliken offered a strong police escort to conduct me across the Clark Street bridge to the North Side, but I preferred to walk across alone. The mob, assembled at the south end of the bridge, did nothing more than indulge in some beastly howling.

From Chicago Dr. Schmidt went to St. Louis where he taught at the "Humboldt Institut," a German medical school. When the Civil War broke out, he joined the Second Missouri Infantry Volunteers, as the regiment's physician with the rank of lieutenant colonel. After his honorable retirement from the army he returned to Chicago, where he was elected coroner in 1864, but resigned in the same year in protest over body snatching practices engaged in by medical schools. In 1879 he was the mayoral candidate of the Socialist party and was thus responsible for putting the Harrison dynasty into the mayor's office.

Unlike most of his compatriotic contemporaries, such as Gustav Koerner, lieutenant governor of Illinois in 1852, who were revolutionary agitators in their youth but turned their back to the Haymarket "conspirators," Dr. Schmidt tried his utmost to save the German labor leaders of 1886 from the gallows. Throughout his life he proved to be a humanitarian who had the courage to stand up for the downtrodden in the face of denouncements and malicious attacks. In public life and as head physician of the Michael Reese and Alexian Brothers Hospitals Dr. Ernst Schmidt attained the respect and admiration of the great majority of his contemporaries. In 1869 he and Dr. Ralph Isham were the first sponsors of the Jewish Hospital, now known as the Michael Reese Hospital, but before that, in 1867, Drs. Schmidt and Wagner chartered the Alexian Brothers Hospital, the first exclusively German-founded hospital of Chicago.

The general training institution of the Alexian Brothers in Aachen, Germany, in an exploratory move in December of 1865, had sent Brother Bonaventura Thelen to Chicago, where he arrived in March of 1866 after an extremely arduous voyage which included ship wreck. Legend has it that on March 31, 1866, he found in Franklin Street the first patient whom he carried home on his back to nurse him to health. In 1867 several additional Brothers were sent from Aachen. They bought a big piece of property between North Franklin and North Market streets close to North Avenue to erect their first hospital, which received its first patients in 1868. After it burned down in the Great Fire of 1871, a much larger one was built which stood until it had to make way for the elevated train. On October 4, 1896 Archbishop Feehan laid the cornerstone for their third hospital on a new lot on Belden and Racine streets. This was not to be their last home, for now the Alexian Brothers Medical Center is located in Elk Grove Village.

Of the hospitals founded by Chicagoans of German descent not only the Alexian Brothers Hospital burned down in the Conflagration of 1871, but also the Jewish Hospital. In its rebuilding the German element also was instrumental. Right after the Great Fire, the real estate developer Michael Reese died. He had emigrated from Germany in 1850 to amass a fortune in California, which he willed to charity. Through the efforts of the doctors Ernst Schmidt and Michael Mannheimer, the executors of the estate agreed to use part of the fortune to erect a new hospital to the memory of Michael Reese. The hospital's first medical staff appointed and headed by Dr. Schmidt consisted of the Drs. Heinrich Banga, Heinrich Gradle, James Hyde, Edwin Kuh and Michael Mannheimer.

In 1873 a group of Germans under the leadership of the doctors Charles Fessel, Heinrich Merkle, Johann Schaller, and Ernst Schmidt formed the German-American Dispensary Society, a charity organization of some 350 members who paid annual dues to buy medical supplies needed by German doctors who gratuitously treated poor ambulatory patients for various ailments. Periodic reports of this society's work in the *Staatszeitung* attest to its effective and indiscriminate treatment of patients with regard to nationalities. On August 3, 1874 the paper gave a survey according to nationalities of the 2,133 patients treated by the society during the period of July 1873 to July 1874: 976 Germans, 480 Americans, 356 Russians and Poles, 119 Irish, 75 English, 67 Scandinavians, twenty-seven Austrians, eleven Dutch, six French, six Italians, six Swiss, three Canadians, and one Australian. Mainly because of financial difficulties the German-American Dispensary Society was forced to cease its humanitarian work on May 1, 1887. In its peak year of 1874 to 1875 it treated over 4,000 ailing, poverty-stricken Chicagoans. The *Staatszeitung* of July 13, 1876 reported that of 2,525 patients treated some 200 syphilis cases were cured. The paper added that most other hospitals in the Chicago area, especially the Cook County Hospital, turned syphilitic patients away.

After the demise of the German-American Dispensary Society several German groups attempted to install additional hospital facilities in Chicago. At first a controversy raged concerning whether they should establish a branch hospital in an already existing one. Several editorials in the *Staatszeitung*, such as the one on June 9, 1878, urged the German Ladies' Society to start a branch hospital in the Cook County Hospital rather than their own building. Finally, in December of 1883 the issue was resolved in that some $250,000 had been contributed by various German-American organizations and individuals for the erection of a separate German Hospital. In 1884 the German Hospital at 242 Lincoln Avenue was able to accept twenty-five patients, but already in 1887 it received new quarters. In 1910 Mrs. Conrad Seipp gave $150,000 for a new building and modernization of the German Hospital, which during the hysterical days of World War I was renamed to Grant Hospital, the name which it still bears.

Chicago benefitted from Germany's "Kulturkampf" between church and state under Bismarck's reign, for some of the persecuted religious orders sought refuge in this city and repaid its hospitality with charitable medical work. For instance, the Poor Handmaids of Christ came in 1875 from their motherhouse in Dernbach to establish a new cloister in Chicago. Already in 1875 the Poor Handmaids of Christ had provided thirty visiting nurses and in 1879 they had opened the city's first day nursery. In addition to that, they must be credited with the founding of several hospitals. On October 13, 1887 the *Staatszeitung* reported that the German-funded St. Elizabeth's Hospital of the Poor Handmaids of Christ, which had just been dedicated, was open to any one, regardless of creed or nationality. The same nuns caused the erection of St. Anne's Tuberculosis Hospital at 49th Street and Thomas Street, which they managed after 1903.

In the meantime the German pastors A. J. Ebert and E. Mathes in 1895 formed the Christian German Aid Society for Epileptics to which German-Americans responded favorably, so that a home for about 100 epileptic patients could be opened in July of 1896 on Church and Lincoln streets two miles west of Evanston. On December 16, 1896, another German-funded and managed hospital opened, namely the St. Agnes Hospital at 693 Halsted Street, which was run by displaced German Franciscan sisters. On August 5, 1911, the *Abendpost* reported on the construction of a new German Evangelical Deaconess Hospital at Morgan Street and 54th Place. By 1919, this hospital, which was forced to drop "German" from its name because of hostile reaction during the frantic war days, appealed to the Chicago Germans for $250,000 contributions in order to enlarge its quarters.

It would be possible to even list all of the Chicago physicians of German descent. Only some of the more prominent ones whose names and accomplishments are mentioned again and again can be cited here. In the second half of the nineteenth century the following doctors of German extraction were outstanding representatives of the various branches of healing: Edward Bert, Bernhard Bettmann, Heinrich Geiger, Gustav Hessert, Jacques Holinger, Karl Hotz, Hermann Loewe, Philipp Matthei, Rudolf Menn, Heinrich Merkle, Ernst G. Miessler, Friedrich Möller, Josef Otto, Friedrich C. Schaefer, Johann Schaller, Friedrich Scheuermann, Nicholas Senn, Hubert Straten, and Theodor Wild. Nicholas Senn (1844-1908), not only was professor of surgery at the College of Physicians and Surgeons, Rush Medical College, and the Chicago Polyclinic, but also served as chief surgeon of the U. S. 6th Army Corps in Cuba during the Spanish-American War. Before he died, he gave his marvellous book collection to the Newberry Library. Just to mention an example of the fame of these German-American physicians, Martha Freeman-Esmond in a letter of June 17, 1893 to Julia Boyd in New York, reproduced in the *Sunday Tribune* of June 22, 1941, praised Dr. Friedrich C. Schaefer, a gynecologist. She pointed out that he had invented many valuable devices widely used in surgery and asserted that, "Dr. Schaefer could operate successfully if he were blindfolded."

Most of these physicians belonged to the first German Medical Society, established in 1857 and defunct after 1875 when Dr. Heinrich Banga, a student of the celebrated Dr. Ignaz Ph. Semmelweiss, presented a paper on the antiseptic treatment of wounds which elicited such a spirited exchange of opinions that further meetings of the society were called off. A second German Medical Society of Chicago, which still exists, was formed on February 13,

1897, by fifteen German-speaking physicians of Chicago. Some of the following information about German physicians of this city is taken from a pamphlet printed for the society's 75th anniversary celebration in May of 1972.

The charter president of Chicago's second German Medical Society was Professor Edwin Klebs (1834-1913), who had come to Chicago in 1894. According to the *Encyclopaedia Britannica*, he was born in Königsberg on February 6, 1834, became assistant to the renowned Rudolf Virchow at the Pathological Institute of Berlin from 1861 to 1866, and subsequently professor of pathological anatomy at Bern in 1866, Würzburg in 1871, Prague in 1873, and Zürich in 1882. Klebs became famous as the discoverer of the diphteria bacillus and the co-discoverer of the typhoid bacillus, which caused F. H. Garrison in his *History of Medicine* to call him, "with Pasteur perhaps the most important precursor in the bacterial theory of infection." Klebs also investigated the bacteriology of gunshot wounds and was the first to produce tuberculosis lesions in animals. Among his many publications, the most important were his two textbooks on pathology in 1869 and 1887. While in Chicago, he was professor of pathology at Rush Medical College and the Chicago Post-Graduate Medical School.

Other famous charter members of the second German Medical Society were the three Beck brothers who contributed a fair share to the advancement of medicine and surgery. Carl Beck was professor of surgery at the Cook County Graduate School of Medicine, Emil Beck was an outstanding radiologist, and Josef Beck was a well-known ear and throat specialist. Some of the most active members during the early years of the German Medical Society were Maximilian J. Herzog, professor of pathology at Loyola University, David Lieberthal, professor of dermatology at Loyola Medical School, and Emil Ries, professor of obstetrics and gynecology at the University of Illinois.

The German Medical Society had to suspend its activities from 1917 to 1919, because many members served in the war and because of widespread anti-German sentiments. After the war the society resumed its functions, especially in supporting their colleagues in war-torn Europe. Many of the relief collections undertaken in Chicago were destined to alleviate the general suffering in Germany and to help erect needed medical facilities there. The society convinced the philanthropist Julius Rosenwald to crown his gifts to Germany with a one-million-dollar donation to Berlin for the erection of a dental clinic. Dr. William Petersen, professor of pathology at the University of Illinois, known for his voluminous publications on the influence of climatic conditions on health, organized a committee for the relief of the children of medical men in Central Europe, which collected substantial amounts for the relief of war victims.

Among the many political exiles who came to Chicago after World War I and especially during the Nazi period were many outstanding medical men from Germany. Franz Baumann, later president of the Chicago Metropolitan Dermatological Society, was arrested in Germany in 1938 but managed to escape with his family to Chicago, where he was supported by colleagues, such as the German-born Rudolf Schindler, who had come to Chicago in 1934. Being known as the inventor of the gastroscope while still in Germany, Schindler immediately became a leading figure in gastroscopy and published the basic textbook on that subject, in addition to many other works on the diseases of the stomach. William Becker, an orthopedic surgeon, became known as the founder of the Self Help Home for the Aged in 1949.

A few more outstanding medical men of German descent ought to be mentioned. They include the presidents of Chicago's German Medical Society, the doctors W. H. Hoffmann, Kurt Ossendorff, Ferdinand Seidler and Johann Siebel. Others were recipients of high honors, such as the doctors Eugen Lutterbeck, Hans H. Reese, Franz Steinitz and Friedrich Wassermann, who received the Officers' Cross of the Order of Merit from the Federal Republic of Germany.

Some of the more prominent Chicago physicians of German background were at the center of various controversies. Barring Governor Altgeld, there probably was no other Chicago German-American who had to bear such hateful attacks of the mob for altruistic motives than Dr. Ernst Schmidt, who stood up for the rights of the "conspirators" of the Haymarket "Riot." As mentioned above, he also had to withstand the brunt of the attacks of the proslavery advocates.

Not until 1916 did another medical man of German extraction come into the limelight of controversy, this time with an especially tragic outcome. The Chicago newpapers of March 20, 1916 stated that Dr. Theodor Sachs, the highly respected head of the Chicago Municipal Tuberculosis Sanitarium, was forced to resign because of a feud with Mayor Thompson. Barely two weeks later, on April 2, 1916, the newpapers reported that Dr. Sachs had committed suicide at Naperville, pleading in a suicide note that the sanitarium remain as it was, "unsoiled by graft and politics—the heritage of the people." The coroner of Du Page County called

Dr. Sachs' death "political murder." He was not the only one, for Dr. Frank Billings, at a memorial meeting for Dr. Sachs in the Auditorium on April 9, 1916, thundered that, "the mayor and his minions sent Sachs to his grave."

In 1929 a medical controversy raged concerning the urologist, Dr. Louis E. Schmidt, one of the sons of the humanitarian Dr. Ernst Schmidt. In April of that year the executive body of the Chicago Medical Association accused Dr. Schmidt, president of the Public Health Institute and the Illinois Hygiene League, of unprofessional conduct in the matter of advertising the services of the Public Health Institute in local newspapers. In a stormy meeting of the 4,500 members of the association, at which Dr. Schmidt was expelled from the organization, some other reasons for the Medical Association's opposition to Dr. Schmidt surfaced. This society took a dim view of Dr. Schmidt's practice of extending medical assistance to patients for either a nominal charge or, as was often the case, for no charge whatsoever. The fact that Dr. Schmidt made enormous progress in the battle against venereal diseases by openly warning against the dangers of VD and by gratuitously treating the afflicted was of no consequence. Several sympathizing colleagues of Dr. Schmidt, such as the Cook County coroner from 1928 to 1932, Dr. Hermann Bundesen, resigned from the Chicago Medical Association. In addition, popular support of Dr. Schmidt was expressed in local newspapers, such as the *Abendpost*, which in a blistering editorial on April 13, 1929, condemned the action of the Medical Association, but this was all of little avail, for the association was relentless in its decision to oust Dr. Schmidt.

This survey of Chicago's medical men of German extraction concludes with a short appreciation of the humanitarian Dr. Otto L. Schmidt, who was born on March 21, 1863 in Chicago as son of the above mentioned Dr. Ernst Schmidt and died in this city on August 20, 1935. Even though no detailed biography of Dr. Otto L. Schmidt exists, testimony of his enormously useful and unselfish life is given in several of the eulogies reprinted in volume thirty-three of the *Deutsch-Amerikanische Geschichtsblätter*, dedicated to his memory, as well as in various other documents.

After Dr. Otto L. Schmidt graduated from the Chicago Medical College in 1883, he served internships until 1885 in the Alexian Brothers Hospital and in the Cook County Infirmary at Dunning. From 1885 to 1887 he engaged in post-graduate work at the universities of Würzburg and Vienna. It is interesting to note that several of the professors under whom he had studied in Europe appealed to Dr. Schmidt for various contributions after World War I to which he generously responded. For instance, in a letter of July 13, 1922, Professor Ferdinand Blumenthal of Berlin sent a "thank you letter" for Dr. Schmidt's contribution of 15,000 Marks to the Berlin Institute of Cancer Research. After 1887 Dr. Otto L. Schmidt was a member of the Alexian Brother Hospital staff and a consulting physician at Michael Reese Hospital and the German Hospital, later known as the Grant Hospital. He was also an instructor of internal medicine at the Medical Department of Northwestern University from 1889 to 1892. Credit must be given to him for introducing about 1893 the first X-ray machine in Chicago. Between 1912 and 1914 he took a leading part in the introduction of the Civil Service Examination system at Cook County Hospital. Though a renowned expert in internal medicine, whose advice was widely sought, he modestly described himself in a contemporary *Who's Who in Medicine* as a "general practitioner."

While Dr. Schmidt's chosen profession was that of healing, he became just as famous as an outstanding historian. After he was elected president of the Mississippi Valley Historical Association in 1926, an honor which formerly had been bestowed only on professional historians of national fame, he was simultaneously head of five important historical bodies, the other four being the Illinois State Historical Society, the Illinois State Library Board, the Chicago Historical Society, and the German-American Historical Society. To mention a few of Dr. Schmidt's accomplishments for Illinois, he played an important part in the purchase of Starved Rock State Park in 1894, in establishing the Cahokia Mounds State Park from 1913 to 1926, in marking the Lincoln Circuit from 1916 to 1932, and in erecting in 1930 a monument to Wild Bill Hickock at his hometown, Troy Grove, Illinois. As far as Chicago's history is concerned, he was instrumental in the successful celebration of the Chicago Centennial in 1918, the All-American Exposition in 1919, the Johnny Appleseed Celebration in 1920, the Saumonauk and the Underground Railway Celebration in 1925, and the Chicago Century Celebration in 1932.

The Chicago Historical Museum contains many donations from Dr. Schmidt, such as over 100 volumes of Lincoln Association books, the so-called Schmidt collection of French manuscripts relating to fur trading in the West from 1735 to 1817, and the large collection of tools, implements and untensils of pioneer life in the "Schmidt Pioneer Room." Moreover, he sponsored many books on national and local history, such as Quaife's books on the Northwest Territory or Zeuch and Knight's book, *The Chicago Portage*, dedicated to Dr. Otto L. Schmidt. The Illinois governor, Henry Horner, characterized him well in his long eulogy in volume thirty-three of *Deutsch-Amerikanische Geschichtsblätter*, stating on page twenty: "Dr. Otto L. Schmidt personifies unselfish citizenship at its best, and he contributed more to historical scholarship than any individual of our time. Moreover, for as long as I can remember, he was my friend."

The unselfish citizenship to which Governor Horner referred could be witnessed in Dr. Schmidt's many substantial contributions in effort and money to alleviate suffering here and abroad, and in the part which he played as member of the board of education in the William McAndrew "trial." As a staunch champion of the defendant's rights, he bore the brunt of the city administration's attack against Superintendent McAndrew, and he finally resigned in sympathy when McAndrew was ousted unjustly because of former congress member Gorman's insidious lies. Though Dr. Schmidt never sought recognition for his diversifed work, the honors bestowed upon him abound. He received various honorary doctor's degrees: from Northwestern University in 1922, from Loyola University in 1930, and from the University of Würzburg in 1933. From Germany he received in 1914 the Order of the Red Eagle Fourth Class, in 1925 the Medal of Honor of the German Red Cross, and in 1928 he was honored with a medal from the "Deutsche Auslandsinstitut." The president of the Austrian Republic awarded him the Golden Decoration of Honor for his post-war relief work.

Chapter 12

The Chicago Germans and Music

In the field of music the Germans have played a prominent role in Chicago's history, listing in their ranks many ringing names of musical performers and institutions that deserve monographic treatment, but can be mentioned only briefly here, if at all. Most likely some of the early German settlers in the Chicago area did find time and had the inclination to practice music, but little is known about their musical activities. The first German musician in the Chicago area whom we know about seems to have been Nicholas Berdell (1802-83), Chicago's first professional musician. He came to Chicago in 1836, after having emigrated from his native Geisselberg in Bavaria to Buffalo in 1834. Soon after his arrival in Chicago he organized a small band with compatriots; including his nephew Charles Berdell, Dr. Valentin Boyer, Jacob Sauter, and Franz Klar; which played at many dances at Joseph Berg's inn on La Salle Street and other places, such as the "Ten Mile House" in South Englewood. In the 1840's he opened a dancing school on the North Side, and in 1852 he became justice of the peace for several years, having his office on the corner of Randolph and Halsted streets.

Many German bands must have been established soon after Berdell's in the 1840's, if we can rely on the testimony of the Virginia lawyer John L. Peyton, who visited and described Chicago in 1848. In talking about "picnicking," Peyton referred to numerous German bands. His comments are reprinted in the December 1954 issue of the periodical, *Chicago*, as follows:

Picnicking was by the by one of the Chicago winter amusements, and they are sometimes very amusing. They are organized somewhat after this fashion. A hotel from ten to fifteen miles in the country is secured for a particular evening and dinner prepared for six or seven o'clock, as the case may be. By this hour sleighs arrive from Chicago, driven by the beaux and freighted with the belles and their chaperons nestling under buffalo robes and other furs. After dinner, dancing commences, the services of one of the numerous German bands in Chicago having been previously secured.

There had been some amateur concerts in Chicago before 1850, such as the first one in Chicago's history by the ephemeral Chicago Harmonic Society on December 11 of 1835. However, the first significant series of concerts in Chicago was held in the Tremont Music Hall under the direction of the German Julius Dyhrenfurth, who had persuaded about a dozen New York musicians to come to Chicago. The 100-by-forty-foot hall housed on October 24, 1850 the first concert of the Dyhrenfurth Philharmonic Society. Eight subscription concerts were to put the organization on a permanent financial basis. The first program follows, reprinted from page 498 of the first volume of Andreas' *History of Chicago*:

1. Potpourri—Fille du Regiment. Orchestra.
2. Song. (With vocal quartette accompaniment.)
3. Violoncello Solo. Carlino Lensen.
4. Comic Song and Chorus . . . . Weinman.
5. The "Chicago Waltz" . . . . Lensen.

Composed for the occasion.—Orchestra.

6. Vocal Trio . . . . Messrs. Davis, Lumbard and Dunham.
7. Polka—French Song. . . . . Lensen.
8. Medley Overtures (Negro Airs). . . . . Dyhrenfurth.

Orchestra.

9. French Grand Chorus. . . . . Weinman.

(With full orchestral accompaniment, arranged from "Preciosa."

In the following years Dyhrenfurth gave "promenading concerts" both at City Hall and at the Tremont Music Hall. But it would be an injustice to remember him only as a promoter of music, for he was at the hub of Chicago's cultural interests for decades, as may be seen from the following account of his life from page 591 of the second volume of Andreas' *History of Chicago*:

Chicago owes a large portion of its musical culture to the influence and example of those, who, though not professional musicians, have possessed an extensive knowledge of music, with more than ordinary amateur's enthusiasm for its cultivation. Among these, the name of Julius Dyhrenfurth will always have great prominence. Identified as he was with extensive financial and educational interests, he yet found the time to encourage musical talent and to promote the success of some of Chicago's earliest musical societies. He was born at Breslau, Prussia, on the 9th of April, 1814. After receiving a liberal education, he engaged in commercial pursuits, and became manager of his firm's trade with England, Spain and Algeria. In 1837, he made an extensive tour of the United States, and was so deeply impressed with the great commercial resources and prospects of the country, that he determined to make it his future home. In 1843, he married, in London, Miss Caroline Thomson, an accomplished English lady, and three years afterward removed to the United States, selecting Chicago as his future home. After a brief and unsatisfactory experience as a farmer, he settled back into financial and commercial pursuits, entering the banking house of R. K. Swift, where he remained for several years. The system of keeping banking accounts at that time was very defective, needlessly laborious, and, at the best, extremely inaccurate. He devised an accurate system of bookkeeping, never since improved upon, and which remains in use by all the banks of the city to this day. The financial crash of 1857 carried with it the fortune of Mr. Dyhrenfurth, and left him, with thousands of others, financially stranded; but with characteristic energy he cast about for a new opening in business, and, believing in his skill as an educator, resolved to open a commercial school. In 1858, he opened his school in Waukegan, but a year or two later removed it to Chicago, where he conducted it, with constantly increasing success, for many years. He greatly enlarged his original plan, after a year or two's experience, and conducted a high school, a young ladies' seminary, and a commerical college; and his ability made them all of the highest character. Among other things, he perfected a new system of bookkeeping, which he published in 1869. It is a system so intelligible and admirable, that it has come into extensive use, not only in Chicago, but throughout the country. He suffered heavily by the great fire of 1871, which destroyed both his home and the buildings occupied by his school. During all the years he has resided in Chicago, he has given largely of his time and means to promote a general taste for music. One of his first efforts was to induce a number of musicians to leave the East, and settle in this city. With these he organized an orchestra, under his personal direction, giving concerts every winter for a number of years. These concerts were among the most fashionable entertainments of Chicago in early days.

Concurrently with Dyhrenfurth's promenading concerts sporadic concerts were presented by the Germania Orchestra, a travelling ensemble which consisted of such outstanding musicians as

Carl Bergmann, Adolph Jaeger, Henry Band and H. Ahner. When this orchestra dissolved in 1853, some of its members, including Bergmann and Ahner, remained in Chicago and provided an impetus to music. Ahner gave popular Saturday afternoon concerts at the Metropolitan Hall at the corner of La Salle and Randolph streets, and some of the others organized the Great Western Band under the direction of Christoph Romanus. This band experienced splits and metamorphoses before it regrouped in 1864 under the name of Great Western Light Guard Band to present popular concerts under various directors for many years. According to the *Tribune* of July 10, 1904, the immensely popular Johnny Hand (1829-1916), who directed it for over fifty years, entertained on July 9, 1904 nearly 100,000 at a concert in Lincoln Park.

With the general influx to Chicago came also outstanding German musicians with great organizing talents. One of them, Hans Balatka (1826-1899), was strictly speaking not German, having been born in Moravia, but he must be mentioned, for he allied himself with the German element to elevate music in Chicago to a high artistic level. After he came for the first time from Milwaukee in 1857, he not only directed several organizations, such as the Philharmonic Society in 1860, but also directed national and international German music festivals of the "North American Saengerbund" in Chicago in the years 1857, 1868, and 1881.

The first music festival in 1857 was a rather moderate affair with 250 singers and a thirty-five man orchestra in which, of the ten participating singing clubs from four states, the three sponsoring ones were from Chicago. But the festival of June 1868 was a grand affair. Thirty-six singing clubs from the United States and eight delegations from Germany provided a mass chorus of 1,200 singers, accompanied by a 100 member orchestra, which held three concerts at the "Rink" on Wabash Avenue and Jackson Street. The financial profit of 4,000 dollars was divided among seven sponsoring Chicago clubs. The music festival of June 1881 was the most magnificent held in America up to its time. A 2,200 member male chorus and a 1,200 member mixed chorus, accompanied by a 150 man orchestra, performed such works as Max Bruch's "Salamis" and Beethoven's "Ninth Symphony." World famous soloists, such as Miss Cary or Herr Candidus were paid $18,700. Madame Peschka-Leutner from Hamburg alone received 5,000 dollars for her appearance. The unfortunate news of President Garfield's ultimately fatal assassination attempt put an early end to this festival. The enterprising Balatka also established the Balatka Musical College in 1879, which still flourished about 1940.

The Chicago Germans have played a prominent role in musical education on various levels. After vocal music had been instituted in Chicago's public schools in December of 1841, many Germans were hired as music teachers, such as Franz Lumbard in 1847 and Christoph Plagge in 1853. With regard to conservatories, besides Balatka, the name of Florence Ziegfeld (1841-1923) must be mentioned. This name now conjures up to most Chicagoans the lavish extravagance of the "Ziegfeld Follies," which were founded by the second generation Florence Ziegfeld and immortalized in at least two movies. But at the turn of the century, when stars like Will Rogers, Fanny Zeisler, W. C. Fields and Ina Clair had not yet made the Ziegfeld Follies a household word, the name Ziegfeld referred to the proprietor of one of the biggest and most significant conservatories in the world, the Chicago Academy of Music, later known as the Chicago Musical College.

Ziegfeld was born on June 10, 1841 in Jever, a small town about thirty miles north of Oldenburg, and came to the United States for the first time in 1858. After completing his studies in Leipzig, Dr. Ziegfeld, declining an offer to direct a newly established conservatory in Russia, came to Chicago in 1863, where he founded the Chicago Academy of Music four years later. At that time this conservatory had 69 students, but by 1905 over 3,350 attended. When Florence Ziegfeld died in May of 1923, the list of honorary pall bearers read like an excerpt from *Who's Who*.

The Chicago Symphony Orchestra, at the present time "the world's best symphony orchestra which has rescued the city from the shadows of Al Capone," according to Claudia Cassidy in *Chicago History's* spring issue of 1972, was founded by the German-born Theodor Thomas and was composed almost exclusively of Germans until World War I. Thomas was born on October 11, 1835 in the small town of Esens, forty miles northwest of Oldenburg, gave a violin concert at the age of six, and came with his family to the United States in 1845. Because he had been performing in many orchestras since his childhood, he never received much of a formal education. Nevertheless, several universities, among them Yale, have conferred on him the honorary "Doctor of Music" degree.

In 1862 he organized the Thomas Orchestra which gave popular concerts in New York's Irving Hall for a long time. Beginning in 1869, he travelled to major American cities, including Chicago, with a fifty-four member orchestra. At that time he did more than any other individual to popularize Wagner's works in the United States. After a stay of thirteen years in Cincinnati, during which he gave many series of concerts in Chicago, he came to live in Chicago permanently in 1890, bringing with him an ensemble of sixty artists, to direct an orchestra known as the Theodore Thomas Orchestra until 1913, when it received its present name. The Theodore Thomas Orchestra performed in the Auditorium until 1904, when the dream of Thomas was finally realized in that his orchestra received a home of its own. The dedication of the magnificent Orchestra Hall, in which Thomas received an enthusiastic ovation, was his final triumph, for a few weeks later, on January 4, 1905, he died.

Upon Thomas' death his former assistant Frederick Stock (1872-1942) assumed the position of conductor, which he held until his death, except for a short span in 1918 and 1919, when war hysteria forced him to resign temporarily. Dr. Stock was born in Jülich, twenty miles west of Cologne, on November 11, 1872. After eight years with the Cologne Municipal Orchestra he joined the Theodore Thomas Orchestra in 1895 as a viola player upon Thomas' request. He was also a composer of note, of whose many compositions, "Symphonic Variations" was conducted in 1903 by Thomas. Among the many recognitions which he received should be mentioned the decoration of "Chevalier" by the French Legion of Honor in 1925 and honorary doctor's degrees from Northwestern University in 1915, from the University of Michigan in 1924, the University of Chicago in 1925, and from Cornell College at Mount Vernon, Iowa, in 1927. As general music director of the Chicago World's Fair in 1933, he demonstrated to many visitors the superb quality of Chicago's musical performers.

Famous artists of German extraction were engaged by Thomas' orchestra. Around the turn of the century the talented Fanny Bloomfield-Zeisler performed many times with his orchestra. On January 23, 1903 the *Tribune* reported that she appeared with the Thomas Orchestra and drew the largest audience of the concert season. This is not surprising, for the audience wanted to see the star who often made newspaper headlines. On November 23, 1902 Chicago papers reported that in Paris an audience had rioted when the Chicago pianist Fanny Bloomfield-Zeisler had attempted to play the "G Minor Concerto" by Charles Camille Saint-Saëns, whom the Paris musicians' union was boycotting. She finished the concert after the police ejected the rioters.

The Chicago Symphony Orchestra attracted many famous musicians to Chicago, both temporarily and permanently. On March 30, 1904 the Chicago newspapers were full of reports that the famous German composer Richard Strauss had arrived in Chicago to rehearse his own works to be presented in concerts during the next few days. It was a gala affair when a few days later, on April 4, Mrs. Potter Palmer opened the art gallery in her home for a concert by Strauss; his wife, the famous singing star Pauline Strauss de Alma; and Paul Maeyer; the proceeds of the concert were to go to the Russian branch of the Red Cross. The renowned contralto, Ernestine Schumann-Heink (1861-1936), made her American debut in "Lohengrin" at Chicago in 1898. The appreciation of her talents by Chicagoans is illustrated strikingly in newspaper accounts of December 18, 1918, which reported that, when Madame Schumann-Heink and two of her sons in uniform were spotted in a box at a performance of the musical "Hitchy-Koo" at the Opera Hall, the show was stopped and the famous contralto obligingly sang several arias to quiet the applause of the appreciative audience. Ironically, most of her compatriots were at the same time considered barbarian "Huns" by many Chicagoans.

Even though Chicago's German element was active primarily in the traditional modes of music, there were some exceptions, as can be seen in George Bushnell's article, "When Jazz Came to Chicago," in the spring 1971 issue of *Chicago History*. Although jazz was the black man's domain when it was practically a Chicago monopoly between 1917 and 1929, a musician of German extraction became a national hit. Leon Bismarck "Bix" Beiderbecke (1903-31), was extremely popular between 1923 and 1925 with his band, "Bix Beiderbecke and the Wolverines." When he died from pneumonia in 1931 the loss of this immense musical talent was mourned by the musical world.

The numerous German singing clubs of Chicago contributed much to the promotion of popular music. Beginning in 1853, the New York Italian Opera Company gave guest performances in Chicago. This was in the wake of an initial attempt by a local group to present operas which ended in disaster when Mr. Rice's First Theatre burned down on July 30, 1850, after the first act of "Sonnambula," the first opera presented in Chicago. But there were also local groups to present operas, among them some German singing clubs. The "Chicago Maennergesangverein," founded in 1850, performed several operas under the direction of Emil Rein, Julius Unger and Heinrich Weinman, among them "Czar und Zimmermann" and "Alessandro Stradella." These operas were presented between 1855 and 1858 in the German House, a center of the German social life which was erected at Wells and Indiana streets in 1854/55, "to escape persecution" from adherents of the nativistic Know-Nothing party. In 1854 another German singing club was founded, the "Freie Sängerbund."

A highlight to which these clubs contributed, with a chorus of sixty singers and an orchestra of thirty members, was the performance of Mozart's "Requiem" in September of 1860 at Bryan Hall, later the Grand Opera House. From the enthusiasm generated by the successful performance of this work the Philharmonic Society originated in October of 1860. It continued to give monthly concerts from 1860 to 1865 in Bryan Hall and later also in Crosby's Opera House, presenting symphonies of such famous composers as Beethoven, Mozart, Haydn and Mendelssohn.

Perhaps the most significant German singing club ever founded in Chicago was the "Germania Maennerchor" which still exists as one of Chicago's oldest clubs. This club had a somber beginning, being conceived at Abraham Lincoln's bier. The Germans had a special affection for President Lincoln and they were crushed by the news of his assassination. Chicagoans of German extraction had the opportunity to express their grief strikingly. When the murdered President Lincoln lay in state at the Chicago Court House on May 1 and 2 of 1865, some 300 German singers chanted dirges. They had been organized by the prominent German Otto Lob. According to a report in the *Staatszeitung* of November 12, 1871, Otto Lob seemed to have been involved in most German singing clubs of the time, for he received national recognition as director of the following German singing clubs of Chicago: "Germania Maennerchor, Concordia Singing Society, Orpheus, Swiss Male Choir, Abendlied Chor," and "Echo Quartett." Of the more than 300 singers, a number decided to form a permanent German singing club, in order to further German music, which had suffered a setback during the unsettled times of the Civil War. On May 31, 1865 this club was organized well enough under its first president, John G. Gindele, to present vocal and orchestral music at the Crosby Opera House.

The "Germania Maennerchor" was a parent, yet in 1865, to the "Concordia Singing Society," which had as its first president Francis A. Hoffmann, a successful banker. Germania was directed by Hans Balatka and Concordia by Otto Lob. Beneficial competition between the two clubs induced them to pursue ambitious goals and thus helped to elevate music in Chicago to a high level. In 1870 the "Germania Maennerchor" performed "Freischütz" and "Alessandro Stradella" in Crosby's Opera House, while Concordia offered Mozart's "Zauberflöte" during the same year. According to the contemporary account of Eugen Seeger on page 287 in his book, *Chicago*, this city has never before seen such well performed operas. Previously, operas had had at the most a forty-member chorus and a thirty-man orchestra, while these two clubs employed in their operas 100 to 120 member choruses and sixty-man orchestras.

The competition of these two clubs was beneficial in yet other ways, in that new singing clubs were formed because of their rivalry. In 1866 at the song festival in Indianapolis, Chicago was represented by five German singing clubs, and new ones were founded with increasing rapidity. In 1868 the long surviving "Senefelder Liederkranz" was formed, and on August 19, 1869, several Germans of the West side founded the influential Orpheus Singing Club.

This club was presided over for many years by Franz Amberg, who was born on September 1, 1837, some twenty miles southeast of Frankfurt on the Main, in the village of Oberndorf. After learning the trade of wagonmaker, he emigrated in 1857 to America, immediately coming to his uncle, Adam Amberg, who had settled in Chicago in 1833. For three years Amberg worked in his trade before he entered the first Illinois cavalry regiment to fight in Virginia and Maryland during the Civil War. He returned to Chicago after three years of service and joined the Board of Trade while he owned a grain business on the West Side. After the Great Fire of 1871 he possessed a lucrative renting stable at 156-158 West Washington Street.

Amberg was a prominent public servant. Governor Oglesby named him member of the Penitentiary Commission for Joliet from 1880 to 1883. In the year of 1888 he was elected city clerk, being the only successful Republican candidate in that year. After an unsuccessful candidacy for city treasurer in 1889, he was named city collector for 1891 and 1892 by Mayor Washburn.

But Amberg's main merit lies in his furtherance of German music in Chicago. Before he had helped to found the Orpheus Singing Club, he was a member of various German singing clubs, joining the "Freie Saengerbund" already in 1858, one year after his arrival in America. He was elected honorary president of the "North American Saengerbund" for the grandious third Chicago German music festival in 1881 and stimulated the foundation of the club United Male Choruses of Chicago which consisted of twelve singing clubs. An inkling of the great appreciation of Franz Amberg may be obtained by reading the report on the music festival of 1881 in the *Staatszeitung* of August 27, 1881. He was enthusiastically praised as the driving spirit behind Chicago's German musical world. It was also decided that medals should be bought for Amberg from the $350 profit of the total income of $116,000, as a token of gratitude.

The devastating Great Fire in October of 1871 put shackles on the development of the Germans' musical culture. All but the Orpheus Singing Club lost their entire possessions and equipment, permitting them to barely survive. Some German singing clubs, such as the "Oratorio Society," were forced to cease their activities altogether. Probably the first German singing club to be founded after the Great Fire was the "Fidelia Club." Heinrich von Oppen, its director for 50 years, recalled in the *Abendpost* of July 8, 1925 that his club was formed sometime in 1872 in George Blein's Tavern at 58 Clybourn Avenue.

Von Oppen had emigrated from Germany in the spring of 1866 as a seventeen-year-old youth on the steamer *Germania*, which required fifteen days for the voyage. He came to his uncle in Chicago who had a cigar business in the Hamilton Hotel at Clark and North Water streets. After his uncle died in 1868, he found employment as the musical director at the National Theater on Clybourn Avenue, the best German theater in Chicago at the time. He also taught piano and violin, performed in various orchestras, and directed several singing clubs, among them the "Fidelia Club," the Swiss Male Chorus, the Harmony Singing Society of Lake View, and the Harugari Union of Musicians. With especial pride von Oppen recalled that at the peace celebration of the Franco-Prussian War in May of 1871 he had worn one of the twenty uniforms from the German crack guards which the German Emperor Wilhelm had sent to the Chicago Germans.

Ten years after the 1871 conflagration, Chicago's singing clubs rallied to a successful third music festival in 1881, but the attempts by Balatka to form a strong central singing society failed, and the mushrooming small clubs were unable to perform highly artistic works. By 1900 there existed over 200 German singing clubs in Chicago, loosely organized under three central clubs.

The number of German singing clubs continued to fluctuate in Chicago's history, new ones were being formed while others dwindled to nonexistence, but few of them transcended mediocrity. One German singing club which attained a reputation for high artistic achievements in its public concerts was the "Chicago Singverein," founded in 1910 to present German musical masterpieces. In the third season nearly 300 voices presented three outstanding concerts, the last one for the benefit of veterans of the 1870/71 Franco-Prussian War, under a board of directors composed of prominent Chicago German-Americans, as the following list shows: President—Charles H. Wacker, Vice President—Ernest J. Kruetgen and Mrs. H. A. Kirchhoff, Secretary—John Koelling,

Treasurer—Karl Eitel, Librarian—Gustav A. Hoffmann, Assistant Treasurer—William R. Ludwig, Musical Director—William Boeppler, and Business Manager—Mrs. Harriet Martin Snow. The office of the club was located in the Steinway Hall building at 64 East Van Buren Street.

According to the biography of the club's renowned musical director in the *Abendpost* of November 27, 1927, William Boeppler (1863-1928) founded the Milwaukee Symphony Orchestra before he organized the "Chicago Singverein" and was the only American citizen to become a member of the Beethoven House in Bonn. During the 1913/14 season the club's public concerts were performed by 600 singers, but the imminent clash of nations prevented the "Singverein's" maximum development. The period during World War I was exceedingly detrimental to German music and singing. War hysteria forced many clubs into suspension of their activities, which some of them did not survive. No German songs could be heard in public in Chicago from 1918 to 1921.

Gradually German songs were heard again in public concerts, as for instance in the Gala Charity Concert by the "Chicago Singverein" in May of 1922. The proceeds were used to feed starving children in post-war Germany and to support Chicago's floundering German Theater. It was a great stimulus for the Chicago German singing clubs when, after a lapse of forty-three years, the North American Singers' Union held its fourth Chicago music festival in May of 1924 to which 151 German singing clubs from all over the United States sent 3,870 singers. The next two Chicago music festivals were held in June of 1938 and in June of 1949. According to the Chicago Recreation Commission, at the 1938 festival more than 10,000 choral singers, representing 186 singing societies, participated in five concerts at the International Amphitheatre. But these figures disagree with the official figures given in the 1949 program of the North American Singer's Union, which gave the official number as 181 attending clubs with 5,882 singers. In view of this exaggeration by the Chicago Recreation Commission, one must be sceptical of their estimate that by 1934 more than 300 German men's, women's, and mixed singing societies existed in Chicago. More realistic figures may be found in the *Abendpost* of July 6, 1935, which gave a survey of at least 452 German clubs in Chicago. Of this number, 92 singing societies were listed, which consisted of 59 male singing clubs such as "Orpheus," twenty-three female singing societies such as "Almira Damenchor," five amalgamated choruses such as "Vereinigte Maennerchöre von Chicago," and five mixed choruses such as "Gemischter Chor Eintracht."

World War II was not nearly as devastating for the German element and German musical culture as the first one. During World War I the Germania Club had to change its name to Chicago Lincoln Club, whereas in the second World War its members were able to conduct their activities in near normalcy. Nevertheless, the number of German singing clubs continued to decline, and even a momentary upward trend after the war, due to a large influx of German immigrants, could not stay the inexorable decrease of interest in German singing. A report in the *Sonntagspost* of March 24, 1974, shows this clearly: When the German singing clubs of the Chicago area sent delegates to Rosco Hall to plan the future 49th music festival of the North American Singers' Union in Chicago, only ten active clubs were represented, namely "Harlem Maennerchor, Schiller Liedertafel, Elmhurst Maennerchor, Rheinischer Gesangverein, Schubert Liedertafel, Schwäbischer Sängerbund, Arion Maennerchor, Schiller Liedertafel von der Südseite, Frohsinn Maennerchor," and "Schleswig-Holstein Sängerbund." Another revealing "sign of the times" for the declining interest of German songs in Chicago may be seen in an account of the 80th anniversary celebration of the "Schwäbischer Sängerbund" in the *Sonntagspost* of April 28, 1974. The concert by the club's seventy members, directed by Ludwig Lohmiller, included many German favorites, such as "Alte Kameraden," but the audience was most appreciative when the American folk song "Cindy" was presented.

Chapter 13

The Chicago Germans' Literature and Theater

In the field of literature and the dramatic arts, Chicago's German element has played a role isolated from the city's general cultural activities. This is understandable in view of the fact that its medium of expression normally was the German language. But in spite of its isolated position, Chicago's German element has played a prominent role in the literary domain, able to obtain the attention of the German-speaking community.

Even today, interest in German-American literature still exists. This is revealed in various articles on German-American authors in such journals as *German-American Studies*, founded in 1968, or publications like Robert E. Ward's 1969 anthology of German literature in America, entitled *Deutsche Lyrik in Amerika. Eine Auswahl.* However, this interest is minimal in comparison to pre-World War I days when war hysteria had not yet dealt a deadly blow to everything German.

Before World War I Chicago was known equally well for the publication and creation of an enormous quantity of German-American literature and for the sustained efforts of its German element to elevate the position of German-American literature. With regard to this, one of the Chicago German element's most ambitious undertakings must be mentioned, namely the attempt by members of the Germania Club to gather the scattered publications of German-American authors and to make selections of their literary works accessible to a wide reading audience. Starting in 1888, the popular German-American poet, Konrad Nies, and his co-editor, Hermann Rosenthal, began to edit volumes of German-

American literature, but their undertaking failed in 1890 after two volumes had appeared. Soon after their unsuccessful venture, the Germania Club of Chicago decided to continue their work on a broader scope by establishing first a repository of all German-American literary works.

The job of collecting the widely dispersed works was relegated to a library committee, consisting of the president, Harry Rubens, and the members, Joseph Brucker, Washington Hesing, Frederick Hild, Dr. Karl Pietsch, and Dr. Gustav A. Zimmermann. In April of 1892 the publication of a survey with representative examples of the gathered material ensued. It had the title, *Deutsch in Amerika. Beiträge zur Geschichte der Deutsch-Amerikanischen Literatur.* According to Harry Rubens, in the preface, the selected examples were taken from several hundred books and booklets, encompassing the gamut of German-American literature.

At least nineteen residents of Chicago were included among the representative authors by the editor Dr. Gustav A. Zimmermann, Superintendent of German Studies in Chicago's public schools. Of course, these nineteen people do not include all of the city's German-American authors. Neither does the following list gleaned from many publications, especially *Deutsch-Amerikanische Geschichtsblätter.* However incomplete this roster may be, it offers an inkling of the large number of German-American authors active in Chicago at one time:

Balatka, Hans
Berens, August
Bertram, Agnes
Binder, Heinrich
Boettcher, Dorothea
Brachvogel, Udo
Brandau, H.
Brentano, Lorenz
Butz, Casper
Dietz, Johann
Dietzsch, Emil
Drescher, Martin
Eberhard, Johann
Eberhardt, Max
Ende, Heinrich
Ernst, Otto
Esselein, Christian
Feistkorn, Wilhelm
Fick, Heinrich
Gauss, E.F.
Gerhardt, Paul
Goebel, Julius
Gross, S.E.
Haering, Theodor
Haupt, Ullrich
Hempel, C.J.
Hercz, Arthur
Hielscher, Theodor
Horn, Fritz
Illing, C.H.
Kinkel, Gottfried
Kurzer, Julius
Lafrentz, Ferdinand
Loebel, Paul
Loewe, H.
Maerklin, Edmund
Mels, A.
Muhlmann, A.
Mueller, Max
Nies, Konrad

Peltzer, Otto	Seebaum, J.A.
Rittershaus, Emil	Stern, Max
Rueckheim, Mathilde	Vocke, Wilhelm
Ruhland, Hermann	Wahl, Christian
Schenck, Leopold	Wiedinger, Karl
Schmidt, Julius	Winckler, Willibald
Schmidt, Ernst	

The majority of these authors remained obscure, and their literary works, often composed for such occasions as weddings, birthdays and similar festivities, cannot be declared great by any criterion. However, there have been some writers among them who, though now forgotten, have attained national and even international fame.

Several of these German-American authors, such as Lorenz Brentano, Casper Butz and Emil Dietzsch, came in the train of the many intellectuals that fled to this country after their unsuccessful uprising against Germany's aristocracy in 1848. To be sure, prior to 1848 there must have been attempts by Chicago area German immigrants to express their experiences in poetic works, but little survives. Thus, the influx of the forty-eighters represents the beginning of German-American literature in Chicago.

Among these forty-eighters one of the most renowned poets was Casper Butz. He was born in Hagen, Westphalia, on October 23, 1825, and had a rather turbulent youth before he became editor of the *Hagener Zeitung*. Because he lent his pen to the 1848 Revolution, he had to seek safety in flight. On his escape to America in 1849 he saw wanted posters alerting police officers to arrest him, a "dangerous revolutionary spirit," for his part in the revolution. He had been singled out as the leader in the storming of the armory at Iserlohn. After he came to Chicago in 1854, he became an outspoken critic of slavery in the *Staatszeitung*. He occupied his first public office, that of state legislator, in 1858. The many offices which he held were crowned with the office of City clerk of Chicago from 1876 to 1878. He died on October 17, 1885 while staying with his two sons in Des Moines, Iowa.

Though prominent in public affairs, Casper Butz became famous as a spirited poet who employed his pen in the fight against slavery and in various other public questions. Most of his innumerable poems on a broad range of topics were published in *Deutsche Monatshefte*, a journal edited by Butz in 1864 and 1865 as a continuation of the journal *Atlantis* by the gifted Christian Esselein, and in two other volumes, *Gedichte eines Deutsch-Amerikaners* (Poems of a German-American), Chicago 1879, and

Grossvater-Lieder (Grandfather Songs), Chicago, 1887. An indication of his literary interests may be seen in the fact that when his library was destroyed in the Great Fire of 1871, Chicago's German newspapers lamented the loss at great lengths.

The following short selections from his works will perhaps provide an inkling of his poetry. No attempt was made to render metric effects in the translations. Upon his escape from Germany, Butz, on board of the sailing vessel in LeHavre, expressed feelings which mirror the lot of innumerable men like him who exiled themselves or were banished for their attempts to create what they thought would be a better, freer Germany. Only a few stanzas from the long poem "Abschied vom Vaterland" (Taking Leave of the Fatherland) can be reproduced here. After describing the agony of departing from everything dear to him to face an uncertain future by seeking exile in a strange land, he addresses the following moving verses to personified Germany:

Wer dich am meisten geliebt, o Land,
An dem unsre Herzen noch hängen,
Den hast du ja immer verfolgt, verbannt
Auf allen Wegen und Gängen. . . .

So leb wohl denn! wir stehen gelehnt am Mast
Und zerdrücken die Trän' unterm Lide;
Doch stehen wir aufrecht, als Männer, gefasst,
Ob's brennend im Herzen auch siede.

Wir sahen dich sinken,—der Freiheit Stern,
Im Blute der besten Brüder,
Wir sahn deinen letzten Glanz von fern
—Doch einst, dann sehn wir dich wieder.

Dann steigst du empor aus der blutigen Gruft,
Um die Nebel des Drucks zu verjagen,
Dann lenkst du gebietend in klarer Luft
Deinen glühenden Sonnenwagen.

Dann staunen die Völker, o! Vaterland—
—Und wir, wir werden nicht säumen . . .
Leb' wohl! wenn wir auch bis dahin verbannt,
Lebst du fort doch in unseren Träumen!

(Who has loved you most dearly, o Land,
Which still captivates our hearts,
That one you have always persecuted, banished
From all ways and paths. . . .

Farewell then! We lean against the mast
And suppress a tear under the lid.

But we stand like men upright, composed,
Even though our hearts ardently burn.

We have seen you fall—the Star of Freedom,
In the blood of the best brothers,
We saw your last glow from afar
—Yet one day, then we will see you again.

Then you will rise from the bloody crypt,
To disperse the clouds of oppression,
Then you will guide imperiously in clear air
your glowing sun chariot.

Then the nations will be amazed, o Fatherland!—
And we, we will not delay . . .
Farewell! Though we are exiled until then,
You continue to enliven our dreams!)

Once in America, Butz expresses in his works the struggle to adjust to altered conditions. He cannot and will not divorce himself from the memories of happier childhood days and from his cultural heritage, but his efforts to fuse two cultures are fraught with seemingly insurmountable difficulties. In a dedicatory poem to Emil Rittershaus, another German-American poet, Butz depicts the lot of the German-American poet whose attempts to wrest a meaningful, lasting expression of existence from grim reality in his mother tongue seem to be a futile, unappreciated undertaking both in his adopted and in his childhood homeland:

Stets ist, im ew'gen Schwinden, Werden,
Des Dichters Los ein Los der Pein,
Doch wohl das härtste Los auf Erden
Ist hier, ein deutscher Dichter sein. . . .
Und Deutschland hat genug der Sänger,
Verbannte Dichter kennt es nicht.

(Always in the eternal waning and waxing,
The lot of the poet is a lot of pain,
But probably the most difficult lot on earth
Is to be a German poet in this land. . . .
And Germany has enough bards,
Exiled poets it does not know.)

Butz was not content with composing idyllic poems praising the beauty of America's landscape or the joys of private life, though he wrote many of them, such as "Am Niagara, 1852" (On the Niagara Falls, 1852) or "Der Grosspapa und sein Enkel" (Grandpa and his Grandchild). He took an active part in many public issues like slavery. In fact, he was an ardent abolitionist who repeatedly lashed out at "America's bane." In his long poem, "Zum 4. July, 1855—Den Deutschen gewidtmet" (Concerning the Fourth of July, 1855—Dedicated to the Germans), he castigates what to him seemed an offensive outburst of chauvinism that contrasted sharply with slavery. After describing different expressions of jingo patriotism in which all over the Union speeches are offered to "Freedom's Might" he contrasts the Independence Day depiction with a scene from a Southern plantation where unfortunate slaves hurl curses at their hypocritical oppressors. Turning to the Germans, he exhorts them to do everything in their power to eliminate this evil and to refrain from celebrating until this goal has been reached. He waxes prophetic in stating that in the future, when the Union will be embroiled in a struggle to eradicate human bondage in the South, the Germans, now despised by the Know-Nothings, will be in the foremost ranks in the Union's efforts to extirpate slavery.

In his poem, "Der zweite Dezember 1859" (The Second of December, 1859), Butz eulogizes John Brown, "who hallows the gallows" through his deed. When Civil War erupted, Butz was a stalwart supporter of the Union. In poems, such as "Virginia," "An Abraham Lincoln" (To Abraham Lincoln), "Deutsche im Bürgerkrieg" (Germans in the Civil War), "Sumter, 1865," and "An Sigel" (To Sigel) he deals with the internecine clash and does not tire of emphasizing how indispensable the Germans were in bringing about the eventual victory for the North. Many an apologetic or even belligerent poem directed at the Know-Nothings, who wanted to curtail the German immigrants' rights or liberties, stresses not only the Germans' important role in preserving the Union, but also their various vital contributions to America's development.

Butz often expresses benign interest in Germany's affairs, even though bitterness about having been forced to flee pervades his poems at times, as in "An Deutschland" (To Germany). Nevertheless, when news of the Franco-Prussian War came to Chicago in 1870, Butz enthusiastically embraced Germany's cause by composing, on behalf of Germany's struggle, a long, somewhat bombastic poem. It appeared in practically all German newspapers here and abroad and was reprinted again and again at times of crises, as during the early World War I days. It begins as follows:

Wenn Wünsche Kugeln wären, wenn Blitz und Donnerschlag
Der längst Verbannten Zürnen, jetzt am Entscheidungstag,

Wie würd' der Donner rollen gewaltig über's Meer
Für Deutschland eine Salve und für sein tapf'res Heer!
Vergessen ist ja Alles, vergessen jede Noth,
Vergessen jedes Urtheil, ob es auch sprach: der Tod!
Für dich, o Muttererde, du Land der Herrlichkeit,
Auch deine fernen Söhne, sie stehen mit im Streit!

(If wishes were bullets, if lightning and thunder [could express]
The wrath of the long-time-exiles, now on the crucial day,
How powerfully thunder would boom across the sea
A salvo for Germany and for its brave army!
Forgotten is all, forgotten every distress,
Forgotten each judgment, though it decreed: Execution!
For you, o Mother Earth, you land of magnificence,
Your distant sons also stand with you in the fight.)

Emil Dietzsch (1829-90) was another forty-eighter who must be mentioned as a well-known author. He was born near Kaiserslautern, the scion of generations of preachers. While he studied pharmacy and philology at the University of Munich, he was drawn into the revolutionary movement and had to flee first to Switzerland and then to America, coming to Chicago in 1853. As soon as he arrived in Chicago, he became one of the most prominent leaders of the German element, building up a profitable business in his pharmacy. When the Conflagration of 1871 destroyed all of his possessions, he devoted himself primarily to public life, serving as coroner of Cook County from 1872 to 1878 and later for several years as deputy sheriff.

His poems were not nearly as bellicose as those of Butz. He addressed himself more to the everyday problems of life which confronted the German immigrant and, perhaps on account of that, became more popular with the masses. As most German-American poets did, Dietzsch expressed a reserved appreciation for America's many positive characteristics, but he fondly indulged in reminiscences of happier childhood days in the fatherland. The following last stanza of his poem, "An mein Vaterland" (To my Fatherland), shows a smoldering yearning for Germany:

Doch wär hier selbst ein Paradies
Mit allen seinen Freuden,
Das Manchen schon vergessen liess
Vom Vaterland das Scheiden:
Ich bin in Freuden und in Noth
Von Herzen deutsch geblieben
Und werd' dich, Deutschland, bis zum Tod
Als treuer Sohn auch lieben.

(Even if a paradise were here
With all its joys,
Which many a man already made forget
The separation from the Fatherland:
I have in joys and in distress
Remained at heart a German
And will, Germany, until death
Love you as a loyal son.)

In poems, such as "Fröhlich Pfalz, Gott erhalt's" (Happy Palatinate, May God Preserve it), Dietzsch did not even shirk dialect to attain a folksy flavor. In his hilarious praise of beer, "Nur keine Biervergeudung" (Whatever You Do, Just Don't Waste Beer), he lets the devil, also addressed with the monstrous epithet, "Schwefelgerücheverbreiter" (Sulphursmellspreader), tempt Luther, who—angered by Satan's impertinent seduction attempts—feels the urge to hurl a container of beer at the infernal visitor, but checks himself in the last second and flings an inkwell instead of the precious cup. Dietzsch also became known as a playwright to Chicagoans, for his melodramatic play, *Die Druiden* (The Druids), was performed on several occasions in Chicago's German theaters. Moreover, he tried his hand at various historical accounts, such as *Kraft und Stoff, aus der Geschichte des deutschen Volkes* (Strength and Matter, Concerning the Story of the German Nation), Chicago, 1884.

Other forty-eighters who rose to prominence as poets should perhaps be mentioned, but the biographies and poetic works of most of them are monotonously similar. Practically all forty-eighters dabbled in literature, but their products usually did not survive them. After the era of the forty-eighters, every so often certain Chicago Germans became well-known to the German community as bards, such as Maximilian Eberhardt, Johann Dietz, Julius Schmidt and Wilhelm Vocke. Johann Dietz (1835-1908) was a printing shop owner whose poem, "Am Grabe Lincolns" (At the Grave of Lincoln), was widely read. His poem "Chicago" was included in Chicago's public school German readers.

Mention must be made of the fact that at least four women poets were represented in Chicago's German element. Mathilde Rueckheim, wife of the owner of the Rueckheim chocolate factory, composed toward the end of the nineteenth century many religious poems which were published in book form in 1900 under the title, *Von seiner Fülle* (Of His Plenty), of which the following stanza from the poem "Gott wird abwischen alle Tränen" (God Will Dry all Tears) may serve as as representative example:

Am Sarge streut man frische Blumen,
Warum denn nur im Leben nicht?
Warum so sparsam mit der Liebe,
Und warten, bis das Herze bricht?
Den Todten freuen keine Blumen,
Im Sarge fühlt man keinen Schmerz;
Würd' man im Leben Liebe üben,
Es lebte länger manches Herz . . .

(At the bier they lavish fresh flowers,
But why not in life?
Why so stingy with love,
And wait till the heart breaks?
The dead ones cannot enjoy flowers,
In the coffin one feels no pain;
If more love were given in life,
Many a heart would live longer . . .)

Agnes Bertram, who was born in Westphalia and lived after 1893 in Chicago as the wife of the Protestant minister E. Bertram, published in the October 1903 issue of *Deutsch-Amerikanische Geschichtsblätter* her first four poems, which are charming in their simple, childlike style, as a few stanzas of "Abendregen" (Evening Rain) will show:

Stiller Abendregen! Wahrer Gottessegen! Rauschest still hernieder, Bringst uns Kühlung wieder.	(Silent evening rain! Truly a blessing of God! You swish down softly, And bring us again refreshment.
Alles war verstorben. Alles schien verdorben. Blümlein hing das Köpfchen; Letzt' nach einem Tröpfchen . . .	All was dead. All seemed ruined. Little flower bent its little head; Gasped for a droplet . . .
Blümlein hebt das Köpfchen, Weinet helle Tröpfchen, Häslein eilet schnelle Zu der kleinen Quelle.	Little flower lifts its little head, Cries clear droplets, Little rabbit hurries To the small spring.
O welch' köstlich Rauschen! Möchte immer lauschen Diesem Gottessegen: Stiller Adendregen!	O what precious rustling! I would like to listen forever To this God's blessing: Silent evening rain.)

A contemporary of hers, Dorothea Boettcher, was born in Schwerin, now East Germany, and came to America in 1876. Coming to the Chicago area, she first taught at Evanston and later in Chicago. At times she consented to a public reading of her poems, as for instance on January 29, 1901, when she recited several of her works to a large audience in the Germania clubhouse. Under the pseudonym of D. B. Schwerin she published the serial novels, *Der Sohn des Bankiers* (The Son of the Banker) and *Die Erbschleicher* (The Legacy Hunters), in the Chicago newspaper, *Freie Presse.* To give one example of her poetry, the first and last strophes of her rhapsodical, nine stanza poem, "Gruß an Amerika" (Greetings to America), are reprinted:

Amerika, o neues Heimathland!
Du Land der Freiheit, Land voll Licht und Wonne!
Sei uns gegrüßt, du gastlich holder Strand,
Sei uns gegrüßt, du goldne Freiheitssonne! . . .

Ziel unsrer Wünsche, aller Hoffnung Strand,
Wird hier die Noth, der Schmerz, die Sehnsucht schwinden?
Das uns verheißne, das gelobte Land—
O, Gott in Himmel, laß es hier uns finden!

(America, o new homeland!
You land of freedom, land full of light and joy!
Be greeted, you hospitable, gracious shore,
Be greeted you golden Sun of Freedom! . . .

Goal of our wishes, shore of every hope,
Will here distress, pain and yearning disappear?
The promised, the pledged land—
O God in Heaven, let us find it here!)

The last poetess of Chicago's German element mentioned here, Caecilie Hammerstein-Illing, came in 1884 to America, the child of Adolph and H. Bloch. She became known as a writer of both English and German literary works. The *Abendpost* of December 16, 1932 reviewed a collection of her novelettes, *Weisser Flieder Novelen* (White Lilac Novelettes), in laudatory terms. The 1935-37 *Yearbook of the Chicago Branch of the National League of American Penwomen* printed her biography on pages 52 to 54, stating that she had published some 400 short stories and other literary works in leading journals in the United States and Germany.

Of the post-forty-eighters, perhaps the most outstanding German-American poet ever, Konrad Nies, must be mentioned, even though he was only a fleeting guest of Chicago's German element, having spent only short and sporadic intervals in Chicago. On November 16, 1928, the *Abendpost* reported that Chicago's German element with concerted efforts was trying to raise money for the indigent family of Konrad Nies, that Mrs. Emma Eitel was auctioning off Nies's poem collection, *Welt und Wildnis* (World and Wilderness), in the Bismarck Hotel. Konrad Nies had been unable to provide for the future needs of his family when he died in 1921, a broken man, after a troubadour-like existence. He moved from place to place in quest of happiness and economic independence, causing Robert E. Ward to call him aptly a "literary knight" on page seven of the 1971 issue of *German-American Studies.*

Konrad Nies was born in 1862 at Alzey, some thirty miles southwest of Frankfurt on the Main, and pursued a promising acting career before he came to America in 1883 to act on the stages of German theaters in various cities. Later he became editor of *Deutsch-Amerikanische Dichtung* from 1888-90 while he taught German in various high schools. After his journal failed, he engaged in several lecture tours throughout the United States and Germany, residing in the intervals in various American cities. During World War I Nies suffered severely in the clash between his native and adopted homelands. Not only was he incarcerated as a pro-German threat and accused of using his illuminated monument in his summerhouse at San Francisco Bay as a beacon for German U-boats in the San Francisco harbor, but he also was fired from the editorship of *The Colorado Herold* when he expressed a friendly attitude toward Germany. As an author he was versatile in producing plays—the first one, *Konradin von Hohenstaufen,* while he was still an actor in Germany—poems, short stories and novels.

Of his poems, several outstanding ones ought to be reproduced here, such as the long eulogy composed for the dedication of the Goethe monument in Lincoln Park on June 13, 1914, but only the last stanza of this lofty poem will be given here:

Wenn uns der Alltag drückt, der nebelblasse,
Wenn uns des Engsinns Staub die Stirn umweht
Und uns durch's Herz, umgellt vom Lärm der Gasse,
Nach Hald' und Höh' ein leises Heimweh geht:
Dann leih' der Jüngling mit dem Blick ins Weite
Uns Führerkraft, wie Goethe sie verliehn,
Dass wir, der Raubgier Aar gezähmt zur Seite,
Lichtwärts ins Zukunftsreich der Menschheit ziehn . . .

When the dreary gray everyday oppresses us,
When the dust of narrowmindedness blows around the forehead
And through our hearts, drowned out by the noise of the street,
Goes a gentle yearning for meadows and mountains:
May then the youth with his gaze into the distance
Give us leading strength, as Goethe has offered it,

That we, at our side the tamed eagle of rapacity,
May move into the light of the future realm of humanity . . .

Of another exceedingly popular poem, "Das deutsche Lied" (The German Song), the first stanza is reproduced as an additional example of his art:

Als wir entflohn aus Deutschlands Gauen,
Durchglüht von jungem Wanderdrang,
Um fremder Länder Pracht zu schauen,
Zu lauschen fremder Sprache Klang,
Da gab zum Segen in die Ferne,
Die Heimat uns ihr deutsches Lied,
Das nun, gleich einem guten Sterne,
Mit uns die weite Welt durchzieht.

(When we escaped from Germany's provinces,
Inspired by youthful wanderlust,
To view the splendor of foreign lands,
To listen to the sounds of foreign tongues,
At that time gave as a viaticum for foreign lands
Our homeland to us her German song,
Which now, like a friendly star,
Accompanies us through the wide world.)

Many of Chicago's German authors wrote plays which were performed in Chicago's German theaters. Understandably, most of these works and their authors passed into oblivion shortly after their maiden appearance. Interesting is an open letter in the *Abendpost* of April 19, 1919 by Conrad Seidemann, director of Chicago's German Theater, to Emil Elsner in which the theater director defended the billing of works by classical German writers. Elsner had previously suggested that the attendance in the financially troubled German Theater would improve if one were to stage the works of "prominent" authors, such as Gustave von Moser and Ludwig Fulda, or of local authors like Otto Ernst. None of these authors was popular in the theatrical history of Chicago's German element with the exception of Otto Ernst (d. 1926), whose play, *Flachsmann als Erzieher* (Educator Flachsmann), was hailed as a delightful comedy in the *Staatszeitung* of April 29, 1901. It was staged periodically after that, as in May of 1926 by students at Waller High School.

It would be nearly impossible to ascertain how many of these ephemeral authors were active in Chicago. An inkling of their large number may be obtained in a perusal of Chicago's German papers' entertainment section. For instance, on April 7, 1879 the *Staatszeitung* reported on two productions by local authors: at Chicago's "Volkstheater" was presented Christian Wahl's comedy, "Man soll den Teufel nicht an die Wand malen" (Speak of the Devil . . .); and in the "Vorwärts Turnhalle" could be seen Paul Loebel's play, "Die Nachfalter von Chicago" (The Nightowls of Chicago). Especially the latter play is full of allusions to local people and deals with current events, replete with public scandals and various other publicity stunts.

In the theatrical history of Chicago's German element, local authors often dealt with current events to attract larger audiences. The temperance question was the object of Julius Kurzer's play, "Die Wasser-Schwachsinnigen" (The Water Morons), which was described in the *Staatszeitung* of April 22, 1872 as a somewhat clumsy attempt to attract crowds. Such locally produced crowd pleasing plays were not able to elevate the position of Chicago's German theater, which always had a precarious existence, though at times ambitiously conceived theatrical undertakings, such as the Schiller Theater in 1892, seemed to usher in propitious times for Chicago's German stage.

It is not known when the first German theatrical production was staged in Chicago. There seems to have existed a German theater as early as 1849, for Conrad Gehrke (1816-98), who came to Chicago in 1848, recalled that he had often visited the "German Theater" which had been established in 1849 by a certain Witmann. In addition to this presumably semi-professional theater, there were sporadic amateur productions of plays and operettas after 1852 by the "Männergesangverein" members, most notable among them Carl Sonne, Henry Wendt, Julius Standau, and Rudolf Schloetzer. Also traveling troupes periodically performed German plays. For instance, in 1852/53 a group directed by a certain Adolph Benroth performed various German plays, among them even Schiller's *Die Räuber*, in Market Hall on South State Street. Tickets amounted to between twenty-five and fifty cents with a small extra fee for reserved seats. Their limited facilities did not even include an adequately operating curtain for the makeshift stage. This troupe did not return the following theater season, but instead a Herr Kurtz from Milwaukee managed a German theater on Canal Street near Randolph Street, which burned in 1854.

In the 1850's, encouraged by the harassments of the "Know-Nothing" advocates, the German element planned the erection of a social center, named "Deutsches Haus," complete with a spacious theater. It was opened early in 1856 with a performance of

Schiller's *Kabale und Liebe* (Intrigue and Love), preceded by a festive prologue by the local poet Casper Butz. Schiller's play initiated a brief, successful series of accomplished plays to appreciative audiences.

However, within two years rivalry and strife began to undermine the success of the auspiciously initiated German theater. John Rittig, formerly the director of a traveling ensemble, who had been asked to serve as the first theater director of the "Deutsches Haus," antagonized many people with his brutally frank opinions and was to be replaced by Alexander Pfeiffer, director of the Milwaukee German Theater. The result of the ensuing intrigues and machinations by various factions was a split in Chicago's first "German Theater." Rittig still continued to present German plays in the "Deutsches Haus" with severely diminished talents. The other members of the ensemble had allied themselves with Pfeiffer to establish a second "German Theater" on the second floor of a large store on Kinzie Street, called the "Kinzie Street Theater." It was opened with an ambitious performance of Goethe's *Faust* with outstanding actors, among them Karoline Lindemann, considered one of the best German actresses at that time. Between the two German theaters evolved a bitter rivalry which, on the positive side, caused a rise in the quality of the theatrical performances but, on the negative side, a precipitous decline in audience.

For a short while, both German theaters offered extremely good performances to nearly empty halls until both of them failed financially. The Kinzie Street Theater vanished and the theater in the "Deutsches Haus" passed through a turbulent era under several directors. The only plays still offered on a regular basis were farces, slapstick comedies, or maudlin tear jerkers which drove away more refined audiences.

When Wilhelm Böttner directed the "theater" he organized a beer fair at which sundry breweries had their products judged by a boisterous clientele. John A. Huck's Brewery was most liberal in providing beer to be tested and was consequently given the distinction "first premium" which was flaunted by this brewery at every possible occasion. In this milieu the theatrical arts did not thrive. The Civil War also put a damper on the enthusiasm for theatrical undertakings, but nevertheless, the German theater vegetated in the "Deutsches Haus" until it was destroyed in the Great Fire of 1871.

In spite of the general decline of Chicago's German theater in pre-fire days, there were occasional highlights. In 1867 there were

Sunday performances, as well as two theater nights during the week. Some outstanding actors and actresses also graced Chicago's German theater with their presence. The famous Fanny Janauschek delighted Chicago's theater goers in 1868 in roles in Schiller's *Kabale und Liebe* and *Maria Stuart*, as well as Lessing's *Emilia Galotti.* In 1870 the talented Marie Seebach won widespread acclaim for several tragic roles in Goethe's *Faust* and several dramas by Schiller.

While the German theater in the "Deutsches Haus" was reeling under various difficulties, several German "Volkstheater," or theaters on a smaller scale, were operated to accommodate the entertainment needs of Chicago's large German element. In 1860 Christian Thielmann and his wife, who had been part of the unsuccessful German theater in the "Deutsches Haus," established a "Volkstheater" on Clybourn Avenue near Division Street which apparently was successful, for even though destroyed in the 1871 Conflagration, it was rebuilt in 1872. Various other German theatrical undertakings were started, in "Aurora Turnhalle" on the West Side, in the "Union Turnhalle," in the "North Side Turnhalle," and various other suitable places.

The one German theater that seemed to have become most important shortly before the 1871 Fire was the Globe Theater. It was located on Des Plaines Street and was under the direction of Gustav Ostermann. With Sigmund and Georg Isenstein, two excellent actors who had absolved their apprenticeships in the "Deutsches Haus" theater, the Globe Theater Company did not hesitate to stage such monumental works as Goethe's *Faust*, and Schiller's *Wilhelm Tell* or *Wallenstein.*

After the 1871 Fire it did not take long before Chicago's German element had a choice of several German theaters. Several theatrical companies, such as the Globe Theater Company and the Thielmann Company survived the fire, and soon new ones also were established. For instance, in the fall of 1872 Louis Kindt started a highly successful season in the "Vorwärts Turnhalle" on West 12th Street. Some of the German theater companies not only changed their names, but also performed at several locations in different parts of the city, making it difficult to keep track of them or to ascertain their exact number.

The German newspapers more or less regularly reviewed between four and five German theaters in Chicago between 1872 and 1892, usually disregarding the smaller theatrical undertakings by local German clubs. On August 31, 1872, the *Staatszeitung* reviewed five plays performed in Chicago's German theaters: at the

"Vorwärts Turnhalle" *Sodom und Gomorrah* was given, in the "Stadt Theater of the West Side" *Die Regimentstochter* (The Daughter of the Regiment), at the "New Chicago Theater" on Clark Street *Die Gebrüder Bock* (The Brothers Bock), at the "National Theater" *Hans Jürge*, and at "Adelphi Theater" *Die zwei Waisen* (The two Orphans).

Usually one of the several theaters took the lead in artistic performance and was identified as "the German Theater" although, until the Schiller Theater was erected in 1892, Chicago's German element did not have a permanent home for its theater. In the 1870's the Globe Theater company, under the directorship of Alexander Wurster, continued to have a good reputation and was identified as Chicago's "German Theater." It moved from "Baum Halle," also known as Burlington Hall, where it was in 1871 and 1872, to "Aurora Turnhalle" in 1873; then to "North Side Turnhalle" in 1874; and, finally, to the Grand Opera House in 1875. Despite the lack of its own house, the Globe Theater company received high praise not only from German newspapers, but also from American papers. The *Tribune* pointed to it as a noteworthy example to be emulated by the English theater, for Wurster did not rely on a vulnerable star system, but had a good all around resident company. However, Wurster splintered his energies too much by accepting the directorship of the German Theater in St. Louis in addition to that in Chicago. In 1879, the theatrical company being on the verge of financial ruin, he had to resign to make way for a new director.

Emil Hoechster, the new director, started to give performances on February 2, 1879, in "Hooley's Opera House." Apparently he had an auspicious start, for a critic in the *Staatszeitung* of February 24, 1879 exclaimed: "Thank God! We have now again a German theater." But Hoechster also failed financially and he was forced to resign in May of 1880. From 1880 to 1883, Georg Isenstein, Alexander Wurster, and Julius Collmer jointly directed the German theaters in Chicago, St. Louis, and Milwaukee. Isenstein alone directed Chicago's German theater between 1883 and 1887.

After 1887 a team of four directors, named William Selig, Heinrich Richard, Friedrich Welb and Albert Wachsner, directed Chicago's German theater until 1911, apparently placing initially much more interest into financial success than into artistic accomplishment. Locally composed crowd pleasers were staged, which rarely happened to be outstanding works of art. All of this caused a reviewer in the *Staatszeitung* of February 13, 1888, to complain: "Today's drama director seems to be only a speculator who counts heads in the theater and dollars in the box." Nevertheless, in 1889, Chicago's German element was treated to several brilliant performances of Schiller's plays, given to honor the great German author's 130th birthday.

These festive performances of Schiller's works and their enthusiastic reception by the public gave the stimulus for a magnificently conceived undertaking, a special, elegant building for the German Theater, which would enable it to compete in every aspect with any other theater. Already in 1890 the plans for the proposed Schiller Building had materialized and its construction could begin. In the fall of 1892 it was dedicated. The Schiller Building, later known as the Garrick Building, considered one of Chicago's thirty-nine architectural landmarks before it was razed in 1961 to make way for a parking lot, had been erected according to the design of Adler and Sullivan at a cost of about $925,000 on Randolph Street between Dearborn and Clark streets. Besides various club rooms, offices and diverse halls, it contained a theater with a seating capacity of some 1,300, which the German newspapers hailed as the most beautiful art temple in Chicago.

In the enthusiasm of the first few highly accomplished performances, Chicago's German newspapers acclaimed the Schiller Theater as an outstanding stage worthy of any German city. The *Staatszeitung* of October 9, 1892, triumphantly stated that Chicago's English newspapers conceded that the German stage was ahead of Chicago's English-speaking stage. For its dedication on September 30, 1892, the German-American poet Julius Gugler composed a festive play, entitled *Die Pioniere* (The Pioneers), which stressed the fact that German culture was a thriving, beneficial force in America's development. For a later performance he wrote the comedy, *For Mayor Godfrey Buehler*, which dealt with the complacency in public life of Chicago's German element. However, the propitious era which optimists predicted for the German element did not materialize. Because of a host of difficulties, mainly economic ones, the Schiller Building was the home of Chicago's German theater for only two years. After 1894 the German theater was forced to give performances again in various other available theaters.

From 1894 to 1896 Chicago's German theater did not even offer performances on Sundays. But after it had rented Hooley's Theater in August of 1897, for three seasons, and later Power's Theater, more favorable times came. Chicago's German element wanted to develop its reeling theater up to its potential. In 1903 a drive was started to reawaken the German element's interest in a good theater, after the German Consul Dr. Walter Wever, Professor Camillo von Clenze of the University of Chicago, and Professor James Hatfield of Northwestern University had stressed the need for a good German stage. From the generated enthusiasm ensued the staging of *Faust* on February 17, 1903, in the Auditorium, before a large audience of some 3,600 persons. The successful production of *Faust* and its favorable reception by the audience prompted the sponsors to stage several other highly publicized classical plays, of which Schiller's works were preferred by the audience. When *Wilhelm Tell* was performed in the spring of 1905 to commemorate the 100th anniversary of Schiller's death, a sell-out audience in the Auditorium was priviledged to view "an examplary performance."

The period from about 1903 to 1911 most likely represents the climax in the development of Chicago's German theater. Schiller's plays were exceedingly popular, but many plays of other outstanding authors were also staged. Lessing's works were performed at least six times, *Minna von Barnhelm* being the favorite. Plays by Grillparzer could be seen at least four times. Only one drama by C.F. Hebbel, *Gyges und sein Ring* (Gyges and his Ring), was performed, but at least twenty-two times works of the now obscure German playwright Hermann Sudermann were staged. Gerhard Hauptmann's plays were also popular. His *Die versunkene Glocke* (The Sunken Bell) was performed at least three times, and when *Hanneles Himmelfahrt* (The Assumption of Hannele) was staged for the first time, about one hundred people had to be turned away. Of course, playwrights who did not write in the German language were also staged in German translations, among them Ibsen and Shakespeare most frequently.

After 1911 Chicago's German theater gradually declined in ever increasing adverse conditions, after an initial upsurge. In 1911 Max Hanisch was called from the Philadelphia German Theater to direct Chicago's German Theater. In order to assure good attendance, Hanisch appealed to Chicago's numerous German clubs to sponsor and support their theater by buying a set number of tickets from the theater and reselling them at a profit to their members. The German element responded well and Hanisch again started daily performances, but he lasted for only two years. During his tenure, the operetta became a favorite genre. Above all, the works of Johann Strauss, especially *Wiener Blut* (Viennese Blood) and *Zigeunerbaron* (Gypsy Baron), were very popular.

After Max Hanisch departed in 1913 as director of Chicago's German Theater several unfortunate factors contributed to the lowering of it to abject depths. The 1913/14 season still offered a few highlights, as for instance when a larger audience than the theater could accommodate came to see Schiller's *Braut von Messina* (The Bride of Messina). But the 1914/15 season could only be described as utterly bleak, in spite of the fact that the German theater was supported by the German element. When a board under John Kölling supervised the German theater, aided by Joseph Danner as playdirector and Wilhelm Arens as business director, the affairs of the German theater became scandalous. Esther Olsen's article, "The German Theater in Chicago" (*Deutsch-Amerikanische Geschichtsblätter*, 1937), which supplied many of the facts in this sketch of Chicago's German theater, describes the 1914/15 season as follows (page 111):

> This season turned out to be a woeful one in the history of the German theater. Although personal sacrifices were made by Horace L. Brand and other wealthy Germans and the 'Columbia-Damenklub' [as well as other clubs] arranged for a performance every month, thus bringing the theater some financial assistance and also new friends, the undertaking proved a sad failure. The artistic niveau became poorer every day, and the monetary situation more miserable. Several of the actors left and were not replaced. Without calling the board together, Kölling dismissed Saltiel, who had succeeded Arens as financial director, and put a certain Mr. Martin in his place. Having been a former advertising agent, Martin knew nothing about the theater, and in addition was rude and coarse of manner. Kölling dismissed Richard Heide, the treasurer, without further ado, and Martin received this position also. This gave him full control over all money affairs. No auditing of the books occurred during this time, and when Brand offered to pay the costs of having them examined at the end of the season, access to the books was denied him. He also made suggestions for the reduction of costs but they went unheeded. Finally, he withdrew from the board as did Hutmann and Krütgen.
>
> When the unpaid actors asked for back wages, Martin answered them only with rudeness. He was also discourteous to members of clubs who arranged for performances and thus many discontinued the practice. Danner was dismissed by him with the assistance of a police officer.
>
> On the 27th of April [1915] the players visited Mr. Singer [editor of the *Staatszeitung*] and asked him to help them obtain about $1,400 back pay. He called Kölling to the conference. Kölling insisted that it was the duty of the actors to help him—they were to play another week, so that he might get money to pay the rent, stage hands and painters; their share of the profits was to be only $267.00.

> That night Kölling determined to dismiss the cast and to make good his expenses by hiring a 'zusammengetrommelte Schmierengesellschaft.' As the players were dressing for the performance, he appeared with his new troupe and commanded them to leave. He even went so far as to call in the police to expedite departure. The actors Zoder and Brückner appealed to the audience which insisted that the regular ensemble should play. The next day police officers surrounded the theater and the players were forbidden to enter. That night fire broke out in the building and thus ended the theatrical undertaking for the season 1914-15, which was a failure in every respect and the saddest in the annals of the German stage.

The hectic war days and the concomitant anti-German sentiments prevented an appreciable improvement in the German Theater. Several different directors tried their luck, actors consented to a cut in salary, sundry organizations and individuals promoted it, such as the famous contralto, Ernestine Schumann-Heink in a benefit concert in 1916, and several Chicago Germans shouldered significant personal sacrifices for it. Nevertheless the German Theater's financial reports invariably showed a deficit. For instance, in the 1917/18 season there was a deficit of $3,160.41 in November, and $3,858.05 in December, which caused the board of directors to contemplate closing the theater "in consideration of the prevailing public sentiment which seemed strongly opposed to performances in the German language." In spite of the board's decision, Conrad Seidemann, the director of the theater, reopened the stage, thus making Chicago the only American city in which a German theater was able to withstand anti-German harassment during the entire war.

The cost of operating the German Theater in Chicago during World War I was high, as the 1919 report covering September 21, 1918 to February 28, 1919 showed. There was a deficit amounting to $9,886.48. Only through the selfless intervention of Chicagoans of German extraction, whose good will apparently was exploited, could the German Theater avoid bankruptcy and general scandal. Interesting is a letter of Dr. Otto L. Schmidt, of March 7, 1919, to Dr. Alexander Wiener in which he referred to a collection for the German Theater for which he had already given $8,400: "Thank you very much for the check of $408.00. The affair is for me also a painfully costly tuition, especially so, since I did not contribute my money out of enthusiasm or because of promises, but in order to prevent the German name from being involved in lawsuits and scandalous newspaper stories."

After the frantic war days had gone by, Chicago's German element was proud of the fact that it hosted the only German theater which had survived the conflict of the nations, and it supported it in many ways, most importantly by good attendance. Benefit fairs and festivals for the German Theater were held quite frequently. On May 28, 1922 the German Federation of Chicago held a May Festival at Riverview Park, the proceeds of which were to go to the theater. Later in the summer of 1922, Charles Appel, the manager of "North Side Turnhalle," arranged a festival for the same purpose.

The German Theater moved from Bush Temple to Victoria Theater at Sheffield and Belmont avenues in the fall of 1922. It had staged between 1919 and 1923 primarily operettas, of which Ascher's *Hoheit tanzt Walzer* (His Majesty Dances Waltzes) attained the record number of forty-one performances, but outstanding dramas and comedies were also staged. As in the entire history of Chicago's German theater, Schiller's plays were most popular. *Wilhelm Tell*, performed at least eight times, was the favorite. Of the more modern playwrights, Sudermann, with twenty-six presentations of eleven plays, was more popular than even Gerhard Hauptmann.

The apparent success of the German Theater after World War I to about 1923 could not stay its inexorable decline, hastened by the success of the cinema; the decline in German immigration; and the fierce competition among different smaller theaters. Revealing is an audit report for March 14, 1923 to October 31, 1923 by the Papke accountant office to Dr. Otto L. Schmidt, president of the Victoria Amusement Company, an undertaking founded to preserve a German theater for Chicago:

> The Company was organized under the laws of the State of Illinois on March 14, 1923, with an authorized capital stock of $10,000, divided into 1,000 shares, each having a par value of $10. The main purpose for which it was called into being was to give Chicago a German theatre. To this end the Victoria Theatre at 3147 Sheffield Avenue was rented, and on April 1, 1923 the first performance was given.
>
> From the very beginning it was thought that a theatre giving German performances exclusively would not be a success financially; therefore it was decided to give German performances on but two days a week, and vaudeville on the other five. Following this plan, German performances were given on Sunday afternoons and evenings of April 1st, 8th, and 15th, and on Monday evenings of April 2nd and 16th. On April 9th a lecture was given instead of a play.

> After April 16th no more German performances were given, as the management felt they distracted too much from increasing the patronage of the vaudeville performances. Therefore, beginning with April 17th the theatre was given over to vaudeville entirely. This policy was pursued until May 6th, when the vaudeville performances were discontinued. After that date only moving pictures were shown; finally, on June 23rd, the theatre was closed altogether. . . . All in all the Company lost $21,650.44 during the twelve weeks of operating the Victoria Theatre.

In spite of these losses, alternately the Victoria Theater and the Bush Temple continued to be homes for the German Theater until 1931, mainly because of personal sacrifices by wealthy German-Americans. Even the declining period of Chicago's German Theater had its bright spots. Difficult times in Europe brought famous stars to Chicago. For instance, in January of 1924 Mrs. Irene Triesch, considered Central Europe's most important tragedienne, played in Strindberg's *Totentanz* (Dance of Death), and was acclaimed as the "German Sarah Bernhardt" in the *Abendpost* of January 25, 1924.

Occasionally certain highly publicized gala performances drew enormous audiences. When the operetta, *Dreimäderlhaus* (Three Girls' House or Blossom Time), by Schubert, was staged in the spring of 1927, many prominent German and American guests attended and scores of people had to be turned away. However, the average performances were poorly attended. The quickly changing directors tried to adjust their billing, which was to no avail. Although the play bills showed that all theatrical genres were performed, the directors seemed to have had most success with operettas, for they were by far most frequently staged. The German stage did indeed sink low, for on December 18, 1927 Mayor William H. Thompson, accompanied by his retinue, made it a boisterous political arena, haranguing against the "British Lion" and against Public School Superintendent McAndrew.

After about 1931 the German Theater in Chicago was kept alive artificially by occasional special commemorative or benefit performances. For all practical purposes the end of Chicago's German Theater came when its last regular director, Rudolf Bach, left the foundering Victoria Company in the middle of the 1931 season. To be sure, the season was guided to an orderly end by the popular actor Angelo Lippich, but in the following two years the German stage of Chicago was entirely inactive. Then on January 15, 1933 the director of "Germania Broadcast," Julius Klein, sponsored Johann Strauss's *Zigeunerbaron* (Gypsy Baron) in the Auditorium, broadcasting it simultaneously. On March 4, 1934 Klein sponsored a production of Lehar's operetta, *Zigeunerliebe* (Gypsy Love), for the benefit of the German Old Peoples Home in Forest Park. The only other performances which were reviewed in the German newspapers were similarly conceived undertakings or gala performances for a special occasion. On April 8, 1934 the comedy, *Im weissen Rössl* (In the Inn to the White Horse), was staged in honor of Angelo Lippich's twenty-fifth year on the stage. Full houses in an afternoon and an evening performance paid tribute to a moribund part of Chicago's German element. There continued to be, of course, theatrical productions in German, as there are occasionally even today, but they were staged by guest ensembles or were short time amateur affairs by sundry German clubs. It is interesting to survey a few statistics, based on Olsen's, "The German Theater in Chicago," to see how many and what kind of theatrical productions were staged in the German Theater during certain time periods:

Period	1861-1870	1911-1913	1913-1914	1914-1915
Total number of performances	381	566	232	216
Operettas	22 (6%)	295 (52%)	51 (22%)	29 (13¼%)
Comedies, farces	204 53½%)	185 (32½%)	84 (36½%)	158 (73½%)
Dramas	155 (40½%)	86 (15½%)	97 (41½%)	29 (13¼%)

Period	1915-1916	1917-1923	1927-1931
Total number of performances	152	1355	309
Operettas	20 (13%)	557 (41%)	216 (70%)
Comedies, farces	63 (41½%)	457 (33½%)	76 (24½%)
Dramas	69 (45½%)	347 (25½%)	17 (5½%)

Of the factors responsible for the elimination of Chicago's German theater, the cinema undoubtedly was one of the most potent. It not only hastened the demise of the German theater, but it also provided a new source of entertainment for the German element. Enterprising individuals had observed the triumph of the new form of mass entertainment and provided the Germans with their own films and movie houses. As early as 1917 Abraham Teitel founded the Teitel Film Company, which specialized in German as well as other foreign films. In the 1920's German films were shown intermittently at various Chicago theaters, but the first movie house which showed exclusively German films and lasted for some time was the "Kino" with a seating capacity of 426 on North Avenue near Halsted Street. From 1931 to some time in the 1960's, except for three years during World War II, it showed only German films without English subtitles. Soon movie houses specializing in German films cropped up all over the city wherever the number of German inhabitants was sufficiently large to support a film theater. Even by 1940 when Naziism and a new war caused anti-German sentiments to come to the fore, four German movie theaters advertised regularly in the *Abendpost*, namely the Kino on 659 West North Avenue, the Little German Theater at 2153 Lincoln Avenue, the Bertha at 4714 Lincoln Avenue and the Music Box at 3733 Southport Street. Of these theaters, by 1956 only the Kino continued to show German films, but in the meantime the 1,400 seat Mozart Theater at 4614 North Lincoln Avenue, prior to 1975 called the Davis Theater, had begun to specialize in German films. While there were still two German movie houses in 1956, today only the Mozart Theater shows German films. They are complemented with showings of other foreign language films in accordance with the ethnically changing community, thus giving indirect evidence for the numerical decline of Chicago's German element.

Chapter 14

Chicago's German Element and Architecture, Engineering, Painting and Sculpture

Chicago's German element has played vastly disparate roles in the realms of architecture, engineering, painting, and sculpture. Among the outstanding individuals in the annals of architecture Chicagoans of German extraction certainly must be mentioned. Their prominent position was stressed by the second generation German architect Arthur Woltersdorf, who had asserted, in the "German Club's" *World's Fair Souvenir Year Book of 1933*, on page forty-eight, that "in the building of Chicago, German-born architects played an important part from the beginning. Frederick Baumann, a Prussian, came to Chicago in 1849 or 1850, the second architect to practice here, John M. Van Osdel being the first."

Actually Baumann came to Chicago on August 14, 1850 after having emigrated from his native Angermünde, now in East Germany, where he was born in 1826. First he worked for the firm of John M. Van Osdel and then in 1852 joined the Burling Company to help design the plans for many business buildings. However, he also contributed much to street widening, sewers, and the "raising of the city" when Chicago's buildings were jacked up several feet to eliminate swampy conditions. He took part in many public affairs as an outstanding member of the community, being, for instance, a member of the first school board from 1857 to 1859. He died in 1920 at the age of 94.

Apparently the next German architect active in Chicago after Baumann was August Bauer, who was born in 1827 at Friedberg, some twenty miles northeast of Frankfurt on the river Main. After he had graduated with honors from the polytechnical school of Darmstadt in 1850, he emigrated to New York, where he gained national recognition for his work on the famous Crystal Palace, the first exhibition hall in America constructed primarily of iron and glass. Immediately after coming to Chicago in 1853, he enjoyed a good reputation as a partner in the Carter and Bauer Company, later of the Bauer and Loebnitz Company, and then the Bauer and Hill Company. Some of the buildings which originated on his drawing board were the churches of St. Peter, St. Paul, and St. Aloysius, the Oxford office complex at 84 LaSalle Street, "North Side Turnhalle," Uhlich's Orphanage, about ten warehouses, residences for Henry W. King, Peter Schuettler, and Washington Hesing, and St. Elizabeth Hospital. As a longtime architect for the public schools of Chicago he designed some thirty elementary schools. Before he died in 1894 he served as president of the Chicago chapter of the American Institute of Architects.

Also in 1853 came the architects Robert Schmid and Otto Matz. Schmid, born in 1827 in the vicinity of Berlin, came to Chicago after having studied architecture in Berlin. First he worked for Van Osdel and Olmsted, then he became independent in 1860 and designed many buildings, especially breweries, before he died in 1876. Matz was born in Berlin in 1830, where he received an education as an architect, before he emigrated directly to Chicago. As an architect for the Illinois Central Railroad he designed the company's main buildings along some 700 miles of track, including the passenger terminal at the foot of Lake Street, the most modern building in Chicago at the time. During the Civil War he served as an engineer in the U.S. Army on the staff of Fremont, Halleck, and Grant, serving with distinction in the Vicksburg campaign. After returning to Chicago in 1864, he resumed his profession. From 1870 to 1871 the Chicago Board of Education appointed him as architect of the public schools. When Chicago's city council requested designs for the Court House and City Hall, Matz's design won a $5,000 award, out of fifty-four plans submitted from all over the country. Among the prominent buildings which he designed before he died in 1919 are the Alexian Brothers Hospital, the Chicago Hospital for Women and Children, and the Criminal Court Building of 1898.

Of the above mentioned German architects, August Bauer started one of Chicago's most important architects on the road to success, namely Dankmar Adler (1844-1900). He was born in Lengsfeld, in the vicinity of Eisenach, in 1844, and emigrated with his family to Detroit in 1854. Coming to Chicago in 1861, he joined the Bauer firm before serving during the Civil War from August 1862 to the end of the war in the First Illinois Artillery Regiment as a topographical engineer. Returning to Chicago, he rejoined Bauer's company, but in 1871 established a partnership with Edward Burling. Their company was exceedingly busy in providing plans for rebuilding Chicago after the Conflagration of 1871. Among other buildings, they designed the *Tribune* Building at Dearborn and Madison streets; several bank buildings, like the First National at State and Washington streets; at least five churches, such as St. James; and many prestigious residences. After 1879 Dankmar Adler alone designed the acoustically nearly perfect Central Music Hall before he joined forces with the gifted Louis H. Sullivan.

The partnership between Adler and Sullivan signified the birth of the "Chicago School" of architecture with the alliterative motto, "Form Follows Function." This concept was embodied in their jointly designed structures, such as the Chicago Auditorium, erected in the middle 1880's. This hall attained national fame with regard to perfect acoustics, unobstructed sight lines, harmonious proportions, and functionally beautiful decorations. It was declared one of Chicago's thirty-nine architectural landmarks. Adler in collaboration with Sullivan designed at least five other landmarks. They are the Wirt Dexter Building at 630 South Wabash Avenue in 1887; the Schiller Building, later the Garrick Building at 64 West Randolph, completed in 1892 and razed in 1961; the Sullivan House at 4575 South Lake Park in 1892; the Meyer Building at 307 West Van Buren Street in 1893; and the Old Chicago Stock Exchange at 30 North LaSalle Street in 1894. The firm was well balanced, Adler being the "scientific man," and Sullivan the "artist." When Dankmar Adler died in 1900, the firm declined.

During Adler's activity in Chicago there were several German architects who designed and supervised the erection of innumerable buildings in Chicago, but they have not attained universal recognition. One of them, Wilhelm Nikolaus Arend, came already in 1854 to join the firm of Van Osdel and Baumann. He had been born in the vicinity of Kassel in 1832 and, after graduating from the polytechnical school at Kassel, he emigrated to America in 1853. Working in Chicago as an independent architect after 1869, he was exceedingly busy, designing the Odd Fellows Hall on Milwaukee Avenue, several business houses and office complexes, and at least five churches, such as those of St. Luke and St. Andrew.

Edward Baumann, born near Danzig in 1838, came to Chicago in 1857 and joined the firm of Burling and Baumann. He designed the "Metropolitan" and the "Ashland" blocks, but he specialized in grain elevators, of which he erected a great number. In 1857 Kurt Gottig also came to Chicago. He had been born at Hamburg in 1829 and was educated at Munich. Having been the architect of the "Altona-Kiel Railroad" in Germany, he became the successor of Otto Matz as architect for the Illinois Central Railroad Company.

Of the German architects that were active in later generations of Chicago's development, several deserve to be mentioned for their contributions. Among them is a student of Adler and Sullivan, the second generation German Heinrich Schlacks, who became well-known as the planner of several Chicago churches, especially of the St. Paul Roman Catholic Church built in 1898. According to the architect Arthur Woltersdorf, "this church was epoch making in that it was a Gothic design carried out in burnt clay products; window sills, mullions, tracery, were all of brick. It was the first church in Chicago to have masonry groin ribbed vaulting with the ribs of terra cotta and the filling of tile." Another German architect who became well-known for superintending the erection of the Masonic Temple and for his designs of Chicago churches was William Brinkmann, also a second generation German, born at Chicago in 1871. The interior of Our Lady of Sorrows Basilica, which Brinkmann designed, has repeatedly been termed one of the most beautiful in America.

The architect Paul Gerhardt, born in 1865 at Döbeln, about twenty-five miles west of Dresden, claimed to be a direct descendant of the famous German poet Paul Gerhardt (1607-76), whose hymns are popular even in American churches of various denominations. He came to Chicago in 1894 to design apartment houses, residences of wealthy individuals, and factories, but he achieved greatest success in his plans for hotels and restaurants. The most famous of his creations include the Hotel Bismarck, as well as the restaurants "Rienzi" and "Pabst Blue Ribbon." Serving as Cook County architect until succeeded by Richard Schmidt in December of 1912, he designed a new County Hospital in 1911 for 1,300 patients.

Another architect who was sought after for the designs of restaurants and residences was Arthur Hercz, who was born in 1866, and came to Chicago in 1892. The Red Star Inn, which only recently yielded to the wrecker's ball, was his work. Hercz was active in many undertakings of Chicago's German element. For the 1918 Pageant of Nations he submitted a short festive play which stressed the importance of the German element in America's development, but which was snubbed because of the prevailing anti-German sentiment.

All of these later architects are outranked by Richard Schmidt, born in 1865 at Ebern, some 100 miles east of Frankfurt on the river Main, the son of the previously mentioned "red doctor" Ernst Schmidt. He designed several hospitals in Chicago and the Midwest, such as the third Alexian Brothers Hospital, the Montgomery Ward Building on Michigan Avenue, at that time Chicago's tallest building, and many other buildings, of which at least three became architectural landmarks. They were the Schoenhofen Brewery, later the Morningstar Building on 18th Street and Canalport in 1902, the Madlener House, later the Graham Foundation at 4 West Burton Street in 1902, and the Chapin and Gore Building at 63 East Adams Street in 1904.

During the Nazi period several individuals of Europe's "brain drain" were architects who became active in Chicago. Among them must be mentioned two foremost names, Walter Gropius (1883-1969) and Ludwig Mies van der Rohe (1886-1969). Gropius was not Chicago-based as was Mies van der Rohe, but he nevertheless left an indelible imprint in Chicago as a consultant and guest professor at the Illinois Institute of Technology. At this institution Mies van der Rohe served as chairman of the architecture department until his retirement in 1958. Besides his academic work, he designed many Chicago buildings, among which the Illinois Institute of Technology campus at 32nd and State streets, erected from 1942 to 1948, as well as the 860-80 Lake Shore Drive Apartments, completed in 1952, attained landmark status.

It would be futile to ennumerate all architects of German extraction who designed outstanding Chicago buildings. Among the most prominent architects would have to be mentioned: L. Guenzel, who in 1907 designed Our Lady of Lebanon Church, an architectural landmark; H. Feick, who in 1912 helped to erect the Edison Shop, later the Hung Fa Village Restaurant, another landmark; Paul Schweiker, who planned the landmark, Third Unitarian Church at 301 North Mayfield Avenue in 1929; and the Keck brothers, who, in 1937, designed the University Building at 5551 South University Avenue, yet another landmark. The Magerstadt House on 4930 South Greenwood Street, a creation of the German-American architect Georg W. Maher, also attained landmark status. The Chicago German D. C. Zimmermann served as longtime State Architect of Illinois.

Many outstanding individuals of Chicago's German element not primarily active as architects, but rather as engineers, supervisors and the like, contributed greatly to Chicago's physical development. When the forty-eighters came to America and Chicago in quest of freedom after their abortive attempts at throwing off the yoke of monarchy in Germany, several outstanding engineers and builders were among their number. One of them was Friedrich Schwemm, one of the earliest bridgebuilders in Chicago, who came in 1851 to this city to erect many bridges.

Another forty-eighter was John Gindele, perhaps the most important builder among them. The following praise heaped upon him in *Garbutt's Biographical Sketches of the Leading Men of Chicago* of 1868 seems richly deserved: "He commenced at the lowest round of the ladder and, by the force of inherent talent and indomitable perseverance, he worked his way up to a high position. We, of Chicago, owe much to his talent."

Born in 1814 at Ravensburg, some ten miles north of Lake Constance, Gindele was intended by his parents for the study of theology, but his natural bent toward building earned him a stipend from his native city to the architects' school at Munich. Soon he attracted the attention of the Bavarian government, which first put him in charge of erecting the public works at Bad Kissingen and then appointed him as superintendent for constructing the canal connecting the rivers Danube and Main. After 1838 he successfully occupied the office of city architect in Schweinfurt, about 75 miles east of Frankfurt on the Main.

Since Gindele had supplied 500 armed men to the cause of the 1848 Revolution, he had to resign his post and was forced to emigrate with his wife and five children to America as a *persona non grata.* Adverse fortunes caused him to lose all of his belongings soon after arriving in the New World. Not knowing English, he was unable to communicate properly and was forced to support his family as a stone cutter in Sherman's marble and stone yard on Lake Street, at a dollar and one-half per day. Soon his language skill improved and with it his occupational success. By 1860 he owned a stone yard for himself and contracted for several buildings, among them the south wing and the tower of the Chicago University. When the board of public works was created in 1861, he was elected commissioner from the South division for six years, serving four years as president of the board and in that capacity also as commissioner of the Illinois and Michigan Canal.

While he was president of the board of public works several great improvements were carried out in Chicago, for which the city council expressed public gratitude to him in resolutions of January 6, 1869. Against vigorous opposition and in spite of overwhelming difficulties, Gindele brought about the constructions of the Lake Tunnel and the "Crib," considered at the time of its construction the "eighth wonder of the world," as well as the LaSalle and Washington street tunnels for which he designed the plans. He also provided the plan to clean the Chicago River by means of a canal to Calumet with pumping works. Gindele was an ambassador of good will to Germany by providing the city of Schweinfurt in 1866 with a feasible plan for regulating the river Main. After the 1871 Fire he helped to redesign the *Tribune* and the McCormick buildings. When he resigned from the board of public works, he was elected Cook County clerk from 1869 to 1872. Being a prominent member of the German element, he was active in various public organizations, helping to found the Germania Club in 1865. When Gindele died on January 31, 1872, eulogies in Chicago's German and American newspapers praised his valuable contributions to Chicago's development.

A. M. Hirsch arrived in 1853, a man who did not occupy high positions, but who nevertheless served the city well as an engineer in the street department. He was born in 1827 near Königsberg and received his education at the technical institute of Berlin before emigrating to America. Coming to Chicago, he obtained work under Chief Engineer Roswell Mason in building the Illinois Central Railroad. In 1856 he entered the service of the city in the street department, where he supposedly drew the first cross section of a Chicago street and introduced many important changes, such as altering the proportion of grades in bridge approaches from a ratio of 1:10 to the ratio of 1:40. W. Strippelmann, a German engineer working for the city's map department, drafted the first "underground map" of Chicago and published an atlas of the city's destroyed areas after the 1871 Fire.

The civil engineer Karl Binder (1853-1903) was responsible for the raising of many Chicago buildings. Born in 1853 at Stuttgart, he graduated from the city's polytechnical school before emigrating to America in 1884. When he came to Chicago in 1889, he joined the Moritz Seifert engineering firm before he made himself independent and helped to erect many of Chicago's prominent buildings. For the Columbia World's Fair in 1893 he raised five buildings, namely the Machine Shop, the Horticultural Building, the Music Hall as well as the Krupp and Hagenbeck buildings. Among the more permanent structures which he erected in Chicago were the main Public Library, the Studebaker and Monk buildings, the Schiller Theater, later the Garrick Building, several University of Chicago halls, several churches, like St. Paul's Lutheran, and a few hospitals, such as St. Mary of Nazareth.

Moritz Lassig (1831-1902) was one of the most important bridge builders of the Midwest in the second half of the nineteenth century. Born at Rocklitz, Saxony, in 1831, he studied engineering at the technical institute of Chemnitz before coming to Chicago in 1851. First he joined the Boomer company and later the American Bridge Company, but in 1876 he founded his own exceedingly successful business at Clybourn and Wrightwood avenues, where he employed some 900 workers. Several large railroad lines, such as the Chicago Northwestern and the Burlington Quincy relied on him whenever a new bridge was to be constructed.

The internationally known "Scherzer Rolling Lift Bridge" was invented and perfected by the second generation Germans William and Albert Scherzer in Chicago. William was born at Peru, Illinois, in 1858, the son of Wilhelm Scherzer, who had emigrated from Germany in 1847. His invention for a bridge between Jackson and Van Buren streets, which, during the passage of ships, was to obstruct the traffic as little as possible, won the prize among many competitors. When he died in 1893, his younger brother Albert, who had been born in 1865, took over his work as head of the Scherzer Rolling Lift Bridge Company, and expanded it considerably by establishing branch offices in European cities. He not only perfected his brother's invention, but he also attained recognition in the academic world through his informative articles in internationally read journals. Among the innumerable bridges which he designed, one should mention the eight-track bridge across the Chicago sewerage and shipping canal, which was at the time of construction the largest moveable railroad bridge in the world.

Of Chicago's German element, Charles H. Wacker (1856-1929) without doubt has done most for the development of the city, though strictly speaking he cannot be called an architect or engineer. A second generation German, he was born in 1856 in Chicago, the son of Frederick Wacker, who had come to Chicago in 1854, and became well-known as a brewer. When his father died in 1884, Charles Wacker became president of the Wacker and Birk Brewing and Malting Company and also of the McAvoy Brewing Company. Through able business transactions he not only became independently wealthy, but was also head or director of several important banks and organizations, such as the Illinois Merchant Trust Company and the Chicago Heights Land Association.

Being gregarious, as is evident from the enormous number of clubs to which he belonged, he had a large circle of friends among Chicagoans from all walks of life. Wacker showed a keen interest in the sound growth of his native Chicago and he did his best to help alleviate social needs. Among other charitable functions he served as president of the Chicago Relief and Aid Society, later called the Chicago Bureau of Charities, of the Chicago Chapter of the American Red Cross, of the Chicago Council of Social Agencies, and of the Illinois Social Hygiene League. As director of the 1893 World's Fair he had absolved his duties very satisfactorily and as vice president and president of the Merchants' Club in 1904 and 1905 he had suggested and caused the execution of many improvements in the city's administration which were widely acclaimed.

When Daniel H. Burnham's plan to transform Chicago into the most beautiful garden city in the world needed to be promoted in the face of stiff opposition, it was a natural and favorably received decision for Mayor Fred Busse to appoint Wacker in 1909 as chairman of the recently created Chicago Plan Commission. For Wacker's outstanding promotional work, the grateful city council decided to name the previously hopelessly congested South Water Street, in honor of the Chicago Plan Commission chairman, the Wacker Drive.

Compared to the great number of outstanding architects, Chicago's German element has furnished only a handful of well-known sculptors and painters. Perhaps the best-known sculptor, Leonard W. Volk (1828-1895), according to page 314 of Albert Faust's *The German Element in the United States*, was born at Wellstown, New York of German parentage. He gave up his trade as a marble cutter in 1848 to open a sculptor's studio in St. Louis. According to page 559 of volume II of Andreas's *History of Chicago*, he completed there the first marble sculpture ever made west of the Mississippi, a highly accomplished copy of Hart's bust of Henry Clay. From 1855 to 1857 he perfected his art in Europe as a protégé of his wife's cousin, Stephen A. Douglas. Returning to America, he opened a studio in Chicago on Clark Street opposite the Sherman House in 1857. A superb life-sized bust of Senator Douglas, executed during his first year in Chicago, made him well-known as an able sculptor. His innumerable other creations, such as the Douglas Monument, the Soldiers' and Sailors' Monument at Rochester, New York, the life mask of President Lincoln, and the Daniel Brainard Bust, contributed to his growing reputation. Among his many activities, beneficial to the flourishing of art in Chicago, it should be mentioned that he helped to establish the Chicago Academy of Design in 1867, serving for more than eight years as its president.

There were a number of sculptors of lesser renown among Chicagoans of German extraction. Artists, such as Carl Beil, Max Mauch and E. H. Würtz, who were mentioned on page 87 of *Chicago und sein Deutschthum* as examples of outstanding German-American sculptors active up to the turn of the century, are now for the most part forgotten. The same fate is shared by Haino Isermann (d. 1899), who was a popular sculptor and whose many creations in marble, bronze and granite grace public places and adorn many graves in the Chicago cemeteries. Another German sculptor, Johannes Gelert, should be mentioned, for he created a few well-known monuments. According to the *Sonntagspost* of November 4, 1973, he was born in Nuebel, Schleswig-Holstein, and created in 1897 the Beethoven bust, and the 1886 Haymarket "Riot" monument. In addition to these two, he also created the Hans Christian Andersen monument, which was dedicated in Lincoln Park on September 26, 1896.

As with sculptors, there is also a dearth of outstanding painters among Chicago's German element. To be sure, several promising German-American painters were active at different times. For instance, in 1916 it appeared that Chicago's artists of German extraction were coming into prominence, for several of them obtained coveted prizes. Emil R. Zettler received the Potter Palmer Gold medal and $1,000 from the Art Institute for his portrayal of "Job." The Norman Wait Harris Silver medal and $500 went to Frederick Frieseke for his picture, "The Hammock," and the Martin B. Cahn prize of $100 was awarded to Walter Ufer. However, these artists, like most Chicago German painters, soon passed into oblivion.

Perhaps the most frequently mentioned example of a German painter is Louis Kurz, who, strictly speaking, was not German, having been born in Salzburg, Austria. He came to America in 1848 and lived in Chicago after 1863 except for a span of seven years spent in Milwaukee. His paintings of religious scenes can be found in churches all over the Union, but he became popular through his paintings of battle scenes from the Civil War, which were eagerly purchased throughout the entire U.S.A. in lithographic copies made by the Kurz and Allison Company. His main work is the thirteen by eighteen foot painting "Washington's Entry into Trenton." With Leonard Volk, Kurz was a co-founder of the Academy of Design. Two sons of Louis Kurz, Louis Jr. (b. 1861) and Frank (b. 1861), also attained a good reputation as artists. Louis was sought after as a painter of portraits and murals. Frank Kurz specialized in portraits and managed the lithographic firm of Kurz and Allison. Already as a nineteen-year-old youth, he created a splendid portrait of the presidential candidate James A. Garfield, which was declared by Garfield the best likeness ever made of him.

Some other early painters of Chicago's German element attained fleeting fame. Carl Brandt came in 1885 to the United States from his native Odenkirchen, in the vicinity of Düsseldorf. He became known as an able painter of religious topics, whose talent is obvious from his works in Chicago's St. Paul's Lutheran Church. Friedrich A. Meyenschein, born at Darmstadt in 1860, emigrated to America in 1880 and came to Chicago in 1890, where he was active as a portrait painter, obtaining much recognition for his portrayal of Governor Yates.

Of the later generations of German-American painters, one should mention Harry Lymann (d. 1933), who immortalized many famous race horses in his pictures; and a number of German-American painters active in the 1930's. Among them were the abstract painters Paul Kelpe and Rudolph Weissenborn, and the fleetingly popular Otto R. Niebuhr, Fritz Becker, Karl Wagner, Kurt Drews, as well as Martin and George Baer, all of whom staged many exhibits of their works in the 1930's. In the 1960's the controversial pop artist, Roy Lichtenstein, came into the limelight for his "Pistol 1964" in the Museum of Contemporary Art's "violence show."

A Selected Bibliography

Note: The innumerable pamphlets, programs, reports, and news releases from many German clubs used in this study are not listed in the bibliography.

Abbott, Edith. *Immigration. Selected Documents and Case Records.* Chicago: University of Chicago Press, 1924.

———. *The Tenements of Chicago, 1908-1935.* Chicago: University of Chicago Press, 1936.

Abendpost and Sonntagspost. Chicago, 1889-date.

Altgeld, John P. *Live Questions: Including Our Penal Machinery and its Victims.* Chicago: Donohue and Henneberry, 1890.

———. *Reasons for Pardoning Fielden, Neebe, and Schwab.* Springfield, 1896.

Amerika-Woche. Chicago, 1973-date.

Andreas, Alfred T. *History of Chicago.* 3 vols. Chicago: A. T. Andreas, 1884-86.

Andree, Karl. *Nord Amerika in geographischen und geschichtlichen Umrissen* . . . Braunschweig: Westermann, 1851.

Angle, Paul M. *A Pictorial History of the Civil War Years.* New York: Doubleday, 1967.

Anon. "A German Family in Chicago, 1856." *Chicago History,* Winter 1956, pp. 309-15.

———. "Chicago and the First World War." *Chicago History,* Summer 1964, pp. 129-44.

———. "Der erste deutsche Ansiedler Chicagos." *Deutsch-Amerikanische Geschichtsblätter,* July 1901, p. 17.

———. "Der 'Gegenseitige Unterstützungs-Verein' von Chicago." *Deutsch-Amerikanische Geschichtsblätter,* 31 (1931), 137-56.

———. "Early Chicago Printing." *Chicago History,* Fall 1947, pp. 268-72.

———. "Michael Diversey and Beer in Chicago." *Chicago History,* Spring 1969, pp. 321-26.

———. "Schwaben-Verein Chicago." *Deutsch-Amerikanische Geschichtsblätter,* 31 (1931), 127-36.

———. "The Gunther Collection." *Chicago History*, Spring 1946, pp. 78-81.

———. "The Opinions of Otto C. Schneider." *Chicago History*, Summer 1961, pp. 111-21.

———. "The Plank-Street City of 1848." *Chicago*, December 1954, pp. 34-35.

Armack, Adolph and Charles Folz. *Nützliches und Belehrendes für deutsche Einwanderer nach den Vereinigten Staaten.* Chicago: German Aid Society, 1887.

Barnard, Harry. *Eagle Forgotten. The Life of John Peter Altgeld.* New York: Duell, Sloan and Pearce, 1938.

Baum, Max. "Chicago und sein Deutschtum. Eine Quellenstudie." *Deutsches Maifest Programm.* Chicago, 1922, pp. 13-20.

Baumann, Friedrich. "Die Baukunst im Staate Illinois." *Deutsch-Amerikanische Geschichtsblätter*, January 1901, pp. 25-32.

Beadle, Muriel. "Nobel Prize Winners." *Chicago Magazine*, Winter 1967, pp. 36-40.

Beinlich, A. B. "The 'Latin' Immigration in Illinois." *Transactions of the Illinois State Historical Society*, 1909, pp. 209-14.

Biographical Sketches of the Leading Men of Chicago. Written by the Best Talent in the Northwest. Chicago: Wilson, 1868ff.

Bishop, Glenn A. and Paul T. Gilbert. *Chicago's Accomplishments and Leaders.* Chicago: Bishop Publishing Company, 1932.

———. *Chicago's Progress. A Review of the World's Fair City.* Chicago: Bishop Publishing Company, 1933.

Bromme, Traugott. *Missouri and Illinois—A Handbook for Immigrants . . .* Baltimore, 1835.

Bruncken, Ernest. "Die Amerikanisierung der Deutschen in den Vereinigten Staaten." *Deutsch-Amerikanische Geschichtsblätter*, January 1908, pp. 37-41.

———. "German Political Refugees, 1815-1860." *Deutsch-Amerikanische Geschichtsblätter*, July 1903, pp. 33-48; October 1903, pp. 33-48; January 1904, pp. 33-59.

Butz, Casper. *Gedichte eines Deutsch-Amerikaners.* Chicago, 1879

———. *Grossvater-Lieder.* Chicago, 1887.

Cachand-Ervendberg, Ludwig. "Das Kirchenbuch der ersten protestantischen Gemeinde von Cook und DuPage County."

Deutsch-Amerikanische Geschichtsblätter, October 1901, pp. 64-78.

Carpenter, Niles. *Immigrants and their Children.* 1920; rpt. New York: Arno Press and the New York Times, 1969.

Cassidy, Claudia. "The Years of Splendor: Chicago's Music and Theater." *Chicago History*, Spring 1972, pp. 4-13.

Chicago Daily News Almanac and Yearbook. Chicago, 1896-1941.

Chicago History. Chicago: Chicago Historical Society, 1945-date.

Chicago Plan Commission. *Forty-Four Cities in the City of Chicago.* Chicago, 1942.

Chicago Public Library. Work Projects Administration. *The Chicago Foreign Language Press Service.* Chicago, 1942.

Chicago Recreation Commission. *The Chicago Recreation Survey, 1937.* Chicago, 1938.

Chicago und sein Deutschthum. Cleveland: German-American Biographical Publication Company, 1901-1902.

Condit, Carl W. *The Chicago School of Architecture. A History of Commercial and Public Buildings in the Chicago Area, 1875-1925.* Chicago: University of Chicago Press, 1964.

Cronau, Rudolf. *German Achievements in America.* New York: Cronau, 1919.

Cunz, Dieter. *They Came from Germany. The Stories of Famous German-Americans.* New York: Dodd, Mead and Company, 1966.

Currey, Josiah Seymour. *Chicago: Its History and its Builders: A Century of Marvelous Growth.* 5 vols. Chicago: S. J. Clarke Company, 1912.

———. "Chicago's North Shore." *Transactions of the Illinois State Historical Society*, 1908, pp. 101-13.

———. *Manufacturing and Wholesale Industries of Chicago.* 3 vols. Chicago: Thomas B. Poole Company, 1918.

Darrow, Clarence. *The Story of My Life.* New York: Charles Scribner's Sons, 1932.

David, Henry. *The History of the Haymarket Affair. A Study in the American Social-Revolutionary and Labor Movements.* New York: Farrar and Rinehart, 1936.

Dedmon, Emmett. *Fabulous Chicago.* New York: Random House, 1953.

Der Deutschamerikaner. Chicago, 1959-date.

Deutsch-Amerikanische Geschichtsblätter. Chicago: Deutsch-Amerikanische Historische Gesellschaft, 1901-1937.

Deutsche Monatshefte. Chicago, 1864-65.

Dietzsch. Emil. *Geschichte der Deutschamerikaner in Chicago.* Chicago, 1881.

———. *Kraft und Stoff, aus der Geschichte des deutschen Volkes.* Chicago, 1884.

Drury, John. *Old Chicago Houses.* Chicago: University of Chicago Press, 1941.

Duden, Gottfried. *Berichte über eine Reise nach den westlichen Staaten Nordamerikas* . . . Elberfeld, 1829.

Dummer, E. Heyse. "Gerhart Hauptmann and the Chicago Stage." *American German Review*, 6 (1939), 17-19.

Ebert, Albert E. "Anfänge des Droguen-Handels und der Apothekerei in Chicago." *Deutsch-Amerikanische Geschichtsblätter*, January 1907, pp. 2-15.

Falbisaner, Adolf. "Das deutsche Lied in der deutsch-amerikanischen Dichtung." *Deutsch-Amerikanische Geschichtsblätter*, April 1902, pp. 33-39.

Faust, Albert Bernhardt. *The German Element in the United States. With Special References to its Political, Moral, Social and Educational Influence.* 2 vols. New York: The Steuben Society of America, 1927.

Fergus, Robert. *Fergus' Directory of the City of Chicago, 1839.* Chicago: Fergus Printing Company, 1876,

Fermi, Laura. *Illustrious Immigrants. The Intellectual Migration from Europe 1930-41.* 2nd ed. Chicago and London: University of Chicago Press, 1971.

Fritsch, W. A., "Christian Esselen." *Deutsch-Amerikanische Geschichtsblätter*, January 1902, pp. 45-47.

Garbutt's Biographical Sketches of the Leading Men of Chicago. Chicago, 1868.

Georg, Adolph. "Aus der Geschichte der Chicago Turngemeinde." *Deutsch-Amerikanische Geschichtsblätter*, July 1905, pp. 42-46.

German Club of Chicago. *World's Fair Souvenir Year Book of 1933.* Chicago, 1933.

German Press Club of Chicago. *Prominent Citizens and Industries of Chicago.* Chicago, 1901.

Germania Club. *One Hundredth Anniversary of Germania Club, 1865-1965.* Chicago, 1965.

Gilbert, Paul Thomas and Charles Lee Bryson. *Chicago and its Makers.* Chicago: F. Mendelsohn, 1929.

Gordon, Milton. *Assimilation in American Life: The Role of Race, Religion and National Origin.* New York: Oxford University Press, 1964.

Gorman, John J. *Report of the Histories now in Use in the Public Schools of Chicago.* Chicago, 1927.

Gould, Benjamin Apthorp. *Investigations in the Military and Anthropological Statistics of American Soldiers.* New York: Riverside Press, 1869.

Grant, Madison and Charles Stuart Davison. *The Alien in our Midst or 'Selling our Birthright for a Mess of Pottage.'* New York: The Galton Publishing Co., 1930.

Hatfield, James Taft. "Deutsche im spanisch-amerikanischen Kriege." *Deutsch-Amerikanische Geschichtsblätter,* April 1902, pp. 43-45.

Hawgood, John A. *The Tragedy of German-Americans. The Germans in the United States of America during the Nineteenth Century—and After.* New York and London: Putnam's Sons, 1940.

Hecht, Benjamin. *Gaily, Gaily.* Garden City: Doubleday, 1963.

Herriott, F. J. "The Germans of Chicago and Stephen A. Douglas in 1854." *Deutsch-Amerikanische Geschichtsblätter,* 12 (1912), 381-404.

Huebener, Theodore. *The Germans in America.* Philadelphia and New York: Chilton Company, 1962.

Illinois Staatszeitung. Chicago, 1861-1925.

Jenks, Jeremiah W. and W. Jett Lauck. *The Immigration Problem.* New York and London: Funk and Wagnalls Company, 1912.

Kapp, Friederich. *Immigration and the Commissioners of Emigration of the State of New York.* New York: The Nation Press, 1870.

Kaufmann, Wilhelm. "Die Deutschen im Bürgerkriege." *Deutsch-Amerikanische Geschichtsblätter,* July 1908, pp. 107-15.

Kenkel, Heinrich. "Der Bau des 'Deutschen Hauses' und die Gründung des 'Theaters' in Chicago." *Deutsch-Amerikanische Geschichtsblätter*, July 1901, pp. 38-43.

Kijewski, Marcia et al. *The Historical Development of three Chicago Millgates. South Chicago, East Side, South Deering.* Chicago, 1972.

Kile, Jessie. "Duden and his Critics." *Transactions of the Illinois State Historical Society*, 1915, pp. 63-70.

Kitagawa, Evelyn M. and Karl E. Taeuber. Local Community Fact Book. *Chicago Metropolitan Area.* 1960. Chicago, 1963.

Koerner, Gustave. *Das deutsche Element in den Vereinigten Staaten von Nordamerika, 1818-1848.* Cincinnati: A. E. Wilde, 1880.

Kogan, Herman and Lloyd Wendt. *Chicago: A Pictorial History.* New York: Dutton, 1958.

Kraft, Oscar H. *Jahrbuch für die deutschen Vereine von Chicago.* Chicago, 1901 ff.

Laughlin, Harry H. *Immigration and Conquest.* New York, 1939.

Lindemann, F. "Die Errichtung des evangelisch-lutherischen Schullehrer-Seminars in Addison, Ill." *Deutsch-Amerikanische Geschichtsblätter*, July 1902, pp. 17-21.

Lindsay, Vachel. *Collected Poems.* New York: McMillan, 1944.

Löher, Franz von. *Geschichte und Zustände der Deutschen in Amerika.* Cincinnati: Eggers, 1847.

Mackay, John Henry. *The Anarchists. A Picture of Civilization at the Close of the Nineteenth Century.* Boston, 1891.

Madigan, John. "Herblock: Public Executioner." *Chicago.* February 1956, pp. 22-26.

Mannhardt, Emil. "Aus alten Illinoiser Zeitungen." *Deutsch-Amerikanische Geschichtsblätter*, July 1904, pp. 45-53.

———. *Deutsche und deutsche Nachkommen in Illinois und den östlichen Nord-Central Staaten.* Chicago: Deutsch-Amerikanische Historische Gesellschaft, 1907.

———. "Die ältesten deutschen Ansiedler in Illinois." *Deutsch-Amerikanische Geschichtsblätter*, October 1901, pp. 50-59, January 1902, pp. 49-54.

———. "Die Anfänge des kirchlichen Lebens in Illinois." *Deutsch-Amerikanische Geschichtsblätter*, April 1901, pp. 24-29.

———. "Die Deutschen in DuPage County." *Deutsch-Amerikanische Geschichtsblätter*, October 1901, pp. 33-40.

———. "Die ersten beglaubigten Deutschen in Chicago." *Deutsch-Amerikanische Geschichtsblätter*, January 1901, pp. 38-46.

———. "Franz Arnold Hoffmann. Ein Führer seines Volkes." *Deutsch-Amerikanische Geschichtsblätter*, July 1903, pp. 56-62.

———. "Gemeinde Chronologie. Chronologische Darstellung der äusseren Entwickelung des religiösen Lebens unter den Deutschen in Illinois." *Deutsch-Amerikanische Geschichtsblätter*, October 1905, pp. 1-62.

———. Über die Mischung des deutschen mit den anderen Bevölkerungs-Elementen in den Vereinigten Staaten." *Deutsch-Amerikanische Geschichtsblätter*, October 1904, pp. 11-21.

———. "Zwei alte Chicagoer, Friedrich Burcky und Nikolaus Berdel." *Deutsch-Amerikanische Geschichtsblätter*, July 1902, pp. 32-33.

Matz, Otto H. "Chicago vor 50 Jahren und die damaligen deutschen Architekten." *Deutsch-Amerikanische Geschichtsblätter*, January 1907, pp. 37-42.

Mayer, Harold M. and Richard C. Wade. *Chicago: Growth of a Metropolis.* Chicago: University of Chicago Press, 1969.

McLean, Geo. N. *The Rise and Fall of Anarchy in America. From its Incipient Stage to the First Bomb Thrown in Chicago.* 1890. rpt. New York: Haskell, 1972.

Nachrichten der Donauschwaben. Chicago, 1955-date.

Nockin, B. J. "Chicagoer Deutschtum in den fünfziger Jahren." *Deutsch-Amerikanische Geschichtsblätter*, October 1901, pp. 59-60.

Novotny, Ann. *Strangers at the Door.* Riverside, Connecticut: Chatham Press, 1971.

O'Connor, Richard. *The German-Americans. An Informal History.* Boston and Toronto: Little, Brown and Company, 1968.

Olsen, Esther Marie. "The German Theater in Chicago." *Deutsch-Amerikanische Geschichtsblätter*, *33* (1937), 68-123.

Pierce, Bessie Louise. *A History of Chicago.* 3 vols. New York: A. A. Knopf, 1937-37.

Pochmann, Henry and Arthur R. Schultz. *Bibliography of German Culture in America to 1940.* Madison: University of Wisconsin Press, 1953.

Pochmann, Henry A. et al. *German Culture in America. Philosophical and Literary Influences 1600-1900.* Madison: University of Wisconsin Press, 1961.

Poole, Ernest. *Giants Gone: Men Who Made Chicago.* New York: Whittlesey House, 1943.

Rattermann, H. A. "Christian Esselen." *Deutsch-Amerikanische Geschichtsblätter,* 12 (1912), 405-61.

Rawidowicz, Simon et al. *The Chicago Pinkas.* Chicago: The College of Jewish Studies, 1952.

Rosengarten, J. G. *The German Soldier in the Wars of the United States.* 2nd ed. Philadelphia: Lippincott, 1890.

Rubens, Harry. *Die Geschichte des Goethe-Denkmales für Chicago.* Chicago, 1913.

Rudolph, Joseph. "Kurzer Lebensabriss eines achtundvierziger politischen Flüchtlings." *Deutsch-Amerikanische Geschichtsblätter,* April, 1907, pp. 89-96, July 1907, pp. 139-47, October 1907, pp. 152-54, January 1908, pp. 21-30.

Rueckheim, Mathilde. *Von seiner Fülle.* Chicago, 1900.

Schaack, Michael J. *Anarchy and Anarchists.* Chicago, 1889.

Schmidt, Frederick R. *He Chose. The Other Was a Treadmill Thing.* Santa Fe: Vegara Printing Company, 1968.

Schrader, Frederick F. *The Germans in the Making of America.* New York, 1924.

Schurz, Carl. *The Reminiscences of Carl Schurz.* 3 vols. New York: McClure, 1907.

Scott, Franklin William. *Newspapers and Periodicals of Illinois, 1814-1879.* Springfield: Illinois State Historical Library, 1910.

Seeger, Eugen. *Chicago. Die Geschichte einer Wunderstadt.* Chicago: George Gregory Printing Company, 1893.

Selby, Paul. "Lincoln and German Patriotism." *Deutsch-Amerikanische Geschichtsblätter,* 12 (1912), 510-35.

Shebs, Robert L. "Mayors of Chicago." *Chicago,* June 1954, pp. 20-23.

Siegel, Arthur. *Chicago's Famous Buildings.* Chicago: University of Chicago Press, 1965.

Silvestro, Clement M. "The Candy Man's Mixed Bag." *Chicago History*, Fall 1972, 86-99.

Simon, Andreas. *Chicago, die Gartenstadt.* Chicago: Franz Gindele, 1893.

Singer, Michael. *Jahrbuch der Deutschen in Chicago.* Chicago: Singer, 1915-17.

Snyder, Jean. "Dining in Chicago. Eine Deutsche Essenfahrt." *The Chicago Guide*, February 1972, pp. 69-74.

Statistical History of the United States from Colonial Times to the Present. Stamford, Connecticut, 1965.

Stuart, William H. *The Twenty Incredible Years.* Chicago and New York: M. A. Donohue, 1935.

Townsend, Andrew Jacke. "The Germans of Chicago." *Deutsch-Amerikanische Geschichtsblätter*, 32 (1932), 1-147.

Uhlendorf, B. A. "German-American Poetry. A Contribution to Colonial Literature." *Deutsch-Amerikanische Geschichtsblätter*, 22/23 (1922/23), 109-295.

Upton, George P. *Theodore Thomas: A Musical Autobiography.* 2 vols. Chicago: A. C. McClurg and Company, 1905.

U.S. Immigration and Naturalization Service. *Annual Report.* Washington, 1971-date.

Vandenbosch, Amry. *The Dutch Communities of Chicago.* Chicago: Knickerbocker Society of Chicago, 1927.

Vise, Pierre de. *Shifts in Chicago's Ethnic Communities, 1960-1970.* Chicago, 1971.

Vocke, Wilhelm. "Einige Betrachtungen über die Stellung der Deutschen in den Vereinigten Staaten." *Deutsch-Amerikanische Geschichtsblätter*, October 1904, pp. 1-10.

Ward, Robert E. *Deutsche Lyrik aus Amerika. Eine Auswahl.* New York: The Literary Society, 1969.

———. "Konrad Nies, German-American Literary Knight." *German-American Studies*, 3 (1971), 7-11.

Waterman, Arba N. *Historical Review of Chicago and Cook County and Selected Biography.* 3 vols. Chicago and New York: The Lewis Publishing Company, 1908.

Wirth, Louis and Eleanor H. Bernert. *Local Community Fact Book of Chicago.* Chicago: University of Chicago Press, 1949.

Wirth, Louis and Margaret Furez. *Local Community Fact Book, 1938.* Chicago: Chicago Recreation Commission, 1938.

Wittke, Carl. *We Who Built America. The Saga of the Immigrant.* 2nd ed. Cleveland: The Press of Western Reserve University, 1964.

Wynar, Lubomyr. *Encyclopedic Directory of Ethnic Newspapers and Periodicals in the U.S.A.* Littleton: Libraries Unlimited, 1972.

Yearbook of the Chicago Branch of the National League of American Penwomen. Chicago, 1937.

Yearbook of the German Club of Chicago Published to Commemorate the 20th Anniversary of its Organization. E. Oscar Stoffels. Chicago, 1933.

Zeisler, Ernest Bloomfield. *The Haymarket Riot.* Chicago: Alexander Isaacs, 1956.

Zglenicki, Leon et al. *Poles of Chicago, 1837-1937.* Chicago: Polish Pageant Inc., 1937.

Ziehn, Bernhard. "Gesammelte Aufsätze zur Geschichte und Theorie der Musik." *Deutsch-Amerikanische Geschichtsblätter*, 26/27 (1926/27), 7-335.

Zimmermann, G. A. et al. *Deutsch in Amerika. Beiträge zur Geschichte der Deutsch-amerikanischen Literatur.* Chicago: Ackermann and Eyller, 1892.

Index